Fly Patterns:
The Expert Selection

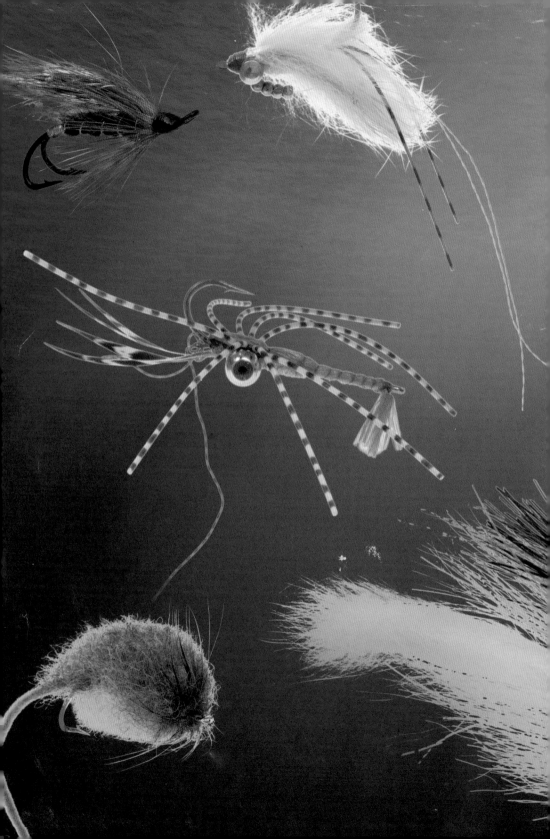

Fly Patterns:

The Expert Selection

200 Failsafe Fly Patterns from
Anglers Around the World

Tony Lolli

APPLE

30127 081071172 7

A QUARTO BOOK

© Copyright 2013 Quarto plc

Published in 2013 by
Apple Press
7 Greenland Street
London NW1 0ND
United Kingdom

www.apple-press.com

ISBN: 978-1-84543-484-7

Conceived, designed, and produced by
Quarto Publishing plc
The Old Brewery
6 Blundell Street
London N7 9BH

QUAR.FTP

Project Editor: Chelsea Edwards
Copy Editor: Sarah Hoggett
Proofreader: Liz Jones
Indexer: Helen Snaith
Photographer: Phil Wilkins
Design: Schermuly Design Co.
Design Intern: Nadine Resch
Art Director: Caroline Guest
Picture Researcher: Sarah Bell

Creative Director: Moira Clinch
Publisher: Paul Carslake

Cut-out work by Modern Age Pte Ltd, China

Printed by Hung Hing Off-set Printing Co.
Ltd, China

10 9 8 7 6 5 4 3 2 1

Contents

Introduction

*Orange Angel
(see page 61).*

There's an old saying, 'Fly fishing is the most fun you can have while standing up'. If that's true, then fly tying is foreplay. It keeps me entertained and ready for the main event – opening day of the fishing season. Fly tying gets me through the winter when there is little fishing to be had. It keeps me connected to the sport I love and links me to the long line of fly dressers who came before me.

When I started tying flies in 1972, my thought was to save some money by tying my own. I soon discovered the unexpected advantage of trying patterns not available from local fly purveyors. What is the unexpected advantage? It was not long before one thing led to another and my materials collection took over the guest bedroom. The collecting activity was as addictive as the tying. It became clear it would be impractical to collect all possible materials, although I went at it earnestly for a few years.

Soon I realized there was a distinction between flies intended to catch fish versus those intended to catch fishermen. However, it took a long time on the water before I could tell which was which. This realization limited the variety of materials I needed. So much so that my collection hardly took up more than several bookshelves and travelling chests.

When I became a fly-fishing guide, I learned some patterns were more effective than others. I also learned some of the simplest patterns were often the most effective. Conversations with other guides confirmed this. As an aside, I learned some guides were unwilling to share any of their secrets while others gave freely of their hard-earned knowledge. I also learned there is no end to learning something new. Every time I watch a fly tier, I see a unique twist (no pun intended) and adapt it to my tying.

I started out as a trout fisher and still prefer fishing for naturally reproducing trout. As I began fishing for different species, I went through the same learning process of tying all over again.

Next, I began to wonder whether effective patterns for the species I was familiar with would work around the world. This question was the genesis of this pattern book: do rainbow trout take similar patterns in England, Argentina and New Zealand? There was only one way to answer the question – start contacting guides from around the world.

During the 12 months of required research, I estimate I made 20,000 initial contacts with professional guides/tiers from around the world. Those appearing in this book have several characteristics in common: knowledge of materials both new and old; a willingness to experiment on the water and tweak their patterns; and a generosity to share their knowledge. Without their contributions, there would be no book. At the same time, this book is the proverbial tip of the iceberg. If you use the reference section listing the tiers' web pages, you'll be well on your way towards greatly expanding your knowledge of how materials and tying techniques interact to result in effective patterns.

Speaking of materials, it should be noted that the possession of some materials is prohibited. The list varies by country. In the US, for example, polar bear and baby seal fur are not to be possessed unless you have written proof the materials were imported prior to the legal prohibition. The good news is there are equally effective alternatives to endangered and protected species.

Ever since the first Macedonian (or Egyptian or Greek) tied a bit of red wool to a hook and caught fish, we've been trying to improve our piscatorial prowess. One would think the limits have been achieved, but thousands of new patterns appear every year. It's impossible, and unwise, to try to tie each of them. If you employ the expertise of the fishers featured in this book, you'll be well on your way towards determining which patterns will meet your needs and improve your success.

Damsel Nymph (see page 122).

Tony Loll.

About this book

This book is split into two sections: fresh- and saltwater. Each fly pattern consists of a set of step-by-step tying instructions, which correspond to an annotated photograph of the finished fly. In addition there is a materials list that sets out everything you'll need to tie the pattern as it was intended by its originator.

Fly directories (freshwater pages 12–129, saltwater pages 130–265)

Name of the guide.

Name of the fly.

Photograph of the finished fly.

This text looks at many aspects and can include the fly's evolution, how best to fish it or the guide's best memory of using it. The species to target with the fly will also be discussed here.

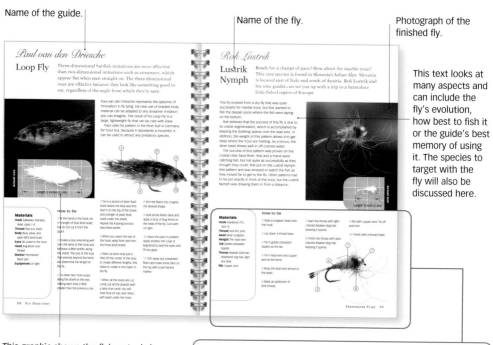

This graphic shows the fly's actual size. There are instances where patterns are shown at a percentage of their actual sizes, but this should still help you to visualize the size of each fly once it is complete.

Actual size: the bold grid represents 1 cm (⅜ in) and each square 1 mm (¹⁄₃₂ in).

50%: the bold grid represents 1 cm (⅜ in) and each square 2 mm (¹⁄₁₆ in).

25%: the bold grid represents 2 cm (¾ in) and each square 5 mm (³⁄₁₆ in).

The materials required to tie each fly are listed here, along with any special equipment that may be needed. A glossary of material terms appears on page 283.

These clear, expert instructions take the reader through the stages of each pattern.

This photograph of the fly is annotated with numbers that correspond to the step-by-step tying sequence.

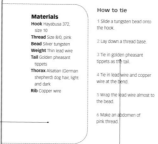

Materials
Hook Hayabusa 372, size 10
Thread Size 8/0, pink
Bead Silver tungsten
Weight Thin lead wire
Tail Golden pheasant tippets
Thorax Alsatian (German shepherd) dog hair, light and dark
Rib Copper wire

How to tie

1 Slide a tungsten bead onto the hook.

2 Lay down a thread base.

3 Tie in golden pheasant tippets as the tail.

4 Tie in lead wire and copper wire at the bend.

5 Wrap the lead wire almost to the bead.

6 Make an abdomen of pink thread.

7 Start the thorax with light-colored Alsatian dog hair, keeping it sparse.

8 Finish the thorax with dark-colored Alsatian dog hair, keeping it sparse.

9 Rib with copper wire. Tie off and trim.

10 Finish with a thread head.

FRESHWATER FLIES 59

Starting and finishing techniques (pages 267–273)

These techniques are covered using step-by-step photographs and instructions.

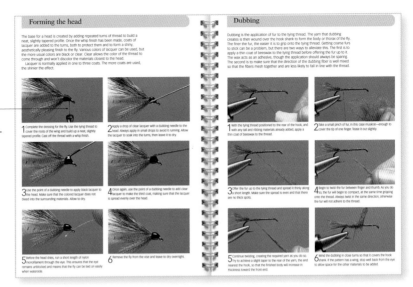

Forming the head

The base for a head is created by adding repeated turns of thread to build a neat, slightly tapered profile. Once the whip finish has been made, coats of lacquer are added to the turns, both to protect them and to form a shiny, aesthetically pleasing finish to the fly. Various colors of lacquer can be used, but the more usual colors are black or clear. Clear allows the color of the thread to come through and won't discolor the materials closest to the head.

Lacquer is normally applied in one to three coats. The more coats are used, the shinier the effect.

1 Complete the dressing for the fly. Use the tying thread to cover the roots of the wing and build up a neat, slightly tapered profile. Cast off the thread with a whip finish.

2 Apply a drop of clear lacquer with a dubbing needle to the head. Always apply in small drops to avoid it running. Allow the lacquer to soak into the turns, then leave it to dry.

3 Once again, use the point of a dubbing needle to apply black lacquer to the head. Make sure that the colored lacquer does not bleed into the surrounding materials. Allow to dry.

4 Apply again, use the point of a dubbing needle to add clear lacquer to make the third coat, making sure that the lacquer is spread evenly over the head.

5 Before the head dries, run a short length of nylon monofilament through the eye. This ensures that the eye remains unblocked and means that the fly can be tied on easily when waterside.

6 Remove the fly from the vise and leave to dry overnight.

Dubbing

Dubbing is the application of fur to the tying thread. The yarn that dubbing creates is then wound over the hook shank to form the body or thorax of the fly. The finer the fur, the easier it is to grip onto the tying thread. Getting coarse furs to stick can be a problem, but there are two ways to alleviate this. The first is to apply a thin coat of beeswax to the tying thread before offering the fur up to it. The wax acts as an adhesive, though the application should always be sparing. The second is to make sure that the base of the dubbing fiber is well mixed so that the fibers mesh together and are less likely to fall in line with the thread.

1 With the tying thread positioned to the rear of the hook, and with any tail and ribbing materials already added, apply a thin coat of beeswax to the tying thread.

2 Take a small pinch of fur, in this case muskrat—enough to cover the tip of one finger. Tease it out slightly.

3 Offer the fur up to the tying thread and spread it thinly along its short length. Make sure the spread is even and that there are no thick spots.

4 Begin to twist the fur between finger and thumb. As you do so, the fur will begin to compact, at the same time gripping onto the thread. Always twist in the same direction, otherwise the fur will not adhere to the thread.

5 Continue twisting, creating the required yarn as you do so. Try to achieve a slight taper to the rear of the yarn, the end nearest the hook, so that the finished body will increase in thickness toward the front end.

6 Wind the dubbing in close turns so that it covers the hook shank. If the pattern has a wing, stop and work back from the eye to allow space for the other materials to be added.

Fly tier information (pages 274–281)

Each fly is pictured in miniature along with biographical information about its tier.

A note on fly-tying materials

Some guides have been very specific in their materials list, while others have been less prescriptive. In addition, some guides have included their preferred brand, but it is not necessary to rigidly adhere to this. These different approaches should allow the reader to select patterns that suit their own ways of working.

The work of guides from over 40 different countries is included here. As such, there are a number of regional products used, which you may be unfamiliar with. The materials glossary (see page 283) should help to explain any unknown terms, so that you can get the necessary materials in your country.

It should be noted that head cement is referred to using various names, but its main function of securing the final threads/materials remains the same. If a guide has not included it in his or her materials list or steps, it still needs to be used, but you can select your preferred brand/type.

Basic tools

As with most crafts, fly tying requires a range of tools designed to make the practitioner's life a little easier. They range from fundamentals, such as a vice and scissors, to optional tools, including the hair stacker and dubbing twister. While it is not imperative to obtain every tool listed here, they will help make the job of producing neat, well-tied flies more achievable.

Vice

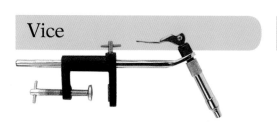

While it is possible to hold the hook with your fingers, a purpose-designed vice will allow you to hold even small hooks firmly and securely. The vast majority of experienced fly tiers wouldn't dream of not using one. Fly-tying vices are available in a range of designs, but they should all have a simple, sturdy action that will hold a variety of hooks firmly in the jaws. The preferred action of many tiers is a lever device that is pressed down once the vice jaws have been adjusted to suit the size of the hook. The jaws themselves should be hard-tempered in order to withstand many years of wear.

Scissors

Another must-have tool. All that is required from a pair of fly-tying scissors is that they have sharp blades that are small enough to work closely around the hook. While it is possible to get away with a single pair, many experienced tiers have two. The first pair is the workhorse, used to cut through tough materials, such as feather stalks, hair and tinsels. The second is kept sharp for the more delicate tasks, such as trimming hackle fibres, and usually has smaller, finer points than the first pair.

Dubbing needle

This simple tool has a number of uses, including teasing out dubbing materials, dividing wing slips and freeing trapped hackle fibres. It can also be used to apply lacquer to the head of a fly.

Hackle pliers

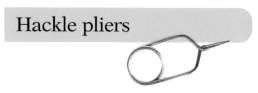

Check that the hook is held firmly by lightly depressing it. If it can still be moved up and down slightly, then the jaws require further tightening.

Bobbin holder

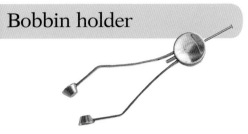

It is possible to tie a fly by removing a length of tying thread from its spool; however, there are a number of advantages to be gained by using a specially designed bobbin holder. The foremost is that it allows the thread to be fed from the spool while it is wound around the hook, reducing waste to the bare minimum. Also, the weight of the bobbin holder, combined with the pressure that the arms exert on the spool, means that it can be released to hang beneath the hook while still retaining tension on the thread. The result is that the thread is prevented from unravelling without resorting to adding a half hitch after every tying procedure.

Hair stacker

When using hair to create wings, achieving the correct density can be a problem. Often the natural position of the hair on the skin means that the prepared wing will taper too much. However, the hair can be stacked so that the tips become level. The hair stacker is a metal or plastic tube into which the bunch of hair is placed, tips first. By tapping the stacker on a hard surface the hairs fall to the bottom, creating a level end to the wing.

Whip-finish tool

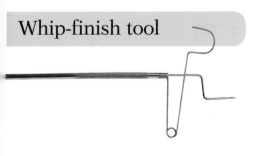

A perfectly good whip finish can be executed with fingers alone; however, some tiers find this specially designed tool to be a great help. Models do vary, but most whip-finish tools have a straight handle with a hook at one end and, lower down, a sprung-wire arm. The tying thread is positioned over the tool's hook and arm and the resulting loop wound around the fly hook.

Dubbing twister

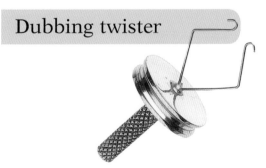

When creating a dubbing loop, it is important to retain tension on the thread loop to keep the fur in position. Hackle pliers can be used, but the dubbing twister is far more efficient. With sprung-metal arms and a heavy circular body, it keeps the thread taut and can be easily spun, twisting the thread and dubbing into a rope.

Freshwater fly directory

Freshwater flies have been evolving since Mesopotamians tied red cloth to a hook. Modern patterns imitate every known food for trout, grayling and salmon, while others look like nothing found in nature. The advent of synthetic materials has given fly tiers more options, and their creations, as seen in this section, border on the incredible.

Rok Lustrik

Lustrik Streamer

Interested in landlocked salmon? Interested in landlocks up to 140 cm (55 in) and 25 kg (55 lb)? I thought so. What's the catch? You'll have to connect with Rok Lustrik in the Julian Alps of Slovenia.

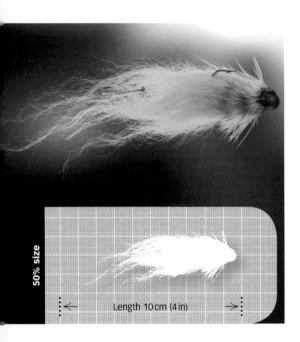

50% size

Length 10 cm (4 in)

The Danube salmon (*Hucho hucho*), a relative of the Mongolian taimen, is found in the Sava River and its tributaries. Prior to the development of this fly, it was not common to catch many of these fish. Now that Rok has developed this streamer, salmon of 13.6 kg (30 lb) are common catches.

Rok believes that the success of this fly is due to the sheep hair, which gives the impression of life no matter how slowly it is retrieved. This characteristic makes it effective for imitating an injured baitfish. It's just the thing to ring the dinner bell for Danube salmon or any other fish.

This fly is fished like any other streamer. It can be stripped across the water fast or slowly, depending on the water conditions. It can also be cast upstream and allowed to tumble along the bottom like a dying baitfish.

The Danube salmon is a challenging fish to catch, but that makes it even more rewarding. The average size caught is 76–102 cm (30–40 in).

Materials

Hook Hayabusa 372, size 10
Trailer hook Size 10 heavy wet fly hook
Thread Size 6/0, black
Weight Lead wire
Connecting wire Stainless steel
Connecting monofilament 9-kg (20-lb) test
Wing Sheep hair on the hide
Collar Elk hair
Flash Crystal flash
Gill cover Grizzly feather fibres
Head Epoxy glue

How to tie

1 Tie in a looped length of stainless steel wire at the bend of the Hayabusa hook for the trailer hook.

2 Tie a length of 9-kg (20-lb) monofilament line to the wire loop. Tie the other end of the monofilament line to the rear hook. The distance between the two hooks should be 4 cm (1½ in). This allows the trailing hook to be hidden by the sheep hairs.

3 Tie wire onto the forward hook shank and wrap it with lead wire.

4 Add crystal flash near the bend.

5 Place the strip of sheepskin at the end of the hook and start wrapping it towards the head.

6 Add a bit more crystal flash along the shank.

7 Tie in elk hair near the hook eye.

8 Trim the elk hair.

9 Add one grizzly feather on each side.

10 Use epoxy glue to form the head.

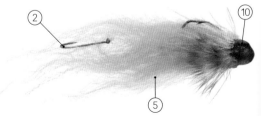

Martin Ångnell

Ångnell's Floating Damselfly Nymph

This pattern can be adjusted for colour and size anywhere that damselfly nymphs are found. It also solves the problem of how to effectively fish in shallow water without getting your fly stuck on the bottom.

Martin Ångnell has investigated how to improve the use of sinking lines and floating flies in still waters for many years. Sinking lines give many opportunities to reach and catch fish in places and conditions where floating lines have limits.

The benefits of this trout fly are twofold: first, it is a floating pattern; second, it imitates an insect that is common in Sweden. It is extremely effective when fishing in shallow water where a sinking pattern is hard to fish because it would foul on the bottom at slow speed.

Fish the fly on a short leader between 30- and 150-cm (1- and 5-ft) long. Use a 6x to 4x tippet and a sinking line. Let the fly jig over the bottom by pulling the line in short twists on a regular basis. Be sure to let the fly float up and stay still at the top of the drift for at least ten seconds, because fish often take the fly when it is standing still over the bottom.

Actual size

Length 3 cm (1¼ in)

Materials

Hook Tiemco 100, sizes 10–16
Thread UNI size 8/0, olive
Tail and gills Olive CDC
Abdomen Olive foam strip, 2 mm (¹⁄₁₆ in) wide
Thorax Olive CDC
Legs Partridge feather, dyed olive; dubbing, dyed olive

Note: You will need a needle for building the body of this fly.

How to tie

1 Place a thin needle in the jaws of the vice for building the body.

2 Use the tip of a CDC to create gills at the tip of the needle. Tie the CDC to the needle tip.

3 Slide the foam body onto the needle, covering the wraps of the CDC.

4 Make thread wraps over the rear half of the foam body to create a segmented effect.

5 Pull the foam body off the needle and tie it onto the hook at the bend.

6 Continue making wraps up the hook shank for the thorax.

7 Midway to the eye, tie in and wrap a partridge feather for legs. Overdub with dubbing.

8 Repeat step 7 twice more and finish at the hook eye.

Mick Hall

Aussie Black Water Beetle

Not every fly is slender, long and lean. Some, such as the Aussie Black Water Beetle, are short and stumpy, like its originator – or at least so he claims. Here's a pattern from Mick Hall, tied to imitate one of the 28,000 species of beetles that inhabit Australia.

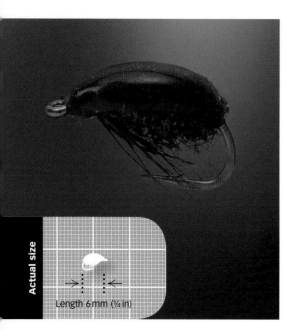

Actual size

Length 6 mm (¼ in)

Mick says that in Australia they have hundreds of streams, most either bush or tree lined. When a breeze comes up in autumn, the beetles fall in and the trout know all about it. In addition, there are heaps of migratory species that fly from one water to the next, some of which find their way into the water. It's a key reason to carry a good selection of these bugs.

In early spring, following a wet winter, Australian streams can overflow and spread out into the surrounding countryside. The trout will also come out of the channels and flooded areas – and when that happens, it's beetle time. At the same time, the margins of the lakes also spread out over new ground and in come the beetles, followed by the trout to feed on them. This time of the season creates a rare opportunity to be able to actually go stalking the margins and hunt your trout.

Materials

Hook Mustad C49 grub hook, size 14
Thread UNI size 8/0, black
Wingcase Black wing quill fibres treated with a flexible cement
Body Spirit River Lite-Brite dubbing, peacock
Legs Moose mane hair
Gloss finish Loon UV Head Finish

How to tie

1 Tie in the black wing quill at the rear of the hook, with the fibres sticking out away from the hook.

2 Dub a body and wrap it forward, towards the eye.

3 Tie in moose mane hair behind the eye, sweeping back towards the hook.

4 Fold the quill over the top of the body and secure at the eye.

5 Coat with Loon UV Head Finish to make a glossy back.

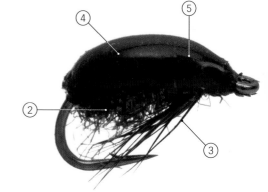

Christof Menz

Backpack Emerger

Fishing the Austrian late season means lots of mayflies will be hatching – but it also means the fish have seen lots of flies during the year and they get shy due to being hooked several times. At this time of the year, often the fish will just take the emergers right in the surface and avoid higher-riding patterns.

Christof Menz is based in Austria, but you'll find him guiding throughout the central Alps of Europe and around the world.

Christof was fishing in October on the Goiserer Traun in the Salzkammergut, a well-known area in Austria, famous for its greyling. The fish were rising to small emergers. However, he couldn't get any to take his flies, so he began thinking about what might be the problem. Finally, he realized that fish were educated and there might be trouble with the size of the fly. He decided to think about tying smaller patterns. However, hooking becomes harder with a smaller hook.

His idea was to turn the hook orientation. He tied his first 'backpack' emerger and the hook was hidden in the wing loop of the fly. The fish could see the extended body, which looked very natural.

His success was really immediate, and Christof uses this fly in all difficult situations when trout are feeding in slow water for emergers.

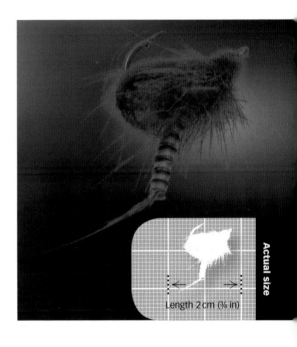

Actual size

Length 2 cm (¾ in)

Materials

Hook Tiemco 2457, sizes 14–18

Silk Dyneema size 10/0, black

Extended body 0.35 mm monofilament

Tail Guinea hen fibres

Thorax Peacock flume, Superglue

Wing CDC feather

Thorax CDC fibres

How to tie

1 Make the extended body by suspending a piece of 0.35 mm monofilament between two vices.

2 Wind a thread base onto the monofilament.

3 Tie in a tail of two guinea-hen feather fibres.

4 Tie in the peacock flume.

5 Apply Superglue to the monofilament, then wrap the peacock flume over the glue. When dry, remove the mono/extended body from the two vices.

6 Put a hook in the vice and make a short thread base.

7 Tie on the extended body and trim the excess monofilament.

8 On the hook, tie in a bunch of CDC fibres facing towards the extended body.

9 Make a dubbing loop for some CDC fibres and wrap the hook shank to make a thorax.

10 Form a wing loop with the first bunch of CDC fibres, turn it forward, and tie it down.

11 Form a head and whip finish.

Length 5 cm (2 in)

Tore Flåten

Bekkoira Special

It's not often that one gets to fish Atlantic salmon in water that has been in private hands since the late 18th century. However, if you contact Tore Flåten, co-owner of Waterproof Flyfishing, he can arrange a trip for you on the River Numedalslaagen in southern Norway.

Materials

Hook Mustad 8052BL, size 2
Thread Size 6/0, orange
Tag Medium oval gold tinsel
Tail Soft fox hair dyed hot orange
Rib Medium oval gold tinsel
Palmer hackle Orange dyed cock
Body UTC holographic silver tinsel
Flash Silver Flashabou
Underwing Orange dyed fox
Overwing Black dyed fox
Front hackle Orange dyed cock

Tore's base camp is in Vestfold, where they fish for salmon from June to mid-September. This is the upper part of the river, and it holds the best fly-fishing areas in this part of Norway.

In general, the River Numedalslaagen is off-coloured and requires an orange fly for success. This led Tore to develop the Bekkoira Special, named for the most beautiful part of the river. Because the river's current is fairly slow, Tore chose soft fibres that would move freely in the current. These soft fibres make the fly come to life and attract the salmon's interest.

This fly is fished in the traditional way, with floating line cast 45 to 70 degrees across and down the river and allowed to dead drift. It is then given a pulsing retrieve as the fly approaches the downstream bank.

How to tie

1 Tie in gold tinsel at the bend and make four wraps for a tag.

2 Tie in the tail equal to one-half of the hook shank's length.

3 Tie in the rib.

4 Tie in the palmered hackle feather.

5 Tie in the holographic tinsel and wrap it towards the eye, making a body. Tie off.

6 Wrap the palmer hackle forward and tie off where the body ends.

7 Wrap the rib forward with five turns and tie off at the end of the body.

8 Tie in four fibres of silver Flashabou at the end of the body 1.5 times the length of the hook shank.

9 Tie in the underwing over the Flashabou, making it 1.5 times the length of the hook shank.

10 Tie in four fibres of Flashabou over the wing.

11 Tie in the overwing above the underwing, making it 1.5 times the length of the hook shank.

12 Tie in and wrap the front hackle ahead of the wing. The fibres should be longer than those of the palmered hackle.

13 Wrap a thread head and varnish it black.

Philip White

Blown-over Dun

Not every mayfly hatches perfectly. Some get trapped in the surface film and are best imitated as emergers or cripples. Others get blown over and present a different profile to the fish. This pattern represents just such an unfortunate mayfly.

Actual size

Length 4 cm (1½ in)

Philip White, of Peak District Fly Fishing, developed this pattern to imitate the large *Ephemera danica* species, which is well known in England. Philip noticed that, on windy days, many emerging flies were blown over and had difficulty drying their wings in preparation for flying away. The trout, too, noticed the struggling naturals and picked them off as an easy opportunity. This fly works well on very windy days, when many duns get their wings trapped. The fish focus on this 'crippled' form. It is especially effective at the early phase of the hatch, when fish are taking the hatching forms and focusing on those individuals having trouble flying.

The imitation is best fished with a slight twitching or 'shiver', imparted by wiggling the rod tip. This gives the impression of a struggling natural. By varying the size and colours, this pattern can be made to imitate almost any mayfly you may encounter.

Philip introduced this pattern at the first International Fly Tying Symposium in Somerset, New Jersey, back in 1993.

How to tie

1 Wrap a thread base to the bend.

2 Tie in the wings, with the tips pointing forward. Make sure one is upright while the other is at 90 degrees so that it can rest on the water's surface.

3 Tie in pheasant tail fibres for a tail.

4 Wrap the pheasant tails forward as a body to the wings.

5 Dub and wrap a thorax on both sides of the wings. The dubbed body helps keep the wings in the desired orientation.

6 Make a small head and tie off.

Materials

Hook Tiemco 100, size 10

Thread Size 8/0, pale yellow

Wings Bull elk hair dyed grey, mixed with some moose body hair to suggest the dark veins in the wings

Tail Five cock pheasant tail fibres tied just shorter than the hook length

Body Three turns of the pheasant tail butts, followed by pale morning dun Superfine dubbing

Thorax Grey squirrel body hair, mainly guard hair but with a little underfur

Martin Ångnell

Ångnell's Floating Cased Caddis

Floating flies are meant for fishing the surface – aren't they? Not always. Martin Ångnell decided to combine a floating fly with a sinking line. The result is that you can fish at any depth without fear that the fly will get hooked onto bottom cover.

Martin says the cased caddis is a common insect in Sweden's Hökensås area. It is a pattern that can be fished throughout the year. Even when the waters are cold, Ångnell's Floating Cased Caddis, on a sinking line and fished very slowly, will interest brown and rainbow trout.

When he was fishing in his home lake, Strandgölen, he noticed a cased caddis climbing up a weed straw. Its case was made of pine needles, and he got the idea of making a floating cased caddis imitation with spun deer hair. Two days later, ice was starting to cover the lake. He attached his new fly to a short tippet. He let the fly sink to the bottom and did not even have time to think when he felt a take. He landed an 3.6-kg (8-lb) rainbow trout. He caught an even bigger rainbow trout on his second cast. On the third cast he missed a take, but on the fourth and fifth casts he caught two more rainbows. He was alone in one of Sweden's most beautiful lakes catching fish on his new pattern!

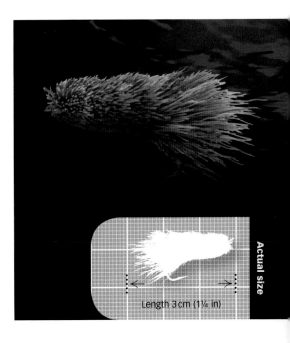

Length 3 cm (1¼ in)

Actual size

Materials

Hook Kamasan B830, sizes 6–14
Thread UNI size 6/0, brown
Larva Olive round-cut foam strip
Legs Partridge feather, the same colour as the larva
Body/case Deer hair

How to tie

1 Tie in at the bend of the hook, but do not cover the shank with thread.

2 Tie in the foam strip as the larva. It should stick out past the bend.

3 Tie in the partridge feather for legs.

4 Spin a deer-hair body from the larva to the eye of the hook. Tie off.

5 Trim the deer head hair into a cylindrical shape. The bottom of the body should be trimmed very short, so that very little deer hair blocks the bend.

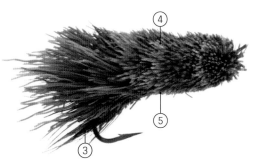

Doug Hintzman

Bonnie Belle

Doug Hintzman is a Spey-casting instructor at Wilson's Sporting Camps on the Miramichi River in New Brunswick, Canada. He wanted a green fly with a good amount of flash and movement, so he added a Mylar body and a wing of softer rabbit fur, rather than the more traditional bear or squirrel.

Actual size

Length 2.5 cm (1 in)

Like most Atlantic salmon wet flies, the Bonnie Belle is cast across the river at a 45-degree angle or so, depending on the conditions, and allowed to swing downstream until it hangs downstream from the angler. Then, take a step downstream and repeat the process.

Since its development, Doug has done extremely well with this fly. The July salmon run in 2011 was exceptional, and he was lucky to be at Wilson's teaching during the best week of the run. He reports having pulls on nearly every other cast.

Doug gave flies to the guides and students and learned of their success, as well. While sharing a pool, Dave caught a grilse and a nice salmon within 15 minutes. EJ Long was guiding the opposite bank and asked which fly he was using. After a change-up, his guest was into a nice fish. EJ shouted over to Doug, 'The Bonnie Belle!'

This is a summer run pattern, but Doug also ties it in red and orange to fish in autumn, at which point it goes by the name of Autumn Belle.

Materials

Hook Partridge Salar black double, number 9
Thread UNI size 6/0, black
Tag Gold medium holographic Holo Tinsel
Body UNI Mylar, green
Wing Black rabbit zonker strip
Flash Green Krystal Flash
Collar Green hen neck
Eyes Jungle cock
Head Black thread

How to tie

1 Start with a thread base.

2 Tie in the tag and wrap it, without running the Mylar further than needed to lock it in.

3 Tie in the Mylar and wrap the body forward, leaving plenty of room at the head.

4 Tie in the zonker strip for the wing.

5 Add two strands of flash to each side.

6 Tie in the hen neck feather collar by the tip and wind forward.

7 Add a jungle cock eye to each side.

8 Whip a neat, small head and apply cement.

Mikael Högberg Robertsdotter

Brown Foam Ant

During the summer months, many streams experience a high influx of terrestrial insects that find their way to the water. When faced with a seasonal bonus, the fish will begin feeding in earnest on these morsels.

Mikael has been tying for 25 years, and his goal is to tie flies that are perfect, using only the best materials. His fishing experience covers streams, ponds and lakes, and he targets trout and grayling.

When Mikael became dissatisfied with dubbed body ants, because they would not float for extended periods of time, he thought about alternatives. He decided on closed cell foam. Not only does it float better than dubbed bodies, but its colour also gives a better impression as it sits in the water's film. Because it does not soak up water, it can be fished much longer than fur-bodied ant patterns. In addition, the Brown Foam Ant has the ability to trigger a strike from fish that are unwilling to take other patterns.

Mikael's method when fishing over brown or rainbow trout is to use a floating line and retrieve with short, light pulls. The fly pushes a little water and the fish often strike when the fly is paused.

He notes that the colour of the fly can be changed to match the variety of ants in various watersheds.

Actual size

Length 2 cm (¾ in)

Materials

Hook Daiichi 1190, sizes 12–16
Thread UNI size 8/0, camel
Body Brown foam strip
Hackle Ginger Metz dry fly cock hackle
Wings Two furnace cock hackle tips

How to tie

1 Take a piece of foam strip and fold it in half. Press the hook through the middle of the foam. Pull the foam along the back of the hook bend and leave it there. One half of the foam will lie above the hook shank and one half will lie below.

2 Start the thread just behind the hook eye and wrap tight turns back to where the body will end.

3 Tie in the Metz hackle where the legs will be, wind a few turns, and tie off.

4 Pull both halves of the foam to make the abdomen, and tie off.

5 Tie in the furnace cock hackle tips as wings.

6 Pull both halves of the foam over the furnace cock hackle to make the thorax, so that the hackles are sticking out

from between the two halves of the foam body. Tie the foam down, leaving room for the foam head in front of the foam body.

7 Pull both the upper and lower foam forward to make a head that covers the hook eye above and below, and tie.

Laszlo Illana

CDC and Elk

Experienced or 'educated' fish require special treatment if you want to bring them in. Laszlo Illana, from Romania, developed just such a pattern to trick trout and grayling that have seen too many flies.

Laszlo is the moderator for the Romanian Fly Tying Forum. He fishes spring creeks in Romania and rivers in the Czech Republic, Slovakia and Poland. He prefers dry fly fishing and, in the early summer, this is effective in fast water. His CDC and Elk fly can be twitched as a caddis imitation to get the fish's attention.

Romania is a beautiful country, with many lakes and spring creeks – but due to fishing pressure, there are few fish and many of them are small. Catch and release is now becoming more common, however, so there are now some bigger fish being caught and released. Lazlo's CDC and Elk pattern is accounting for a considerable number of the larger fish he finds.

Materials

Hook Daiichi D04, sizes 10–18
Thread UNI size 8/0, grey
Body Grey CDC
Underwing Grey CDC
Wing Elk hair
Thorax cover Grey foam strip, 1 mm wide
Thorax Black CDC

How to tie

1 At the bend, tie in a grey CDC feather by its tip. Twist the feather into a rope and wrap it up the shank as a body, three-quarters of the way to the eye.

2 Tie in another grey CDC feather as an underwing sticking out beyond the bend.

3 Tie in a wing of elk hair the same length as the CDC underwing.

4 Tie in a short length of foam.

5 Tie in a black CDC feather. Twist into a rope and wrap a thorax. Trim.

6 Pull the foam over the thorax and tie in. Trim.

7 Make a small thread head.

Tore Flåten

Brufoss Special

Necessity, they say, is the mother of invention. Tore Flåten, co-owner of Waterproof Fly Fishing, needed a brighter fly. The brown floodwaters of the Numedalslaagen River made it impossible for him to see his favourite Atlantic salmon fly, the Thunder and Lightning.

Tore decided on brighter colours and softer materials that would shed water when the fly was picked up for the back cast, making it lighter for easier casting. He selected fine, orange-dyed squirrel tail.

The first day out, the pattern accounted for two salmon, one landed and one lost. Tore's father, a salmon fisher for more than 20 years, and others who fish the Brufoss area, all started having success with the fly, so it became known as the Brufoss Special.

Actual size

Length 4.5 cm (1¾ in)

Materials

Hook Mustad 8052BL, size 8

Thread Black

Tag Medium oval gold tinsel

Body Dubbed black seal wool

Rib Medium oval gold tinsel

Wing Orange squirrel tail with four fibres of thin flash inside the wing

Hackle Orange cock, tied as palmer hackle all around

Head Black varnish

How to tie

1 Wrap a thread base from the eye to the bend.

2 Tie in gold tinsel at the bend and take seven turns to make the tag. Tie the tinsel off, but do not trim.

3 Dub a body and wrap it forward towards the eye, leaving room for the wing.

4 Wrap the tinsel forward over the body in wide, open turns. Tie off and trim.

5 Tie in the wing, making it 1.5 times as long as the body and at a 45-degree angle.

6 Tie in and wrap a collar from the orange hackle.

7 Make a thread head to push the hackle along the wing.

8 Varnish the head.

Leif Ehnström

Sililegs Chamois Dragon Nymph

There's something to be learned if only we pay attention. Leif Ehnström, from Sweden, turns his observations into working patterns.

Materials

Hook TMC 200R nymph hook, sizes 4–8

Thread Dyneema size 6/0, black

Underbody Small piece of thin, semi-hard plastic and Zap-A-Gap adhesive

Eyes Beads and Red Amnesia line, burnt

Weight Lead-free wire

Abdomen Strip of chamois leather glued and wound over the underbody, and medium-brown waterproof marker pen

Legs J. Son Sweden stonefly legs

Thorax Fur dubbing to match the colour of the abdomen

Wingbuds Loon Soft Head

The dragonflies are an important food for rainbow trout in the spring. Leif made this fly as realistic as possible. Adding to the realism is the chamois. When it gets wet and a little slimy, it looks great in the water.

He fishes it near the bottom in shallow bays, where the bottom grass has not yet grown up in the springtime. He lets the fly sink to the bottom and then retrieves it as fast as he can, with short pulls. Be aware, the fish attacks hard and viciously. The first time he used it he lost two before he managed to be a little cooler when striking.

In 2011, during his first trip for the season, there was 10 cm (4 in) of snow on the ground. He anchored in a small bay and rested with a cup of coffee and a ham sandwich. Looking into his fly box, he saw the big dragonfly he had made in the winter. He put it on a sinking line and made a cast, retrieving it with short, fast strips. There was a stop and, after a second, the shake of a nice rainbow. Ten casts and four fish later, he rowed to shore and took a break to have some more coffee and warm up.

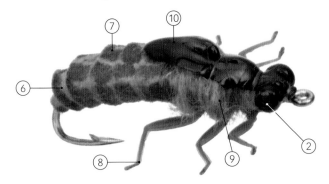

How to tie

1 Make the underbody from a piece of plastic cut to a boat shape; the length should be equal to that of the hook shank.

2 Make eyes using two glass beads and Amnesia line burnt at the ends.

3 Tie on the eyes.

4 Tie in some wire weight behind the eyes. Wrap the wire about half the length of the shank.

5 Use Zap-A-Gap to hold the underbody in position on the hook shank.

6 Tie in the chamois strip at the bend. Apply more Zap-a-Gap to the underbody and wrap the chamois strip to the eyes.

7 Colour the top and bottom of the abdomen with a medium-brown waterproof marker pen.

8 Tie in stonefly nymph legs on the underside of the thorax.

9 Wrap the fur dubbing around and between the legs to form the thorax.

10 Cut out a wingbud shape from plastic and coat it with Loon Soft Head. When dry, peel off the coating and colour it with a medium-brown waterproof marker.

11 Tie on the Loon Soft Head wingbud, securing it behind the thorax and at the eyes.

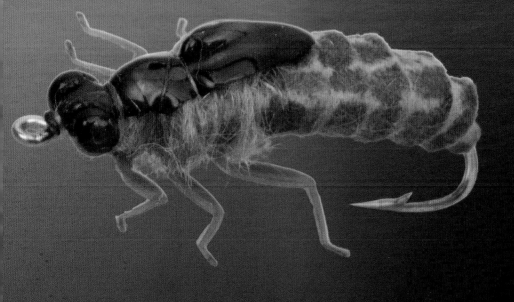

Length 3 cm (1¼ in)

José Manuel Ruiz Pérez

Cholo's Orange Emerger

Could combining foam and CDC fibres result in an unsinkable mayfly pattern – or is that too tall an order? Not any more. Cholo's Orange Emerger does all that and fools educated trout as well.

José Manuel Ruiz Pérez – 'Cholo' to his friends – owns Moscas Orbigo, a supplier of innovative fly-tying materials and patterns. He is also a guide and is affiliated with the Spanish and Japanese International Fly Fishing teams.

Cholo's experience has taken him across Spain and much of Europe in search of fishing opportunities. His series of emergers was designed to present convincing imitations of emerging mayfly to fish that have been fished over for much of the year.

He reports that the use of foam keeps the fly tracking true, as it floats without drag. Although the pattern is small, the angler and the trout can easily see its orange colour. In addition, it sits high on the surface – as do the natural emergers just before they fly away. This encourages the fish to take them without hesitation.

This is an exemplar rather than a specific pattern; it can be matched in colour and size to mimic any mayfly on any water.

Materials

Hook Tiemco 100, size 16
Thread UNI size 8/0, orange
Tail Natural-colour CDC fibres
Body Orange feather fibres
Eyes and wing sac Orange foam
Wings Natural-colour CDC fibres
Hackle Grey Metz hackle

How to tie

1 Wrap a thread base to the bend.

2 At the bend, tie in tail fibres slightly shorter than the hook shank.

3 Tie in orange feather fibres and wind a body halfway to the eye.

4 Tie in orange foam, with the end pointing towards the bend. Fold it forward, towards the hook eye. At the front end, trim the foam short. Wrap the end of the foam so that the eyes stick out on either side by using figure-of-eight wraps.

5 Between the wing sac and the eyes, tie in CDC fibres and divide them left and right with figure-of-eight wraps.

6 Between the wings and eyes, tie in a short hackle and make three turns. Tie off and trim.

Jason Cooney

Cooney's Mudeye

Jason Cooney of FLYmad Fly Fishing needed a dragonfly nymph that would float low enough on the surface to convince brown and rainbow trout on the lakes of southeastern Australia. What he developed will also work wherever these nymphs are found.

Cooney's Mudeye is especially effective when the dragonflies are migrating as part of their hatching process. At such times, they hatch by the hundreds. When fish have easy access, casts must be made ahead of cruising fish so that they will come upon the fly naturally. They will not chase a fly when so many are available.

The switch to closed cell foam from feather wings allows for a low-riding silhouette with a wing that will not flare. The Mudeye can also be fished on the bottom if used with a full sinking line.

Jason reports that in the summer dragonfly nymphs are more active during the dark of night. His preferred method is to skulk along a lake's shoreline after dark and cast to fish searching for shallow-water emerging nymphs. He casts to a sighted fish and makes a couple of short retrieves, leaving a very small wake that attracts the fish's attention. This technique requires you to fish familiar waters for your own safety.

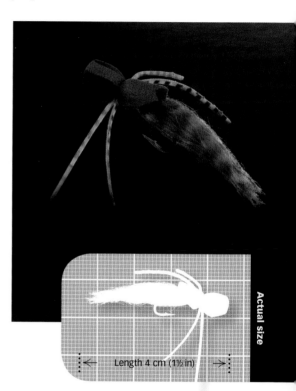

Actual size

Length 4 cm (1½ in)

Materials

Hook Tiemco TMC 2457, size 6
Thread Size 6/0, dark olive
Tail Olive acrylic fibre teased out and segmented with marker pen
Wingcase and head Olive closed cell foam
Marker pen Dark bronze
Legs Fine rubber
Adhesive Superglue

How to tie

1 Tie in the tail just behind the eye and segment with the marker pen.

2 Tear the tail to length to create an uneven edge. Do not cut it.

3 Trim the foam to shape and leave a tab for tying in. Tie in the foam, then trim the tab at the point where the tail was tied in.

4 Tie in rubber legs at the same point.

5 Add a drop of Superglue to protect the thread wraps.

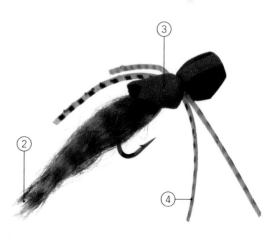

Mick Hall

Compressed Aussie March Brown Emerger

Some tiers stumble upon effective patterns; some use years of experience to design flies that will perform well immediately. Mick Hall is one of the latter and he has received numerous honours in the world of fly tying.

Materials

Hook Mustad C49s grub hook, size 10 or 12

Thread Size 10/0, brown

Tail A few strands of Medium Pardo Coq de Leon

Ribbing Fine copper wire

Wings Enrico Puglisi Trigger Point wing fibres, dark brown

Body Brown dubbing blended with Spirit River medium hare's fur dubbing

Post Brown Enrico Puglisi Trigger Point fibres

Compressing foam Soft Evasote foam, 2 mm (1/16 in) wide and 1.25 cm (1/2 in) long

Hackle Whiting Farms brown/grey dun

Mick is a big fan of parachute-hackled flies, because they float better: they have more hackle on the water and they sit low in the water's film. In many instances, the first part of the fly that is seen by a trout is its wings standing upright, which is a key trigger point. The concept behind the design of this fly is balance and profile; be it in riffle water or windblown lakes, the fly must sit right to avoid refusals.

The soft foam that Mick prefers for this pattern actually compresses the hackles so that they become more effective, with more hackle sitting in the surface film. At the same time, the foam flattens the wings; this enhances the fly's profile with a more natural-looking wing, rather than a round post. On a lesser scale, the foam also helps with flotation.

Watching the emerger float, you will notice that the tail end of the fly actually sits just under the surface, fully supported by the hackle. The grub hook helps accentuate this. Mick normally uses a fluorocarbon tippet, tying on the fly using a Palomar knot so that the tippet section near the fly also sits under the water.

How to tie

1 Tie in the tail at the hook eye.

2 Tie in the ribbing.

3 Tie in the wings, with the butt facing back towards the eye, and support them with a few wraps of thread. Position the wings directly above the barb.

4 At this same point, tie in ten strands of Trigger Point. Wrap the base so it stands up next to the wing base.

5 Dub and wrap a body.

6 Rib the body with four turns and add a few turns of thread around the post. Do not use a lot of fibres for the post; you need a little transparency.

7 Secure the foam to the side of the post facing you.

8 Take the foam around under the hook, pulling firmly, and secure it to the other side of the post. This will spread the wing fibres, giving a skinny profile. Do not trim the excess foam.

9 Tie the hackle to the post, with the underside of the hackle facing you. Wrap at least four turns of hackle from the top of the supported area. Wind carefully back down the post and tie off. Trim the excess hackle.

10 Trim the foam close to the hackle so that it folds back on itself; this in turn compresses the hackle. It is best not to cut too closely, because you need the foam tags to fold back.

Mark H. V. Corps

Corr Shrimp

Not all patterns are 'by the book'. Mark H. V. Corps experiments at his vice each year and the resulting flies are extensively tested. Some are never fished again; some find a home in his fly box; and some, like the Corr Shrimp, become favourites due to their success.

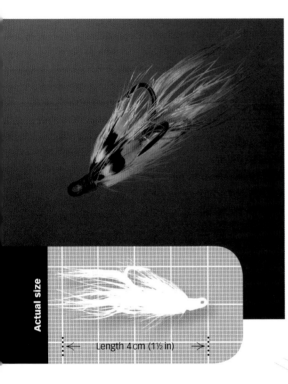

Actual size

Length 4 cm (1½ in)

Mark fishes this pattern for Atlantic salmon and sea trout in rivers and lakes across Ireland. No reason why it shouldn't work wherever these species are found.

On a lake, Mark usually uses this as the tail fly on a team of three or four flies. On rivers, he uses two flies with the Corr Shrimp on point. His standard technique (with a good river flow) is to cast across the river and let the fly swing around. In slower water, some hand lining with a very slow retrieve works best.

This pattern is one of his six 'go-to' patterns. Using the old adage, 'bright day – bright fly', the Corr Shrimp works best on dull days. It can be very effective for fresh grilse, and Mark is sure this success is related to the green body.

Materials

Hook Sizes 6–14 treble
Silk Red
Tail Golden pheasant red breast feather
Rib Silver wire
Body Green Mylar
Middle hackle Grizzly
Front hackle Grizzly
Cheeks Jungle cock feathers
Head Red thread

How to tie

1 Tie in a golden pheasant breast feather at the bend and wind it as the tail.

2 Tie silver wire at the bend.

3 Tie in green Mylar and wrap a body.

4 Rib the body with the silver wire.

5 Ahead of the body, tie in and wind two hackles.

6 Tie in two jungle cock feathers, roof style, side by side, for the cheeks.

7 Wrap a thread head and finish with varnish.

Mark H. V. Corps
Elaine Shrimp

The Elaine Shrimp was discovered during one of Mark's experiment sessions, and it has turned out to be his best fly for spring salmon.

While fishing the Delphi River in western Ireland, Mark saw several salmon milling around in a deep hole. After an hour of nymphing, he had no success and switched to the Elaine Shrimp. On his second cast a fish took the fly, ran upstream and threw the fly. As Mark was stripping the fly in, another Atlantic salmon took the fly and ran upstream.

Following the contest, Mark landed the fish – 8.5 kg (18 lb, 10 oz) and the largest salmon caught at Delphi since 1986.

He's keeping the fly as a go-to pattern whenever spring salmon are being targeted.

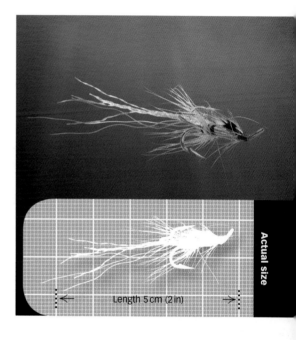

Actual size

Length 5 cm (2 in)

Materials

Hook Sizes 6–14 treble
Thread Size 6/0, red
Tail Three strands of pearl Crystal Flash
Rib Fine gold wire
Body Gold Mylar
Middle hackle Long yellow cock
Front hackle Short orange cock
Cheeks Two jungle cock hackles
Head Red thread

How to tie

1 Lay down a thread base to the bend.

2 Tie in three strands of pearl Crystal Flash 1.5 times the length of the overall hook.

3 Tie in fine gold wire for the ribbing.

4 Tie in gold Mylar, wrap it forward (allowing the red thread to show) and tie off. Halfway, stop and tie in the yellow hackle. Make two wraps, tie off and trim. Advance the gold Mylar.

5 Wrap the ribbing forward and tie off.

6 Tie in the orange hackle. Make two turns, tie off and trim.

7 Tie in the jungle cock hackles, roof style.

8 Make a red thread head.

Length 10 cm (4 in)

Sacha Putz
Dark Queen

Tube flies have been around for several years and their versatility is well accepted. The Atlantic salmon fishers were the earliest advocates of this tying technique. As a result, most existing tube patterns are used for Atlantic salmon.

Materials

Hook Ken Sawada treble sized to the tube fly

Thread Wood duck UTC Ultra 70

Tube 2 mm (1/16 in) plastic inside a brass tube

Tag Fine silver tinsel and red UNI yarn

Body Gold and black glitter thread

Ribbing Red and copper twisted wire covered with a black schlappen feather

Underwing A small number of brown and ginger fox hairs with a few fibres of gold Angel Hair

Back hackle Badger hackle and tan/brown mottled marabou feather

Main wing Black fox hair with a few fibres of red Angel Hair

Front hackle Orange/brown grizzly marabou feather

Eyes Two jungle cock feathers

Sacha Putz, from Germany, needed an Atlantic salmon and sea trout pattern that would move seductively in slower currents. He also wanted the versatility offered by tube flies. Depending on conditions, the hook can be switched out from a treble to a double or even a single point.

He noticed that many of his previous flies lacked movement in calmer currents. His solution was to mix some marabou with fox hair to give extra movement and, at the same time, make a fly that was stronger and would hold up better to the leaping salmon and hard-pulling sea trout.

These patterns have proven their effectiveness in the Morrum River in Sweden and the River Moy in Ireland, where Sacha fishes them any evening throughout the season.

Sacha's first time out with the Dark Queen remains burned into his memory. Standing in a salmon river after dark, he was fishing a double-handled rod. With nothing to be seen, there came the fish's strike and long run marked by the reel's brake. Not once, not twice, but six times the Dark Queen did his bidding and he landed all six fish.

How to tie

1 Tie in the tag of silver tinsel and red yarn.

2 Wrap the body.

3 Wrap the ribbing, followed by the black schlappen feather.

4 Tie in the underwing, including a little flash of gold Angel Hair.

5 Tie in the back hackle.

6 Add the main wing.

7 Add the front hackle.

8 Make a small thread head.

9 Tie in a jungle cock feather on each side.

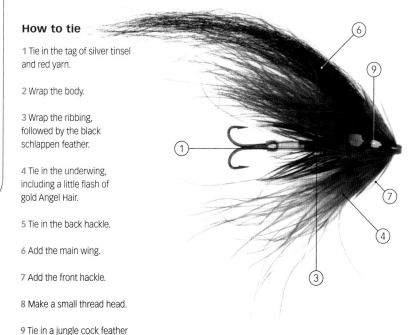

Misako Ishimura

Eboshi

Tenkara, the ancient form of simplified fly fishing, started during the Japanese equivalent of the Middle Ages. Contemporary masters of the art are revered as teachers, and many use fly patterns that have been in existence for 2,000 years.

Materials

Hook Gamakatsu S10-B, sizes 12–14

Thread UTC size 70, black, and Danville size 6/0, red

Post Enrico Puglisi Sparkle Blue Magic and Icelandic sheep's hair dyed orange

Hackle Partridge body feather and brown cock hackle

Head and butt Red thread

Body Black thread and peacock herl

Ribbing Small-to-medium gold wire

Misako, a member of the Japanese International Fly Fishing Team, wanted to improve on the Tennyo fly of Master Somajijii (a Master *Tenkara* teacher), so she developed the Eboshi (Japanese for 'old hat') to express her admiration for him. The addition of a post improves the visibility for both fish and fisher. The added wire rib weights the fly just enough for the hook to ride lower in the water, improving hook-ups.

Misako has used the Eboshi for iwana, yamame and grayling in the Nakatsu River in the Tanzawa Mountains in Kanagawa Prefecture. She has also used it in the Willowemoc River in New York's Catskills for browns and rainbows.

This is how she described a memorable event with the Eboshi: 'There was a fairly big rock in the mountain stream, and I saw a fish two feet behind. I drifted the regular *Tenkara* fly upstream of the rock and had the current move it to the shadow. It seemed to move a bit too fast and the fish ignored it.

'I changed to the Eboshi, cast it to the front of the rock, and gave a little slack. The fly dropped to the water, then started to go down along the current. I saw my fly well because of the post. When the fly was almost past the fish, it turned. Then I took a short breath and set the hook. I felt my line straighten with the weight. The trout took Eboshi!'

How to tie

1 Wrap the red thread tightly from the eye to where the bend starts.

2 Change the thread from red to black and make the post with Enrico Puglisi Sparkle Blue Magic.

3 Tie in an Icelandic sheep-hair post in front of the previous post.

4 Add five wraps of thread ahead of the posts to make it stand firmly.

5 Behind the post, tie in the partridge feather and the cock feather by their tips.

6 Wrap the partridge and cock feathers four times, with the dull side of the feathers facing towards the eye. They should form a wide cup around the shank, as if the hackle cup is holding the post and the eye.

7 Wrap the thread back to the red butt and tie in the gold wire.

8 Wrap the thread and make a tapered black thread body, ending behind the hackle.

9 Rib the body with the gold wire, ending behind the post.

10 Tie in the peacock herl behind the post and make two turns. Tie off.

Adrian Pop

F-Fly

Everyone loves a winner. Adrian Pop was the 2010 and 2011 National Fly Tying Champion of Romania. He offers a standing invitation to fly fishers to join him – as long as you're not afraid to fish the waters of Transylvania, home of Dracula.

Actual size

Length 2 mm (1/16 in)

Adrian is a PhD student at the Horticulture University, Klausenburg, and he started fly fishing and tying in 2002. One can only imagine what he will accomplish in a few years.

Adrian fishes many rivers near his home, including the Crisul Repede, Hell Valley, Dragon Valley, Somesul Rece, Somesul Cald, Aries and Tirnava The F-Fly has proven its value on browns and grayling.

Adrian developed the F-Fly because, in autumn, there are a lot of very small and almost iridescent flies. Grayling and trout take this fly very well.

His best day fishing the F-Fly was on the Hell Valley on a day in early winter. He reports catching more than 20 grayling during several hours of fishing.

Materials

Hook Varivas dry fly hook, sizes 14–20
Thread size 6/0, red
Tail Brown feather fibres
Body Spectra Flash
Legs Brown saddle hackle
Wing Two brown CDC feathers

How to tie

1 Tie in three brown feather fibres on the hook as a tail.

2 Tie in the Spectra Flash and wind a thin, translucent body.

3 Tie in the brown saddle hackle and make one turn for the legs. Tie off.

4 Tie in two CDC feathers to form the wing.

5 Make a head with red thread and finish with head cement.

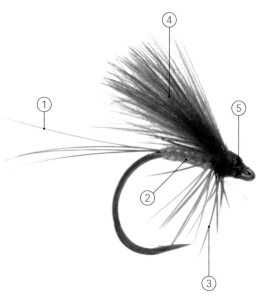

Masamitsu Kasuya

Foam Emerger

Sometimes, less is more – much more. Masamitsu Kasuya developed a fly made of one material – yellow closed-cell foam.

Masamitsu is a member of the Japanese Fly Fishing Team. He reports that this pattern is effective for rainbow trout, iwana and yamame in his home water, the Kosuge River in the Yamanashi Prefecture of Japan.

The idea for this pattern came to Masamitsu when he found that usually wary trout were jumping at his yellow strike indicator. A New Zealander friend suggested he try 'adding a hook'.

Masamitsu often casts behind holding trout, and finds that they will turn back and take the fly before it is swept away from their holding position. He attributes the plopping sound and bright colour as the trigger for this fly. Fish seem to take it without hesitation in order to return to their holding positions. The small size of the fly makes it easy for the trout to take and hook-ups are more likely than not.

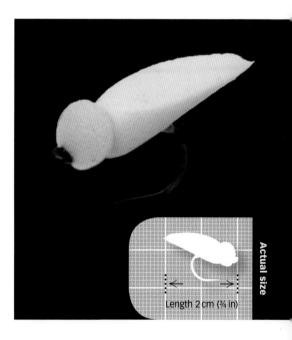

Actual size

Length 2 cm (¾ in)

Materials

Hook TMC 206BL, size 12 or 14
Thread UNI size 6/0, light cahill yellow
Body Closed-cell foam, 4 mm (⅛ in) in diameter
Adhesive Alpha Mate
Coating Nail polish

How to tie

1 Wrap the thread tightly from the eye to the bend and back two-thirds of the way towards the eye.

2 Cut the foam diagonally and tie it in where the thread stops.

3 After the fifth wrap, pass the thread under the rear of the foam and trim it, without making a knot.

4 Invert the fly and apply the instant adhesive to the thread wraps.

5 Coat the bottom of the foam that will come in contact with the water with nail polish.

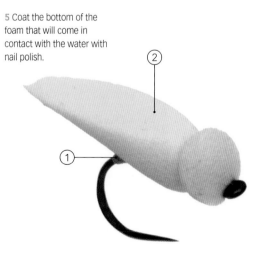

Lawrence Finney

Finney Woven Wire Nymph

What kind of spark does it take to create something new? Sometimes it takes dynamite; at other times, a simple conversation will do. Whenever fly tiers gather there is discussion aplenty to spark the creative juices.

Materials

Hook Kamasan B170, size 10

Silk Size 8/0, black

Tail and wingcase Cock pheasant tail fibres

Body UTC 0.2 mm wire, silver and gold

Flash Peacock Mylar

Lawrence Finney owns Finney's Flies in Moira, County Armagh, Ireland. In addition to his expertise behind the vice, he has fished the rivers and lakes of Ireland, from the River Lagan for brown trout to the River Mourne for wild salmon, the Whitewater for sea trout and Irish loughs such as the Erne, Sheelin, Corrib and Conn.

The wire woven pattern was developed in 2009 at the Spring Fly Fair in Newark, Nottinghamshire. Lawrence was talking with other tiers about how lead-wrapped Hare's Ears had a tendency to get ropy, with the lead eventually showing through the dubbing. It occurred to him to design a pattern that used weighted materials for the body: coloured wire was his choice of material.

He wove wires around hooks, creating a multitude of variations. By using cock pheasant tail fibres as a wingcase and legs, he improved the patterns. Brightly coloured patterns such as the teal blue and silver nymph have taken the east coast of Ireland by storm and accounted for record numbers of sea trout.

The main reason why these patterns work is that the woven wire gives a unique segmented effect to the body and also creates a weight that sinks it at a fast rate. The result is ideal for getting down deep at the head and tail of pools.

How to tie

1 At the bend, tie in the pheasant tail fibres as a tail.

2 Tie in two different colours of wire, then whip finish to enable the weave; in this case, the wires are silver and gold for the mayfly nymph. Have the silver wire facing towards you and the gold wire facing away.

3 Bring the gold wire over the silver and under the hook.

4 Now bring the silver wire over the hook.

5 Bring the gold wire under the hook, over the silver wire and back under the hook, so that the wire faces away from you. Repeat this three-quarters of the way along the hook to give a gold segmented effect on the top and a silver segmented effect under the hook.

6 Start the thread ahead of the abdomen. Tie in some peacock Mylar.

7 Tie in a bunch of cock pheasant feather fibres with the tips facing towards the bend, just slightly beyond the tail, and build a bit of a thorax with the tying thread.

8 Bring the cock pheasant fibres forward and tie in securely to form the wingcase.

9 Divide the fibres in half, tie back one half and secure them at the side as legs. Do the same with the other half on the opposite side.

10 Pull the Mylar over the thorax and tie down.

11 Whip finish and cement the head.

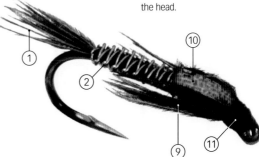

Fox Statler

Fox's Mudbug

Fox Statler, from Salem, Arkansas, has been guiding the White River and the North Fork of the White for over 20 years. He does his research before he develops his flies, and this pattern for big trout is no exception.

Materials

Hook Daiichi 1750, sizes 4–8
Thread UNI size 8/0, green
Weight .035 mm lead wire
Back and tail Medium olive Swiss Straw
Antennae Two mini speckled olive tarantula legs
Pinchers Golden pheasant body feathers dyed olive
Eyes Gold I-Balz
Body Tan sparkle yarn
Legs Four medium speckled yellow centipede legs

Big fish often eat scary things like big crayfish that will draw blood if they get the chance. Fox Statler observed how often trout ate big crayfish and figured out how to take advantage of what he learned. The resulting

Mudbug is a pattern with lots of movement to entice larger trout. Unlike many of the more static crayfish imitations, the Mudbug is constructed to wave the 'free lunch' banner in front of big, hungry trout.

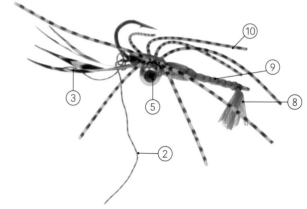

How to tie

1 Start the thread at the beginning of the hook bend. Tie in the Swiss Straw on the inside of the hook bend in the centre.

2 On the back of the hook, tie in the two strands of centipede legs about 5 cm (2 in) from one end, making four antennae – two antennae 5 cm (2 in) long and two antennae 2.5 cm (1 in) long.

3 Tie in the two golden pheasant body feathers for the pinchers so that they hang off the hook bend on each side.

4 Wrap six wraps of wire onto the hook shank for the body.

5 Tie in the appropriate size of I-Balz at the base of the pinchers. Before gluing the eyes, move the lead wire up against the eyes and secure with thread.

6 Remove the pattern from the vice, lay it on a flat surface with the hook point up, and adjust the hook so that it is perpendicular to the eyes. This adjustment will ensure that the pattern runs hook point up.

7 Tie in the sparkle yarn just behind the lead wire, then wrap the thread to the hook eye.

8 Tie in the Swiss Straw tail at the hook eye.

9 Wrap the sparkle yarn over the lead wire around the eyes and the base of the pinchers, then reverse directions and wrap the yarn to the hook eye. Tie off and trim.

10 Wrap the thread forward until just in front of the eyes. Rotate the vice so that the hook point is on top. Tie in the four medium strands of centipede legs material centred over the eyes. Use a 'crossing' pattern to make four legs of equal lengths. The thread should end up just behind the eyes of the pattern.

11 Open the Swiss Straw so that it will cover the back,

making the outside shell. Bring the straw over the back and place the first wrap of thread just behind the eyes. Advance the thread so that the second wrap of the thread over the straw is at the end of the lead wire. Then continue wrapping the thread over the straw, segmenting the remainder of the body and tail. Trim the straw at the hook eye and whip finish between the tail and the hook eye.

12 Open the tail of the mudbug to form a wide, flapper tail. Coat all the straw with glue.

Length 6.5 cm (2½ inches)

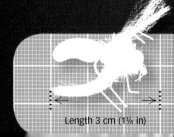

Actual size

Length 3 cm (1¼ in)

Paul van den Driesche

Foam Wasp

Paul van den Driesche is an innovative fly tier from the Netherlands. Foam Wasp is a semi-realistic dry fly.

Materials

Hook TMC 2487, size 10

Silk Size 6/0, black

Body Black and yellow craft foam, 1 mm (1/32 in) thick, strung on about 7.5 cm (3 in) of monofilament

Legs Yellow broom bristles

Thorax Yellow ostrich herl with yellow craft foam over the ostrich

Wings White floating yarn

Feelers Thin broom bristles or monofilament

Adhesives Bug-Bond and Superglue

Marker pen Permanent black

Equipment UV light

Having started out as an exact imitation 'show fly', the construction of the Foam Wasp requires many detailed steps. Paul recommends this pattern for stocked trout in reservoirs on sunny days.

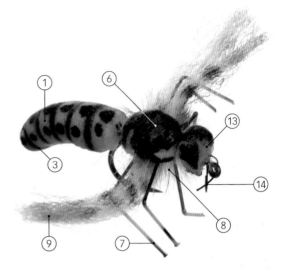

How to tie

1 Use a belt hole punch to make six yellow and five black foam disks. String them on 1.8-kg (4-lb) monofilament in alternating colours. Leave 1–2 mm (1/32–1/16 in) of monofilament sticking out of the last small yellow disk for a stinger.

2 Use Superglue to glue the disks together.

3 Using a black marker pen, draw a thin line on the topside of the body and small dots on the side on each yellow disk.

4 Apply Bug-Bond over the disks to seal the colour.

5 At the bend, tie the monofilament on the hook to make an extended body.

6 At the same point, tie in a strip of yellow foam, 4 mm (1/8 in) wide and 2.5 cm (1 in) long, extending to the back of the hook.

7 Tie in three broom bristles on the bottom side of the hook for the legs.

8 Tie in a yellow ostrich herl in between the first two pairs of legs.

9 Tie in a 5-cm (2-in) strand of floating yarn just behind the front legs. The floating yarn should be tied in the middle, so that one strand creates both wings.

10 Tie in another ostrich fibre and hackle, and wrap them in front of the legs, making a furry thorax.

11 Fold the foam strip over the thorax, tie it down right in front of the front legs, and cut off the surplus. This should push the wings sideways; with a little pull, they should extend to the back of the fly.

12 Leave about 2 mm (1/16 in) of space behind the eye of the hook at this point.

13 Make a head from one extra yellow foam disk. Make a cut straight through the middle to about three-quarters of the way up, so that both sides stay attached to each other. Then cut away a tiny piece from both sides of the cut at an angle, so that you end up with a triangular shape with a rounded top and a cut from the bottom to about three-

quarters up to the top of the disk. With a little imagination, you can see the shape of a head and the jaws of the wasp. Open up this cut with tweezers and place the disk over the hook shank at a 90-degree angle. The round top should be on top of the shank. Secure the disk with a drop of Superglue.

14 To make the feelers, repeat the same process as for the legs (see step 7).

15 Coat the foam on the thorax with Bug-Bond and put a drop in between the head and the thorax to secure the head capsule. Cure with UV light.

Giuseppe Re

Gold Bead Krystal CDC

Early-season flies need some flash to trigger a strike. Standards such as the Pheasant Tail Nymph and Gold Ribbed Hare's Ear are used everywhere that trout are found. The Gold Bead Krystal CDC is a flashy replacement for these standard patterns, but with a look all of its own.

Actual size

Length 3 cm (1¼ in)

Giuseppe Re owns the Nymphomania School. As the name may or may not suggest, Giuseppe is big on nymphs.

He was looking for a nymph to use at the beginning of the season. Normally, a stonefly pattern is the best choice – but not in Italy.

A plentiful nymph in freestone rivers is the clinging nymph. Giuseppe chose to imitate these and began thinking about a flashy form. The main feature is the flash wing, which grabs the fish's attention. The amount of flash is enough and that's why he does not include the gold ribbing found in the Hare's Ear. The tungsten gold bead provides weight and more flash. The addition of the CDC feather gives the fly more movement and traps micro air bubbles. The two different colour tones of the dubbing and the wide silhouette of the fly give a good impressionistic imitation of the real insect.

This pattern has been extremely successful with rainbow trout and has been tested in many rivers all over Europe and the US.

Materials

Hook Standard wet fly, sizes 8–14

Thread Danville size 6/0, tan

Head Gold tungsten bead

Weight Lead wire sized to hook

Tail Brown hackle fibres

Abdomen Light-coloured hare dubbing

Wing Pearl Hareline Ice Dub

Thorax Dark-coloured hare dubbing

Collar Natural-coloured CDC feather

How to tie

1 Slide the bead onto the hook.

2 Cover the hook shank with wraps of lead wire and push it into the end of the bead.

3 Cover the lead wraps with thread to form a smooth body.

4 At the bend, tie in brown hackle fibres as a tail longer than the hook shank.

5 Dub light hare dubbing and wind it, creating an abdomen three-quarters of the way to the bead.

6 Tie in Ice Dub as a wing. Trim it so that it reaches the bend of the hook.

7 Dub a spiky thorax of dark hare dubbing. Wrap it ahead of the wing.

8 Ahead of the thorax, tie in a CDC feather by the tip. Make three wraps. Tie off.

John Gordon

Gordon's BWO Hackle Stacker

John Gordon wanted to improve his odds on blue-winged olive (BWO) rivers across the Rocky Mountains in the U.S. and Canada. What he developed will work on all species of trout anywhere that BWOs are found.

John, from Colorado Springs, Colorado, wanted a fly that did not float high but would sit in and dimple the surface film. This pattern represents an insect as it is hatching – the stage between emerger and dun. Because of the fly's pronounced thorax, it sits in and dimples the surface. From a fish's point of view, it has a different 'footprint' in the surface film and makes for an easy target.

This pattern is fished as a dry fly with floatant and a longer leader. This fly can be hard to see and distinguish among the naturals on the water. If you have difficulty locating your fly on the water, you can use two flies – a high-visibility parachute for ease of sighting and a trailing Hackle Stacker, 60 cm (2 ft) below.

Actual size

Length 1.5 cm (⅝ in)

Materials

Hook Tiemco 900BL, size 20

Thread UNI size 8/0, olive dun

Tail Coq de Leon, medium pardo

Abdomen Kreinik silk dubbing, olive

Wing post 7x mono tippet

Wing Whiting grizzly saddle hackle

Thorax Kreinik silk dubbing, olive

Head UNI size 8/0, olive dun

How to tie

1 Create a small thread ball above the hook barb. Then tie in five to seven Coq de Leon feather fibres for tailing.

2 Place a very small amount of olive silk dubbing for the abdomen. Wrap about two-thirds of the hook length towards the eye.

3 Double over 15–18 cm (6–7 in) of 7x tippet, creating a loop. Tie in the two tag ends well and add a drop of head cement. This will be your post.

4 Tie a saddle hackle on the side away from you, parachute style. The 7x mono tippet will become the post. To hold the post up, insert one finger inside the mono loop. Use a saddle hackle: the stem on a neck hackle is too thick and will not wrap as well.

5 Starting at the base and working your way up the mono post for about four wraps, wrap the hackle anticlockwise, then work three wraps back down the post. Tie off and trim the hackle as close as possible.

6 Dub a large thorax, using olive silk dubbing. You want the thorax to be round and very tight. Build up a nice, tight ball by creating an x pattern when wrapping the dubbing.

7 Pull the monofilament post forward over the thorax. Stroke back the hackle fibres and place a few thread wraps to secure the monofilament post in front of the eye. Pull the monofilament post to tighten the hackle over the dubbing-ball thorax. Do your final tie-off and trim off the remaining post.

8 Add a little olive silk dubbing for a head and whip finish.

David Murray-Orr

CDC Emerger

Improving a fly pattern, like building a better mouse trap, will have people busting down your door. In this case, David Murray-Orr's door is in New Zealand, on the Mataura River, NZ's only true 'match the hatch' river, in the province of Southland.

On the Mataura River, brown and rainbow trout feed mainly just in and under the surface film. They look as though they are feeding off the top but they are, in fact, feeding on the emerging nymphs. David wets the body so that it sinks in the film and is supported by the CDC. Trout take it as an emerger or even as a dun, so it covers a number of different bases.

David said another guide used to fish this fly in the English shuttlecock style, but it was difficult to see. He lifted the wing and cut the butts off to form a shoulder. The result was easier to see, and for that reason the trout picked it up earlier because of the higher wing profile. The shoulder also floated it better.

David fishes it during a dun hatch; some trout will take it as a dun, but mostly the trout are feeding on the emergers. David reports that when the trout are taking duns, they will also take emergers – but when they are on the emergers, they won't look at the duns.

Materials

Hook Tiemco 900BL, size 16 or 18
Thread UNI size 8/0, black
Body Dubbed hare's ear
Wing Three mallard CDC feathers

How to tie

1 Tie in the thread and wind to the tail of the hook.

2 Dub the body up to near the hook eye and form a small thorax.

3 Place three CDC feathers on top of each other and tie in just in front of the thorax.

4 Lift the wing and do several turns behind the eye and in front of the wing to make the wing stand up at about 45 degrees.

5 Tie off either behind or in front of the wing.

6 Trim the butts to form a shoulder.

7 Trim the wing and slightly shape, as in a mayfly wing.

Giuseppe Re

Grayling Jig Fly

Innovation is where you find it. The Grayling Jig Fly is a style rather than a specific pattern. Its colours and sizes can be changed to meet your nymphing needs anywhere that grayling are found.

The most interesting aspect of this fly is the use of a jig hook, which allows the fly to swim upside down. This particular feature lets the fly fishermen fish very close to the bottom. Most importantly, it almost never hangs up on the bottom structure.

Giuseppe's dressing is very impressionistic and can imitate a variety of insects. He prefers to use it in relatively small sizes and in light colours. The specific colour of the dubbing mix used for this fly has been tested for a long time and it works better than other colour combinations. It probably imitates small caddis larvae or other light-coloured nymphs.

Giuseppe has also used this pattern in Slovenia and Austria. He keeps one box dedicated to this fly and has been rewarded with hundreds of grayling.

Actual size

Length 2 cm (¾in)

Materials

Hook Jig hook, sizes 12–16
Thread Size 8/0, red
Bead Gold
Tail Pheasant tail fibres
Body Cream fur mixed with a little yellow flash
Rib Fine silver tinsel
Thorax Coarse brown fur

How to tie

1 Slide a gold bead onto the hook and start the thread behind the bead.

2 Wrap a thread base to the bend.

3 Tie in the tail equal to the overall hook length.

4 Tie in the silver tinsel at the bend.

5 Dub and wrap the body to the bead.

6 Wrap five turns of tinsel and tie off.

7 Dub the brown fur and wrap a thorax, keeping the guard hairs sticking out.

8 Finish the fly with several wraps of red thread showing behind the bead.

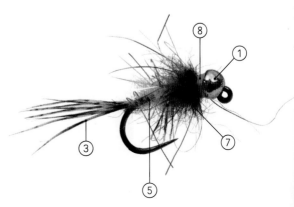

Mikael Högberg Robertsdotter

Grey and Blue Zonker

Mikael Högberg Robertsdotter, from Sweden, developed this fly for early-season fishing in both lakes and ponds. It is especially effective for browns and rainbows in the still waters of Fisklösa and Sundsjön.

50% size

Length 7 cm (2¾ in)

Mikael needed a pattern for the spring when the water is coldest. The zonker strip and soft gadwall fibres move enticingly, even when retrieved very slowly. Mikael fishes the Grey and Blue Zonker on a slow-sinking line. He attaches the fly to the short tippet with a loop, so that it can move around freely. His retrieve is short pulls separated by pauses, giving the lethargic trout time to take the fly.

Testing this pattern convinced him of its effectiveness. While on his home water, he made two consecutive casts and landed two fish. That day he caught and released six trout, each weighing 1 kg (2¼ lb) or more – not bad for a cold, spring day with an experimental fly.

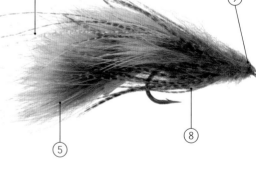

Materials

Hook Maruto 177, sizes 8–10

Thread UNI size 8/0, grey

Rib UNI French oval silver tinsel, XS

Wing Hends Z-11 zonker strip rabbit fur, grey

Body UV Ice Dub grey, Oracle Flash dub F3-600 515, and Adams Fly Rite dub #26 grey

Flash Four pieces of smolt blue Krystal Flash

Hackle Gadwell feathers

How to tie

1 Wrap a thread base to the hook bend.

2 Tie in the tinsel at the bend.

3 Tie in the rabbit-fur strip behind the eye.

4 Dub the mixed body fur with flash. Wrap a body forward, behind the rabbit-fur strip.

5 Pull the rabbit-fur strip back over the body and tie down at the bend, with the remainder sticking out beyond the hook.

6 Wind the tinsel forward, over the rabbit-fur strip, with five well-spaced turns. Separate the rabbit fibres out of the way at each place the tinsel crosses the rabbit strip, so that none of the rabbit fibres are caught under the tinsel.

7 Tie in the flash, making it the same length as the wing.

8 Tie in and wrap two turns of the hackle feather.

9 Dub a small head from the body materials and tie off.

Howard Henley

Howard's Fly

You're out fishing and some elephants come wading in and make the water all muddy. Don't you just hate it when that happens? Now what do you do? Well, Howard Henley from Nyeri, Kenya, has just the solution.

Howard's Fly was originally tied with the idea of incorporating a lot of white and black, because two favourite flies in most Kenyan waters are the Kenya bug (black) and the coachman (white). Henry and his clients use this fly for rainbow trout when all else fails.

Henry's son tied this pattern at a very young age, and he amazed everybody with its success. Family fishing trips were most often in the rivers that originate in the Aberdare Mountains. Elephant, buffalo, rhino and lion are all present near these rivers. On this particular day, elephants waded in and they muddied the waters. Howard was not to be discouraged and he continued using the largest fly in his box. (Most of my friends run like little girls if the bugs get too thick. I can only imagine what they'd do if an elephant showed up.) Howard fished on and was rewarded with a brown trout weighing 900 g (2 lb).

Actual size

Length 3 cm (1¼ in)

Materials

Hook Size 10 long shank nymph
Thread Size 8/0, black
Head Gold bead
Tail White ostrich tail or wing feather
Weight Thin lead wire
Body Black ostrich feather
Rib Live Glow
Wing White ostrich tail or wing feather

How to tie

1 Slide a gold bead onto the hook.

2 Lay down a thread base.

3 Tie in a tail of white ostrich feather.

4 Tie in a length of Live Glow at the bend.

5 Wrap a thin underbody of lead wire.

6 Tie in a black ostrich feather and wrap it forward, making a body.

7 Rib the body with Live Glow.

8 Tie in a wing of white ostrich. Trim the excess.

9 Make a head and cement.

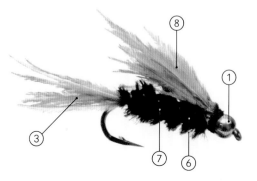

Juan Ramirez

Juan's Hopper

The relatively recent development of foam-bodied flies has resulted in patterns looking like insects affected by nuclear contamination. While their size and shape are the stuff of horror films, there is no arguing with their trout-catching ability.

Juan Ramirez guides for the Angler's Covey in Colorado Springs, Colorado, and designs flies for the Montana Fly Company. When he talks, it's worth paying attention.

Juan had five criteria in mind as he developed this pattern. It had to be his own, and not a slight variation of existing patterns; simple and attractive; buoyant enough to float not only a heavy hook, but also a tungsten dropper fly; visible to clients even under low light conditions; and durable enough to stand up to many fish before coming apart.

He uses this pattern from early spring to late autumn. It serves as an indicator in the spring in low, clear water. Juan always drops another fly off the back of the hopper. He uses a heavy tungsten dropper, representing the seasonal bug or bugs, and later follows that with a midge or smaller mayfly nymph.

As the season progresses and water levels fluctuate, Juan changes the droppers accordingly. As more fish look to the surface, more fish eat the dry fly. As more stoneflies appear, more fish are taken on the surface. He often fishes a stonefly nymph dropper at this time in order to double his chances.

Materials

Hook TMC 5262, 2x long hopper hook
Thread UTC 140 denier, tan
Body Tan and brown 2 mm (¹⁄₁₆ in) foam, two pieces of each, Chernobyl taper
Underwing Mottled web Montana Fly Company wing material, stonefly wing cut
Flash Midge-sized pearl Krystal Flash
Wing Cow elk hair
Legs Barred round rubber legs
Indicator Hot pink Gator Hair
Adhesive Krazy Glue

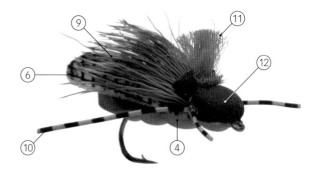

How to tie

1 Wrap a thread base from the eye to the bend.

2 Pierce through the tan foam and tie it in at the bend. The tail extends 6 mm (¼ in) beyond the bend. Glue the foam to the hook.

3 Lay the brown foam on top of the shank and secure with four thread wraps in the same spot as before, making sure that the tips of both foam strips match in length. Add a drop of glue to the thread wraps.

4 Advance the thread one-third of the distance towards the eye and make a second segment of the body. Glue the thread wraps as before.

5 Advance the thread and make the third segment. Glue as before.

6 Tie in an underwing of web material that extends to the end of the foam-body tips.

7 Advance the thread to the hook eye and form the head. Cut a small hole in the brown foam. Wrap it in place with thread.

8 Tie in the pearl Krystal Flash.

9 Tie in the elk-hair wing.

10 Tie in rubber legs on each side.

11 Tie in some Gator Hair as an indicator.

12 Pull the brown foam over the head and secure it with thread and glue.

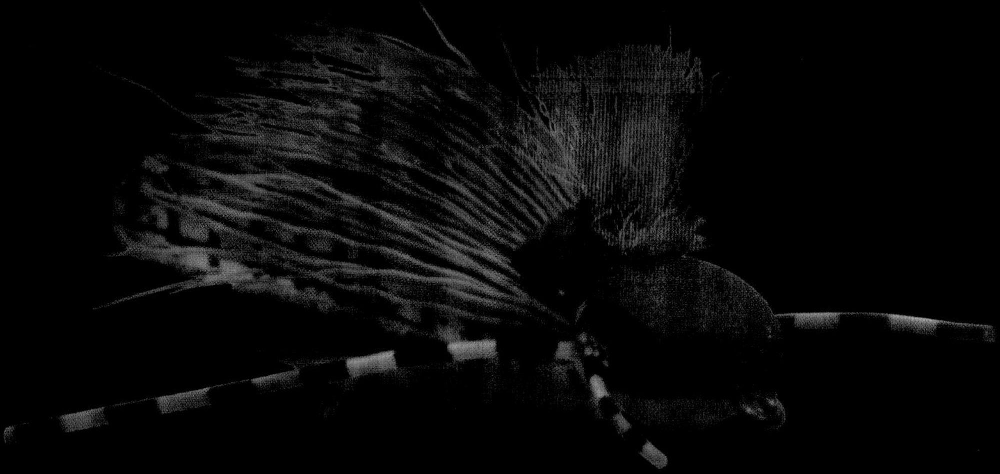

Actual size

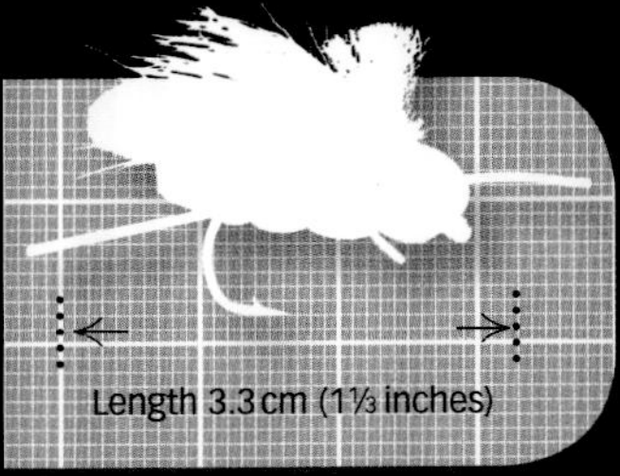

Gary Hyde

Horsehair Klinkhammer

What's old is new again. Once upon a time fly tiers were limited to natural materials, one of which was horsehair. Now, Gary Hyde of West Yorkshire Fly Fishing Services is once again making use of this plentiful material.

Gary says the use of a lighter-coloured thread – for example, yellow – can give a much paler appearance to the fly and works well when imitating a yellow mayfly or yellow sally.

Horsehair is a great material, giving a nice, segmented body on the fly. It's especially good on the Klinkhammer, as it doesn't easily absorb water, thus keeping the fly very buoyant.

Gary reports on one of his best days fishing using the Horsehair Klinkhammer and tungsten-head nymph combination. He was fishing for grayling on the River Nidd, a river in the Yorkshire Dales. It was a very cold day and his rod rings kept freezing up. However, he had over 60 fish – mostly on the nymph, but a surprisingly large percentage took the Horsehair Klinkhammer.

Actual size

Length 6mm (¼ in)

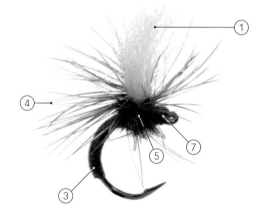

Materials

Hook Tiemco 212Y, sizes 21–15

Thread UNI size 8/0, olive or black

Wing post Polypropylene

Body Horsetail hair dyed olive or black

Hackle Saddle grizzle, olive or black

Thorax Peacock herl

How to tie

1 Tie in the wing post just back from the eye of the hook, then tie in the horsehair just below the wing post and secure to the hook.

2 Wrap thread over the horsehair to the bend and back up to the wing post.

3 Wind the horsehair back up the hook, using touching turns back up to the wing post, then tie off and secure with the thread.

4 Tie in the grizzle hackle directly behind the wing

post on the shank side of the hook.

5 Tie in the peacock herl, also behind the wing post. Wrap the peacock herl around the hook, three turns behind the wing post and one in front. Trim.

6 Wind the grizzle up the wing post, making four turns.

7 Finish by wrapping a small thread head.

Kelly Laatsch

Laatsch's Attractor Stone Fly

A British Columbia forest ranger once told me to fish only close to the bridge and not to walk through the stream-side woods. Why? Because there were grizzlies with cubs in the woods. From that point on, I couldn't tell you if my dry flies floated or not: it's hard to fish looking over your shoulder.

However, Kelly Laatsch from Kimberley, British Columbia, owner of the St. Mary Angler Fly Shop, did pay attention. He noticed that traditional stonefly patterns did not float very well in rough water, so he added foam to increase floatability.

The early July stonefly hatches come off when the water is often high and rough from spring run-off. Kelly has used this trout pattern on the St. Mary and Elk rivers. It will work on most free stone rivers in your area, too.

One reason for the Attractor Stone Fly's success is that you can add quite a bit of movement to give it the look of a real stonefly fluttering on the surface. Kelly finds that you have to move the fly quite a bit to get the trout's attention. But when they hit, there's nothing gentle about the take – so be sure your tippet is sized accordingly. His favourite tactic is to cast along the shore edges and skitter the fly over the deeper water.

This durable pattern is adaptable and can be tied to imitate many different stoneflies.

Actual size

Length 4.5 cm (1¾ inches)

Materials

Hook Tiemco 2302, size 6
Thread Size 6/0, brown
Body Brown foam
Overbody Pink foam
Legs Tan and brown/ white round rubber
Post High visibility yellow foam
Flash Gold Crystal Flash

How to tie

1 Lay down a thread base.

2 At the hook bend, tie on the brown foam.

3 Lay four pieces of gold Crystal Flash on top.

4 Cover the brown foam with pink foam. Tie down.

5 Advance the thread.

6 Pull the brown and pink foam forward and tie down.

7 Repeat steps 5 and 6, creating two more segments.

8 Between the third and fourth segments tie two lengths of tan and brown/ white round rubber legs.

9 On top of the legs, tie on a post of high visibility yellow foam.

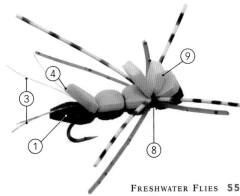

Adrian Pop

Olive Epoxy Minnow

You would expect a national fly-tying champion to develop something exciting. Adrian Pop, from Romania, does not disappoint. His Olive Epoxy Minnow has landed several species of fish, and its durability is proof of his careful development efforts.

Adrian created this fly after noticing many small, iridescent minnows being chased by gamefish. He happened to be on Gilau Lake, home of trout, chub and perch, all of which have taken the Olive Epoxy Minnow.

Adrian wanted to develop a minnow that looked very natural. He noticed several characteristics of Gilau Lake's small minnows: nearly transparent bodies, lots of shine and prominent eyes.

Following some experimentation, he tied this fly. In two hours he caught one trout, three chub and seven perch. This gave him confidence in the pattern. He went on to develop a range of colours that work well for different predatory fish. He had the best success imitating trout minnows with black, olive or blue backs. Each colour was accomplished by using different colours of dyed calf tail.

Materials

Hook Varivas wet fly hook, sizes 6–14

Thread UNI size 6/0, olive dun

Tail Orvis Spectrablend dubbing, olive

Monofilament 1.8-kg (4-lb) test

Dorsal band Calf tail dyed olive

Ventral band Calf tail dyed orange

Body Silver holographic tinsel

Coating Fast-curing epoxy glue

Eyes Hend's Epoxy Eyes

How to tie

1 Tie in the tail made from Spectrablend dubbing.

2 Tie in the monofilament at the tail.

3 Tie in eight olive calf-tail fibres on the upper part of the hook, at the bend, with the natural ends extending past the bend of the hook.

4 Repeat step 3 on the bottom of the hook with eight orange calf-tail fibres.

5 Tie in holographic tinsel at the tail and wrap it forward over the calf-tail fibres, stopping at the hook eye. Take care to keep the olive fibres on top and the orange fibres on the bottom.

6 Wrap the monofilament forward over the calf-tail fibres and tinsel.

7 Make a small head from the tying thread.

8 Use fast-curing epoxy glue to secure the eyes on each side of the fly. Applying the eyes before the final step makes it easier to form the epoxy into the desired shape.

9 Cover the entire fly with fast-curing epoxy glue, shaping it into a teardrop shape that is wide at the head and tapers towards the tail.

Mick Hall

Red-Orange Spinner

In the Central Highlands of Tasmania lies a World Heritage Area that contains more than 3,000 small interlocking lakes and tarns, all of which contain wild brown trout. The lakes are shallow and the trout feed along the shorelines. At times they are so close to the shore that their backs are out of the water!

This pattern is the spinner stage of the Aussie March Brown. The male is slightly darker than the female and has a reddish hue. The female is a true orange, with both sexes being approximately the same size.

Mick Hall says they actually swarm out over the surface during the day to mate, rather than forming columns as you would normally expect. They often become prey to dragonflies, swallows and ducks, as well as trout. They are more active on still days, and if the wind comes up they go to ground, hiding in streamside foliage.

Mick is well known in the international fly-fishing community. He is a pro Team Member for Mustad of Norway, Jarvis Walker and Whiting Farms. He also worked with the Enrico Puglisi Company to develop EP Trigger Point. He has also been invited several times to judge international fly-tying competitions in various countries.

Actual size

Length 3 cm (1¼ in)

Materials

Hook Mustad R72 2x long, sizes 12–14

Thread Black 6/0

Wings Quick Silver Enrico Puglisi Trigger Point fibres

Tail Medium Pardo Coq de Leon fibres

Body hackle Light brown Whiting Farms hackle size 18 or smaller, four turns

Body Spirit River Golden Stone dubbing

Hackle Whiting Farms saddle hackle, furnace for the male and light brown for the female

How to tie

1 Wrap a thread base from the eye of the hook to the bend.

2 Tie in the wings near the eye, keeping them sparse so that they are translucent.

3 Tie in ten stiff Coq de Leon hackle fibres at the bend.

4 Behind the wings, tie in the body hackle by the tip.

5 Dub a body and wrap it forward to the wings.

6 Tie in the hackle behind the wings and make four turns.

7 Take three turns of saddle hackle behind the wings and three turns in front of the wings.

8 Make a small thread head and finish.

Paul van den Driesche

Loop Fly

Three-dimensional baitfish imitations are more effective than two-dimensional imitations such as streamers, which appear flat when seen straight on. The three-dimensional ones are effective because they look like something good to eat, regardless of the angle from which they're seen.

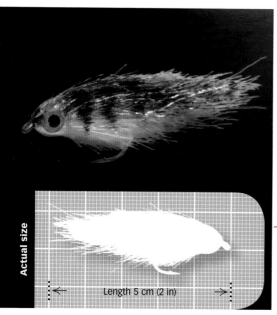

Actual size

Length 5 cm (2 in)

Paul van den Driesche represents the epitome of innovation in fly tying. His new use of braided body material can be adapted to any streamer imitation you can imagine. The result of his Loop Fly is a large, lightweight fly that can be cast with ease.

Paul uses his pattern in the River Kyll in Germany for trout but, because it represents a mouthful, it can be used to attract any predatory species.

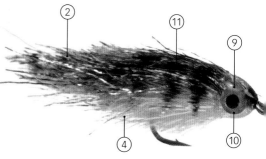

Materials

Hook Saltwater stainless steel, sizes 1–5
Thread Size 4/0, black
Body Blue, silver and pearl Bill's Bodi-braid
Eyes 3D, sized to the hook
Head Bug-Bond over thread
Marker Permanent black pen
Equipment UV light

How to tie

1 At the bend in the hook, tie in a length of blue Bodi-braid, but do not cut it from the spool.

2 Create a loop extending well over the bend of the hook and tie down a little further along the shank. The size of the loop that extends beyond the bend will determine the length of the fly.

3 Tie down two more loops along the shank to the eye, making each loop a little smaller than the previous one.

4 Tie in a strand of silver Bodi-braid where the blue was first tied in on the top of the shank and a length of pearl Bodi-braid under the shank. Repeat the looping process described earlier.

5 When you reach the eye of the hook, whip finish and trim the three Bodi-braids.

6 Now cut each loop just a little off the centre of the loop, to create different lengths; this helps to create a nice taper in the fly.

7 When all the loops are cut, comb out all the strands with a fairly fine comb. You will have blue on top, over silver, with pearl under the hook.

8 Trim the fibres into roughly the desired shape.

9 Hold all the fibres back and apply a drop of Bug-Bond on the head of the fly. Cure with UV light.

10 Place the eyes in position. Apply another thin coat of Bug-Bond to seal the eyes and fill any gaps.

11 Trim away any unwanted fibres and draw some bars on the top with a permanent marker.

Rok Lustrik

Lustrik Nymph

Ready for a change of pace? How about the marble trout? This rare species is found in Slovenia's Julian Alps. Slovenia is located east of Italy and south of Austria. Rok Lustrik and his nine guides can set you up with a trip to a heretofore little-fished region of Europe.

This fly evolved from a dry fly that was quite successful for marble trout, but Rok wanted to fish the deeper pools where the fish were laying on the bottom.

Rok believes that the success of this fly is due to its visible segmentation, which is accomplished by keeping the dubbing sparse over the lead wire. In addition, the weight of this pattern allows it to get deep where the trout are holding. As a bonus, the silver bead shows well in off-coloured water.

The success of this pattern was proven on the crystal-clear Sava River. Rok and a friend were catching fish, but not quite as successfully as they thought they could. Rok put on the Lustrik Nymph test pattern and was amazed to watch the fish as they moved far to get to the fly. Other patterns had to be put exactly in front of the trout, but the Lustrik Nymph was drawing them in from a distance.

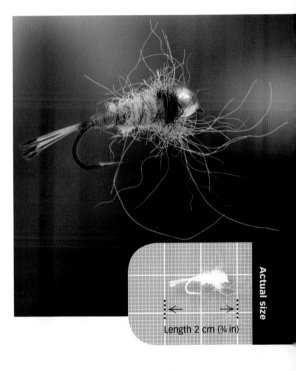

Actual size

Length 2 cm (¾ in)

Materials

Hook Hayabusa 372, size 10
Thread Size 8/0, pink
Bead Silver tungsten
Weight Thin lead wire
Tail Golden pheasant tippets
Thorax Alsatian (German shepherd) dog hair, light and dark
Rib Copper wire

How to tie

1 Slide a tungsten bead onto the hook.

2 Lay down a thread base.

3 Tie in golden pheasant tippets as the tail.

4 Tie in lead wire and copper wire at the bend.

5 Wrap the lead wire almost to the bead.

6 Make an abdomen of pink thread.

7 Start the thorax with light-coloured Alsatian dog hair, keeping it sparse.

8 Finish the thorax with dark-coloured Alsatian dog hair, keeping it sparse.

9 Rib with copper wire. Tie off and trim.

10 Finish with a thread head.

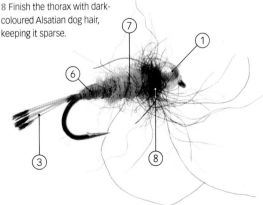

Pontus Eriksson

Flipside Mayfly

The form of this pattern follows its intended function – to quickly get deep in fast water where mayflies are found. The pattern is lightly dressed, so that it will not be swept away by rapid currents on its way to the bottom.

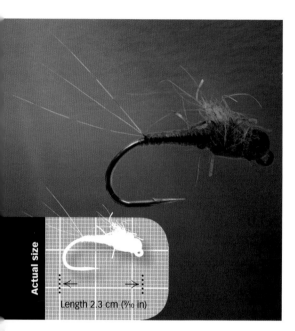

Actual size

Length 2.3 cm (⁹⁄₁₀ in)

Pontus Eriksson, from Sweden, says that there are two important ingredients that account for the Flipside Mayfly's seductiveness. First is the body quill used for the abdomen, which results in a more realistic, hollow, glowing appearance. Second, the thin Coq de Leon tail fibres do not catch any water. This allows for a quick descent to the bottom, resulting in longer fishing time during every drift.

Pontus reports the most effective technique for this fly is to fish it with a traditional Czech nymph style and a 2.7-kg (6-lb) leader tippet. Manipulation of the drift is best when the fly is fished no more than a rod's length away, giving greater control of depth and speed. Using a short line also means setting the hook is a quicker possibility. When you cannot wade any deeper but still have water that you want to cover, use a strike indicator to keep the fly from sinking too deep and getting stuck.

Materials

Hook Hends HJ120, sizes 8–14

Thread UNI size 8/0, black

Weight Tungsten bead head and lead wire

Tail Coq de Leon

Abdomen Hends BQ-10 body quills

Thorax back Flexi Body

Legs Flat black Diamond Braid

Thorax Natural hare's ear dubbing

How to tie

1 Put on four wraps of lead wire to build up the thorax. Secure it with thread wraps and continue wrapping until the shank is covered.

2 Tie in three Coq de Leon fibres as a tail, separating them with the tying thread and making them point at three different angles.

3 Wrap thread up and down the shank, with the thread making a smooth, tapered body up to the point where the wire is tied in. Clip off the tying thread.

4 Tie in the body quill and wrap towards the tail and back again, completely covering the thread underbody. Secure the body quill by tying in with thread.

5 Turn the hook over in the vice.

6 Tie in a 3–5-mm (⅛–³⁄₆₄-in) strip of Flexi Body, pointing towards the bend of the hook. It will be folded over the thorax later.

7 Clip the Diamond Braid so that you have loose fibres resembling legs, and mix it with some hare's ear dubbing. Build a dubbed thorax with this mixture.

8 Fold the strip of Flexi Body over the dubbed area and tie it in just behind the bead.

9 Make a whip finish and rough up the thorax with a dubbing brush.

Sacha Putz

Orange Angel

Sacha Putz from Hemer, Germany, likes the versatility of tube flies. He's not alone. Many Atlantic salmon fishers like the ability to remove a bent hook from a still serviceable fly. After all, there's the investment of time and materials in every fly – so why not get the most out of your time at the bench?

Sacha believes the fly is especially active, even in calmer currents, and this action is attractive to the salmon. His experience on the Morrun in Norway is one that he will long remember. Using the Orange Angel he hooked a fish and had it on for 15 minutes before he lost it. The following day, back at the same location, he hooked and landed an 8.6-kg (19-lb) fish. Another angler came by and Sacha asked him to take a picture of the fish. The angler said the fish had been caught before, because he saw the broken leader hanging from its mouth. On closer inspection, Sacha saw his Orange Angel in the fish's mouth. He had caught the same fish twice!

Length 10 cm (4 in)

50% size

Materials

Hook Ken Sawada treble, sized to the tube

Thread UTC Ultra, 70 denier, wood duck

Tube 2 mm (¹⁄₁₆ in) plastic inside a brass tube

Tag Fine silver tinsel and red UNI wool yarn

Body SLF dubbing, burnt orange

Ribbing UNI twisted silver tinsel and a light orange schlappen feather

Underwing Orange and red fox hair with shrimp-coloured Fluo Fibres, copper-coloured Angel Hair fibres and grizzly orange mottled marabou with two longer jungle cock at the side

Back hackle One dark orange schlappen hackle

Wing Orange fox hair with light brown tips, red Angel Hair fibres and shrimp-coloured Fluo Fibres

Front hackle Dark orange mottled marabou feather

Eyes Jungle cock feathers

How to tie

1 Tie in the tag of tinsel and red wool at the bend.

2 Wrap the body.

3 Wrap the ribbing.

4 Tie in the underwing and include a little flash.

5 Tie in the back hackle.

6 Add the main wing.

7 Add the front hackle.

8 Make a small thread head.

9 Tie in the jungle cock feathers on each side.

Pontus Eriksson

PCL Nymph

The combination of soft CDC fibres and stiff seal fur makes this pattern effective. The PCL Nymph is a generic style and can be adapted to imitate the colour of caddis naturals anywhere in the world.

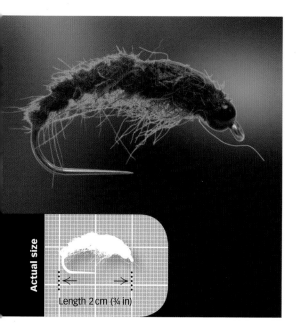

Actual size

Length 2 cm (¾ in)

Pontus Eriksson wanted an effective caddis nymph for trout in the fast streams of Sweden. Over the years, a couple of versions of this fly have been tied. During the process, Pontus has come to prefer CDC as abdomen material and seal fur as dubbing for the thorax. The seal fur fibres are transparent and quite stiff, and do not stick together when wet. The CDC abdomen holds air bubbles that give a lively appearance in the water. Too many flies look great dry, but when wet they can lose their volume and texture.

Pontus says PCL Nymphs are best fished on a short line with a Czech nymph style or by using a strike indicator at longer distances. A way to trigger fish with this fly is to lift it from the bottom with the Leisenring lift, to imitate a hatching caddis fly.

Lighter PCL Nymphs can be fished as standard nymphs. Letting this fly pattern drift just below the surface can also imitate a hatching caddis fly, a technique at its best when the fish is already actively eating hatching insects.

Materials

Hook Skalka G Czech nymph hook, sizes 8–12

Thread UNI size 8/0, black

Weight Small black tungsten bead

Rib Hends BQ-10 body quills

Abdomen Natural brown CDC

Thorax Seal dubbing (or substitute), black

Thorax shield Brown poly yarn

How to tie

1 Slide a tungsten bead onto the hook.

2 Wrap a thread base from the eye to halfway down the bend.

3 Tie in the rib at the bend.

4 Dub an abdomen of CDC and wrap halfway to the eye.

5 Wrap the rib forward and tie off at the front edge of the body. Trim off.

6 Tie in a length of brown poly yarn where the rib ends.

7 Dub a thorax with seal fur all the way to the bead, but leave a small gap for the final steps.

8 Fold the poly yarn over the thorax and secure it with thread wraps.

9 Rough up the CDC and seal dubbing. Trim the fibres so that they are longer in front and tapering to shorter at the rear.

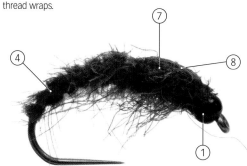

Nick Toldi

Peute

Talk about simplicity: how about a fly with just one material?
As a bonus, it has a remarkable story behind its name.

Nick Toldi, from Paris, France, describes the Peute as a dry fly to try when all else fails. It imitates nothing in particular, but has the characteristics of something alive. It may suggest several shapes of bugs, sedges or butterflies.

But what about its name? In the late 1940s, Henri Bresson was returning with a heavy fishing creel when he came upon a starving Gypsy fortuneteller and her daughter. Bresson offered the woman his fish. She was so grateful that she gave Henri an ugly fly. She explained that her father had been a famous poacher and this was the only pattern he used.

Some time later, Henri and his friend were having one of those days when nothing would entice the trout. Henri saved the day by using the fly gifted to him by the Gypsy. His friend could not believe that a *peute* (slang for stupid, ugly-looking, dirty – in other words, a really unattractive girl) could have saved the day.

Actual size

Length 2 cm (¾ inch)

Materials

Hook Orvis Premium or equivalent, size 14, 16 or 18
Thread Prewaxed size 6/0, light cahill yellow
Hackle Hen mallard breast feather

How to tie

1 Starting and ending at the eye, lay down a thread base.

2 Strip off the webby fibres of the hen mallard breast feather.

3 Tie it in by the tip.

4 Cut off the short ends of the tips that stick out from the thread.

5 Take three turns, wet fly style.

6 Pull all the fibres back towards the bend so that the fibres surround the hook shank. Tie off and trim.

7 Make a head at the tie-in point, so that the fibres are held in place as an envelope around the shank.

8 Whip finish.

9 Trim all the fibres at the same time, so that they end slightly beyond the rear of the bend.

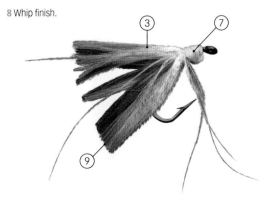

David Murray-Orr

Quill Emerger

David Murray-Orr, who owns Southland Flies & Guides in New Zealand, says that the Mataura River brown and rainbow trout can sometimes be so fussy that he needs to carry more than one style of emerger pattern.

Actual size

Length 2 cm (¾ in)

David says the trout in the Mataura River feed mainly on emergers and cripples in preference to the duns, so he is forever trying to come up with new emerger patterns. This fly represents a more advanced stage of the emerger.

The trailing CDC fibres are a good way to represent a shuck, as the body sinks into the surface film. The profile of this pattern in the water looks just like an emerging mayfly with its shuck still attached.

Timing is important in selecting a fly. David fishes it just before and during a dun hatch. Knowing when a hatch is about to begin is the sign of an accomplished guide. Guides base their 'guesses' on extensive experience in order to get their clients into fish.

Fishing the Quill Emerger involves no guessing. The penchant for selective trout to be fussy about sloppy drifts can be predicted. For this reason, David's creation must be fished upstream or across with a dead drift.

Materials

Hook Tiemco 2457, size 16 or 18
Thread UNI size 8/0, black
Body Stripped peacock herl
Wing and shuck Three CDC feathers
Thorax Dubbed hare's ear fur

How to tie

1 Tie in thread and wind just past the curve of the hook.

2 Tie in the stripped peacock herl and wind up to under where the thorax will be.

3 Tie in three CDC feathers, with the butts facing towards the eye.

4 Dub a thorax at this point.

5 Bring the CDC over the thorax, but let several loose fibres of CDC trail over the back of the hook to form the shuck.

6 Tie the CDC off in front of the thorax and then lift the CDC wing up by tying off in front of it and behind the eye.

7 Trim the CDC wing to suit and do the same for the shuck.

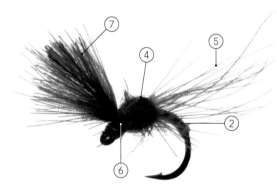

Leif Ehnström

Red Eye Corixa

How many of us have experimental flies that we never take the time to try out? Leif Ehnström had the good sense to try this pattern and now it is one of his go-to flies.

Leif lives in Sweden and fishes for rainbows, browns, grayling and Arctic char all over the country. His Red Eye Corixa is a water boatman imitation. Corixa are abundant in most of the still waters of Sweden and make up a major part of the fishes' diet.

Leif admits that he does not know much about the life patterns of Corixa, but he tied some imitations and they sat in his fly box, untried, for several years. Early one spring, Leif was casting streamers for rainbows on a small lake. With dusk approaching and no fish to show for several hours of casting, he saw some activity near shore and opened his fly box in anticipation of changing flies. He saw the little red eyes looking back up at him, so he tied one on. Five casts and five trout convinced him to keep using the experimental fly.

He fishes the Red Eye Corixa just under the surface with a very slow retrieve.

Actual size

Length 2 cm (¾ in)

Materials

Hook Mustad 94142, sizes 10–14

Thread Dyneema size 8/0, black

Eyes Amnesia line, red, melted

Weight Non-lead wire

Body Yellow acetate floss and acetone

Paddle legs Rubber legs

Back Hen saddle hackle, soft glue

Light Silver tinsel

Varnish Bug-Bond

How to tie

1 Melt the ends of red Amnesia line and tie them in just behind the hook eye for the eyes.

2 Tie in non-lead wire and wrap it around the front half of the hook shank.

3 Cover the whole body with acetate floss. The body should taper from thin at the tail to thicker near the eyes.

4 Put acetone over the floss, making the floss melt into acetate plastic.

5 While it is still soft, flatten the body using pliers.

6 At the midpoint of the body, tie in a pair of rubber legs.

7 Coat a hen saddle hackle with soft glue and tie in at the tail.

8 Tie in two pieces of silver tinsel at the same point.

9 Fold the hackle and tinsel over the back of the fly and tie in at the head.

10 Coat the back with Bug-Bond.

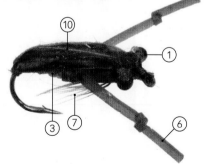

Pepe Perrone

Reversed Frog

Need a fly to awaken the predatory instincts of hunting fish? This is it. Although it was originally designed for tiger fish in Argentina's Pampas region, it can be tried anywhere larger fish cruise heavy cover in search of swimming frogs.

Materials

Hook Mustad 33632, size 10
Thread Size 6/0, orange
Weed guard 0.60 mm nylon monofilament
Tail Black marabou feather tips with Krystal Flash
Legs Orange hackle feathers
Body Spun and trimmed deer hair, dyed dark green and orange
Collar Untrimmed, spun deer hair, dyed olive
Head Spun and trimmed deer hair, dyed green and orange
Adhesive Instant glue

Pepe needed a fly for fish that are cruising in lagoons. Such locations always have ample vegetation, especially following flooding. Previously, existing flies could not be fished in such areas, because they were constantly hooking the vegetation. Pepe says the design for the Reversed Frog came to him in a dream.

The effectiveness of this pattern comes from its design, allowing it to be fished where frogs are found and predators hunt. When the fly is worked with small jerks, the head gives a tiny sound like that of a frog feeding on insects.

Pepe's preferred method is to cast from open water towards the shallows. A slight movement of the wrist is enough to make the fly sound off, but not enough to move it out of the target zone. The culmination is the explosive strike as the gamefish takes the frog in shallow water.

How to tie

1 At the bend of the hook, tie in the nylon monofilament with the loose end pointing past the bend.

2 Tie in a pair of black marabou feathers and six pieces of Krystal Flash at the bend.

3 Tie in orange hackle legs at the bend. Alternatively, tie each feather into a knot.

4 Reverse the hook in the vice, so that the point is up.

5 Starting at the bend, spin deer hair along the shank, alternating dark green and orange to create stripes in the body. Spin the hair two-thirds of the way to the eye. Trim the hair so that the side opposite the hook point is shorter than the hair on the point side.

6 Spin olive deer hair to form a collar. Trim the bottom side close, leaving longer hair on the hook point side.

7 Spin a head of dark green followed by orange deer hair. Trim both colours shorter on the side opposite the hook point.

8 Loop the monofilament so that it circles back and encloses the hook. Tie the loose end at the hook eye, with the end running through the hook eye. Melt the end of the monofilament so that it cannot slip out from under the threads.

9 Cover the head wraps with instant glue.

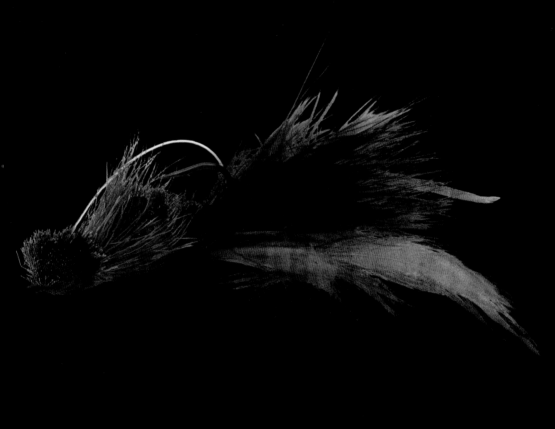

Length 12.5 cm (5 in)

Laszlo Illana

Yellow Spider Variant

Some people think of fly tiers as hidebound traditionalists, unwilling to experiment. Not so. Here's an example of using modern materials to outperform the originals.

Actual size

Length 13 mm (⅝ in)

Laszlo Illana fishes for trout and grayling in Romania, the Czech Republic, Slovenia and Poland. The 'traditional' body material for a wet fly such as this imitation of an emerging mayfly would be dubbed fur. Laszlo chose Body Glass because it makes a translucent, yellow-tinged body and looks like a natural emerging insect. In addition, the Body Glass is hollow so it floats the wet fly in the surface film like a trapped mayfly emerger trying to escape the surface tension. Many emergers get trapped in the film and cannot escape as winged adults. They are very vulnerable and trout do not have to invest much energy chasing them down, so they are readily taken by trout and grayling. The soft collar of Hungarian partridge pulses and gives the appearance of a swimming insect as it makes its way towards the surface.

Laszlo generally fishes this pattern in tandem with a small Czech nymph as the point fly. He casts across the stream and works the fly with small twitches as it floats downstream.

Materials

Hook Mustad wet fly, 1x short, micro barb, sizes 12–18

Thread UNI size 8/0, white

Body Body Glass, yellow

Thorax Grey muskrat underfur

Collar Hungarian partridge fibres

Adhesive Superglue

How to tie

1 Trim the end of the yellow Body Glass to a taper. Tie it in at the bend.

2 Apply Superglue to the underside of the hook and wrap six close turns of Body Glass towards the eye. Leave room for the thorax and head.

3 Dub and wrap a small thorax.

4 Tie in a partridge feather and make one wrap. Tie off and trim.

5 Wrap a small thread head and trim.

Fabrizio Gajardoni

Gaja's Olive Emerger

The special feature of this pattern is that the extended body sits in the water while the rest of the emerging fly sits on top. It looks like a blue-winged olive mayfly caught in the surface film in the act of emerging from a nymph to a winged adult.

Fabrizio Gajardoni wanted an early season pattern for grayling on the Brenta River, Italy. In March, the fish are rising only for a few hours, from noon to 3.30pm. The hungry fish key in exclusively on the blue-winged olive emergers.

Fabrizio started with a standard parachute style but added an extended body made from soft, multifibre dental floss. This extension sits under the water and mimics the emerging blue-winged olives.

On one of his early tests with this pattern, Fabrizio caught and landed nine big grayling in under two hours. He credits the natural balance of the submerged body and floating dry hackles and thorax with presenting a realistic imitation of the emerging blue-winged olives.

Actual size

Length 2 cm (¾ in)

Materials

Hook Tiemco 2487, sizes 14–18

Thread UNI size 8/0, rusty brown

Extended body White dental floss coloured tan with permanent marker pen, and two fibres of brown speckled Coq de Leon hen

Marker pen Promarker sandstone 0928

Tail Four fibres of brown speckled Coq de Leon hen

Adhesive Bug-Bond Lite

Wings Dark dun Enrico Puglisi Trigger Point

Hackle Sandy dun

Thorax Dubbing mixture of tan and March brown Enrico Puglisi Trigger Point

Equipment UV light

How to tie

1 Take a 10-cm (4-in) piece of dental floss and colour it with a tan marker pen.

2 Insert two fibres of brown speckled Coq de Leon hen into the floss. Leave them as long as the body.

3 Add a very small drop of Bug-Bond Lite glue at the back end and fix with a UV lamp for three seconds.

4 Run the hook point into the extended body and out again, so that the extended body reaches beyond the hook bend. Tie in place at the midpoint of the shank.

5 Wrap wings onto the shank, in front of the extended body. Stand them up with cross wraps. Trim to length.

6 Tie in a single sandy dun feather at the wing base and make four turns, parachute style. Tie off and trim.

7 Wrap the thorax material behind and in front of the wings. Tie off.

8 Make a small thread head.

Mark H.V. Corps

Tara

Tara, Mark H.V. Corps' six-year-old daughter, watched him tying salmon flies. To encourage her interest, he asked her what materials to use and she gave him the benefit of her opinion. The resulting creation has taken salmon, and is excellent for fresh grilse and sea trout from rivers and lochs across Ireland.

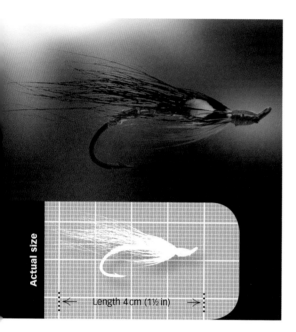

Actual size

Length 4 cm (1½ in)

Mark's most memorable day with this fly was on the River Suir. He was fishing with a journalist from *Trout & Salmon* magazine on the Kilsheelin beat. The journalist had the choice as to where to start. He told Mark to start towards the bottom of the Castle Run while he would start at the top.

Mark started with a traditional pattern, the Collie Dog, on point and a Tara as a dropper. As the fly swung across the stream, he had a gentle take and lifted into the fish. 'Any size?' the journalist asked. Mark said he thought it was 3.5 kg (8 lb) or so.

The fish slowly came up stream. It was quiet for five minutes and then turned and slowly ran for about 90 m (100 yd). Halfway down the run a large tail came out of the water, causing Mark to re-estimate the size of the fish.

The fish fought hard and after about half an hour it reluctantly came close enough to net. It weighed 10.6 kg (23 ½ lb) and was Mark's largest ever Atlantic salmon. After being weighed and photographed, it swam off to continue its journey.

Materials

Hook Sizes 6–14 hooks, tubes or Waddington shanks
Thread Size 6/0, red
Body UNI Mylar, peacock
Rib Medium silver oval wire
Hackle Cambridge blue tied in as the throat
Wings Black squirrel or stoat fur
Cheeks Jungle cock feathers
Head Red 6/0 thread

How to tie

1 Layer the hook with red thread.

2 At the bend of the hook, tie in the Mylar and then the silver wire.

3 Tightly wind Mylar onto the head and rib with silver wire.

4 Tie off at the head. Tie in the throat hackle.

5 Tie in the black fur wings.

6 Add the cheeks.

7 Build up the head, and varnish.

David Gamet

Turkey Biot Yellow Sally

David Gamet, from Rapid City, South Dakota, is the manager, instructor and guide for Dakota Angler and Outfitter. Although it sounds like a new sandwich, this fly works well on rainbow, brown and brook trout.

In early and midsummer, hatches of little yellow Sallys bring fish to the surface. The ovulating pattern, tied with an egg sac, works well when the females return to lay eggs. This pattern also works well without the egg sac when the adults are blown onto the water during windy afternoons.

Whereas other patterns seem to be too bulky and overdressed, the incorporation of an egg sac, good wing profile and a lightweight body make this fly very productive.

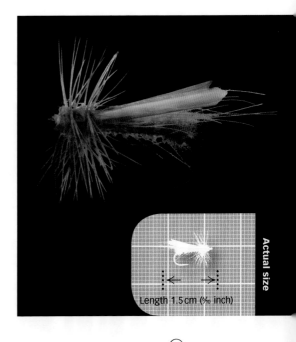

Actual size

Length 1.5 cm (⅝ inch)

Materials

Hook Daiichi 1110, sizes 14–18

Thread Gudebrod 10/0 BCS 42, light yellow

Rib Yellow thread

Egg sac (optional) Fine & Dry Dubbing, stonefly orange

Underwing Pale yellow CDC

Wings Two turkey biot quills, dyed pale morning dun

Hackle Pale yellow

Abdomen Turkey biot quill, dyed pale morning dun

How to tie

1 Lay down a thread base to the bend in the hook.

2 Tie in yellow thread for a rib.

3 At the bend, tie in a biot quill.

4 Dub an egg sac (optional).

5 Wrap the quill forward as an abdomen.

6 Rib the body with the thread and tie off.

7 Tie in the pale yellow CDC as an underwing.

8 Tie in two turkey biot quills, splayed out, as wings. Tie in by the tips and trim to round out the edges.

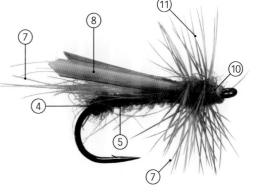

9 Tie in a yellow hackle.

10 Make a thorax of yellow dubbing.

11 Wind the hackle over the thorax. Tie off and trim.

12 Make a small head and whip finish.

Jean-Paul Dessaigne

Futura Mayfly

Taking an unusual path to a new style, the Futura's developer took advantage of the shape of a unique hook. Jean-Paul Dessaigne saw in the shape of the Tiemco T400 the essence of a natural mayfly's angular shape, and used this built-in feature to create an effective style of mayfly.

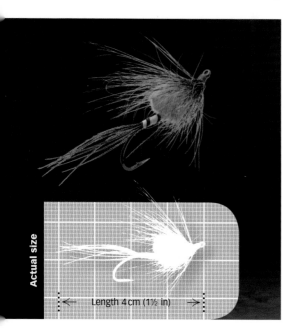

Actual size

Length 4 cm (1½ in)

The straight-shanked, traditional dry fly hook does not imitate the natural's bent shape when it sits upon the water's surface. How much more effective, Jean-Paul Dessaigne thought, could an imitation become if it has the general shape of the natural it intends to imitate?

Unwilling to stop with simply a realistic body shape, Jean-Paul went on to arrange the fly's fibres so as to mimic characteristics of the mayfly's profile. The only difficulty he mentioned was finding Coq de Leon fibres of sufficient length. However, he assures us that the search is worthwhile in terms of what the fibres add to the fly.

When fishing the Futura for brown and rainbow trout on his home waters, Jean-Paul uses the classic drag-free drift by casting up and across the river's current.

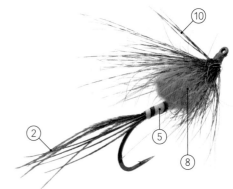

Materials

Hook Tiemco T400, size 12
Thread 12/0, tan
Tail Pheasant tail fibres
Abdomen Yellow foam
Rib Peacock herl
Thorax Yellow CDC and yellow hare dubbing
Wing Coq de Leon flor d'escoba

How to tie

1 Lay down a thread base from the hook eye to the bend.

2 Tie in eight pheasant tail fibres as a tail. It should be as long as the hook shank.

3 Cut a narrow strip of yellow foam and tie it in at the bend.

4 Remove the fuzz from a peacock herl by gently rubbing it with a pencil eraser. Tie the herl in at the bend.

5 Wrap the foam halfway to the eye and tie off. Trim the excess.

6 Wrap the rib forward in open turns. Tie off and trim the excess.

7 Tie in two CDC plumes on top of the hook at the end of the body. Stroke the CDC fibres to the rear.

8 In front of the CDC, make a dubbing loop of hare dubbing and wrap a large thorax.

9 Trim the hair on the bottom of the fly.

10 Tie in a Coq de Leon hackle, wrap it several times, and tie off. Trim the fibres off the bottom of the fly.

Jean-Paul Dessaigne

Boxite

Sometimes an old material is used in a new way, resulting in an innovative tying technique that can be adapted to create new forms of many existing fly patterns.

Jean-Paul Dessaigne found a piece of moose mane hide and noticed the coarse fibres. The moose is a large animal and its hair is proportionately large and coarse. He began to think about using the fibres in such a way as to take advantage of the hair's roughness.

He understood that the profile of a natural mayfly, when seen from the trout's perspective, is a mixture of individual fibres and refracted light caused by the legs as they enter or sit upon the water. The refracted light is often a trigger that results in the trout taking the fly. If one was able to convey this refracted light in a new way, it might provide the impetus for tempting trout. Jean-Paul's Boxite accomplishes this illusion and, at the same time, creates a fly that floats well.

Actual size

Length 2 cm (¾ in)

Materials

Hook Daiichi 1180, size 14
Thread Berkley Nanofil
6 mm (¼ in)
Tail Dark moose mane hair
Abdomen One white moose mane hair and one dark moose mane hair
Thorax Hare's ear natural
Wing Hare body fur

How to tie

1 Lay down a thread base from the eye to the bend of the hook.

2 At the bend, tie in a tail of six moose mane fibres, using enough tension to allow them

to splay out. The tail should be as long as the hook shank.

3 Wrap the thread forward over the mane three-quarters of the way to the eye and trim off the excess mane.

4 Return the thread to the bend and tie in one white hair and one dark hair.

5 Wrap over both hairs to the point where the mane ends. Wrap the hair to form a striped abdomen. Trim off the excess hair.

6 Pull out a pinch of hare body fur that includes both guard hairs and underfur.

7 Cut some coarse guard hairs and add them to the body fur.

8 One-third of the way back from the eye, make a spinning loop of the thread and twist the fur in the loop.

9 Make six wraps of the loop to create a thorax. The individual fibres should stand off at 90 degrees to the shank. Tie off and trim the excess loop.

10 Wrap a small thread head in such a way that it forces the hare fibres to slant backward over the abdomen. Cement the head.

Pål Andersen

Andersen Multipurpose Pupa (AMPP)

The key to this fly is that it breaks through the river's surface film and keeps floating. The combination of a copper rib for weight and a closed-cell foam post help the fly to appear as an emerging midge trapped in the surface film.

Actual size

Length 1.25 cm (½ in)

Pål Andersen, from Hokksund, Norway, owns Fly Fish Norway. From his earliest fishing years he loved to fish in the spring soon after ice out. At this time of year the only flies available to fish are midges.

The midges hatch in great numbers, and it's difficult to get the fish's attention. At such times, long leaders (often three times the rod's length) and 8x tippets are necessary.

A day on the Gudbrandsdalslågen River demonstrated the AMPP's potential under completely different conditions. In August 1994, after a long, hot, dry period, the river's surface was covered by flying ants and fish began rising in huge numbers. After trying all available ant patterns with no results, Pål switched to the AMPP for its inaugural cast. The fish responded immediately. By the time it was over, the AMPP had accounted for 40 grayling weighing up to 1.8 kg (4 lb) and brown trout up to 2.7 kg (6 lb).

Materials

Hook Knapek P midge pupae, size 16
Thread Giorgio Benecchi Ultrafine size 12/0, black
Rib Copper wire
Tail White Antron
Body/thorax Black Fly-rite
Post White foam
Head Black thread

How to tie

1 Lay down a thread base from the eye to the bend of the hook.

2 Tie in the copper wire for ribbing.

3 Tie in a short section of white Antron for a tail. It should be one-quarter of the length of the hook shank.

4 Move the thread to within one-quarter of the shank away from the eye and tie in a post of white foam.

5 Return the thread to the bend. Dub some black Fly-rite and wring-wrap the body to the eye, covering the thread where the foam is tied in. The body should be thin at the rear and fatter near the eye. Trim off the excess.

6 Wrap the ribbing forward to the eye and tie off. Trim the wire.

7 Trim the foam post to 6 mm (¼ in) in length.

8 Make a thread head and cement.

Mike Algar

Dunce Cap Bowser

The old saying is that big fish need big flies. This is probably true, because after trout attain full size, they prefer to eat smaller fish rather than insects. It's a matter of getting more benefit from a big meal.

Mike Algar owns Freestone Fly Fishers in Calgary, Alberta. His home water is the Bow River. This fishery is renowned for its large rainbow trout. The combination of large predator fish and a large streamer pattern have brought Mike success for himself and his clients.

Mike describes the Bowser as one of his secret weapons for the trophy trout of the Bow River. It fishes best on a fast strip but often gets eaten on a dead drift or while it is sinking.

Apparently, it cannot be fished incorrectly. That's a good thing. On a recent outing on a small spring creek, it accounted for five brook trout between 30 and 40 cm (12 and 16 in).

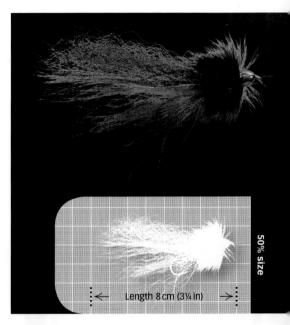

50% size

Length 8 cm (3¼ in)

Materials

Hook Tiemco 5263, size 2
Thread Danville flat waxed nylon, 210 denier, black
Cone Head 6-mm (¼-in) black nickel
Underbody Pearl EP Fiber under rainbow EP Flash
Body Grey SF Flash under black SF Flash
Collar Black mink fur strip

How to tie

1 Thread the cone head onto the hook and wrap the hook shank with thread about one-third of the way down the shank.

2 Turn the hook upside down and tie in a clump of pearl EP Flash.

3 Turn the hook so that the fly is right side up again. Tie in a smaller clump of rainbow EP Flash.

4 Repeat these last two steps until there is approximately 1 cm (⅜ in) between the flash tied in last and the cone head at the top of the hook.

5 Add the black and the grey SF Flash.

6 Turn the fly upside down once again, tie in a sparse clump of the grey hair, and lock it into place.

7 Turn the fly right side up once again and do the same with a slightly larger clump of black hair. Lock it into place with the thread.

8 Tie in the black mink strip fur side down and at a 45-degree angle to the rear. Pull the strip taut, wrap it anticlockwise towards you six times up to the cone head, and tie off. Trim the remaining mink strip.

9 Cement the thread wraps.

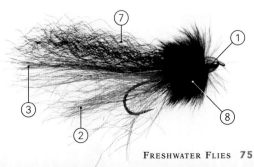

Marcelo Malventano

Realistic CDC Emerger

In many places, caddis flies comprise the trout's main diet. On heavily fished waters, the trout become selective and can discriminate between naturals and imitations. In such situations, a new pattern is required for success.

Materials

Hook Daiichi 1160, sizes 14–18
Thread UNI size 8/0, olive
Overbody Translucent Fino Skin
Body Caddis green natural dubbing
Marker pens Olive and yellow
Wing case and wing One olive CDC feather
Parachute Black ostrich fibre

Marcelo Malventano, from Patagonia, Argentina, knew that the microfibres of CDC can float a fly without the need for adding floatant. The microfibres trap air and, in addition to floating the fly, mimic the air bubbles often found on emerging caddis flies. This, in addition to Marcelo's unique method for creating a translucent body, makes his Realistic CDC Emerger a go-to fly.

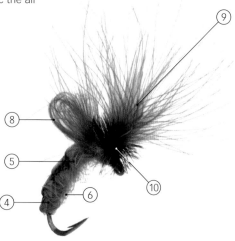

How to tie

1 Starting in the middle of the hook shank, wrap a thread base to the bend.

2 At the bend, tie in a 6-mm (¼-in) wide strip of Fino Skin so that it hangs out over the bend.

3 Dub the rearmost segment of the body into a round shape. It should cover one-eighth of the length of the shank.

4 Pull the Fino Skin over the first segment and tie it down in front of the segment.

5 Repeat the process, creating a series of six body segments, each covered by the Fino Skin. The final segment should leave room for the wing and head.

6 Colour the Fino Skin with the olive marker, being sure to get it down into the space between the segments. Be careful not to colour the dubbing that lies beneath the Fino Skin. Colour one segment at a time and let it dry for one minute.

7 Colour one segment at a time with yellow marker. After each stroke, blot the marker pen on paper to remove the olive that the yellow marker has picked up. The yellow will pick up some of the olive and resulting in graduated colour, from dark at the edges to faintly tinted at the centre. The dubbing colour will show through the top centreline of each fibre. Go on to the next segment and repeat until you have five segments.

8 Tie in the olive CDC feather in front of the abdomen, with the concave side down. Gently pull the plume forward and tie it in, creating a loop of fibres.

9 At the same place, tie in a second olive CDC feather. Wrap thread around the base of the feather, creating an upright post.

10 Tie in a black ostrich fibre and wrap it four times around the CDC post. Tie off and trim the excess.

11 Make a green dubbed head and a small thread head. Cement the thread.

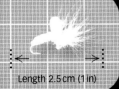

Length 2.5 cm (1 in)

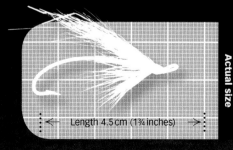

Length 4.5 cm (1¾ inches)

Glyn Freeman
Sewinmeister

Although the Sewinmeister (Seatrout Master) was developed for night fishing for sea trout on the River Eden in Cumbria, it seems to work on all rivers that have migratory fish in the UK, Norway, Iceland and Argentina.

Materials

Hook Bartleet low water, size 6 or 8
Thread Size 6/0, black
Tag Gold wire
Butt Fluorescent red floss
Body Gold holographic tinsel
Rib Gold wire
Collar Red hackle fibres
Wing Black squirrel hair
Topping Flashabou
Cheeks Jungle cock feathers

Glyn Freeman, owner of Cumbria Fly Fishing, wanted a slim pattern that would be effective at dusk and into the night. The silhouette had to be correct for fishing against a dark sky and with only a little flash. Patterns that were heavier dressed tended not to work as well.

The Sewinmeister is fished nearly always with a sink tip and 3-m (10-ft) leader on a seven-weight forward-floating line. The fly is cast across the current. The rod is then pointed downstream. When the current grabs the tension on the fly line, a very slow but steady retrieve figure-of-eight is done right to the rod tip. The secret is getting the speed of retrieve correct.

There have been quite a few red-letter days with this fly, many evenings with both sea trout and salmon showing an interest, and some very big double-figure fish in the daytime on the Rio Gallegos in Argentina.

Glyn's real pleasure is giving the fly to others to try. He does not know whether it is simply a matter of confidence, but the Sewinmeister seems to work for them also.

How to tie

1 Wind thread halfway down the hook shank.

2 Tie in four turns of gold wire tag, leaving enough for the ribbing.

3 Tie in a small red fluorescent butt twice the length of the tag over the gold wire and bend the wire back.

4 Wind the thread back up to the eye and tie in the gold holographic tinsel.

5 Wind the tinsel down to the butt and back up to the eye, and secure.

6 Wind gold wire ribbing in even turns to the eye, and secure.

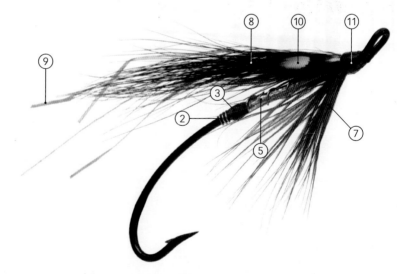

7 Tie in red hackle fibres extending just beyond the tag. Wind three turns, but do not pull down. Secure the hackle fibres.

8 Tie in black squirrel hair wings extending just beyond the bend of the hook. Dab a drop of varnish to the butt end to secure. The hackle should show as an underwing.

9 Tie in three strands of Flashabou for the overwing.

10 Tie in the jungle cock feather cheeks. Varnish the head.

Pål Andersen

Heggeil Streamer

When the maiden voyage of an experimental fly yields many fish and then two days later results in second place in a national championship, it's a fly that deserves your attention. When it is an easy tie, there's no excuse for not having several in your fly box.

Actual size

Length 2.8 cm (1⅛ in)

Pål Andersen, from Hokksund, Norway, lives two minutes from the River Drammenselva, one of Norway's best rivers for big wild brown trout and Atlantic salmon.

This fly is based on a very old Norwegian wet fly pattern called the 'Heggeil fly'. This streamer version uses different materials and colours, but is true to its ancestry in that it catches fish.

Pål fishes this fly in rivers, lakes and saltwater and finds that it works in most depths and at most retrieving speeds. He often counts the seconds after the cast in order to determine at what depth the fish are holding.

The Heggeil Streamer imitates baitfish, and the species that seem to prefer this fly include brown trout, sea trout, Atlantic salmon and rainbow. It has been successful all over Norway, northern Sweden, Iceland and Poland. It is also very good in some places for char and big grayling.

Materials

Hook Knapek N, size 4/0
Thread Giorgio Benecchi Ultrafine size 12/0, black or red
Tail Golden pheasant tippets
Rib Copper wire
Body (lower ¾) Flat silver tinsel
Body (upper ¼) Peacock herl
Hackle Brown cock hackle
Wing Siberian squirrel tail hair
Eyes Jungle cock feathers
Head Black

How to tie

1 Wrap a thread base from the eye of the hook to the bend.

2 Tie in 15 golden pheasant tippets as a tail.

3 Tie in the copper wire rib.

4 Tie in flat silver tinsel and wrap it forward three-quarters of the way to the eye.

5 Wrap the ribbing to the end of the tinsel and tie it off. Trim off the excess.

6 At the end of the tinsel, tie in peacock herl and wrap the remaining one-quarter of the hook shank. Trim off the excess.

7 In front of the body, tie in the brown cock hackle and make two wraps. Tie off and trim the excess.

8 On top of the hackle, tie in a wing of squirrel tail hair that reaches the end of the tail fibres.

9 Tie a jungle cock feather on each side as eyes.

10 Make a thread head and cement.

Jack Simpson

Root Beer Leech

During the late autumn, winter after ice-over and early spring, just after the ice disappears, the stillwater rainbow trout's preferred larger protein diet consists of small, brown freshwater leeches. This pattern mimics the subsurface neutral buoyancy of the micro leech.

Jack Simpson owns Sandpiper Fly Fishing on Williams Lake in British Columbia, and does a great deal of his fishing on stillwaters. He reports that the Root Beer Leech is fished either with a floating or clear intermediate sinking line, depending on the depth of the lake.

The cast is made towards the reeds at the shoreline into a depth of 30–90 cm (1–3 ft). Jack then counts as the fly sinks at a rate of 45 cm (18 in) per second. Jack begins with a 10-cm (4-in) strip-and-pause retrieve when the fly is near the bottom. You should expect to snag weeds occasionally, because that's where leeches hide and trout go searching for them.

The best day with the Root Beer Leech in Jack's own words: 'Early May of 2009, immediately after ice-off. Second strip, I hook a log. Then the log takes off and nearly spools me – three times. Twenty minutes, he's done – and so am I: a beautiful, huge, 8-kg (18-lb) rainbow trout.'

Actual size

Length 3 cm (1¼ in)

Materials

Hook Mustad C53S, size 12
Thread Size 8/0, black
Body Root-beer-coloured Czech glass beads, size 11/0
Tail Black, brown and golden brown stacked marabou fibres

How to tie

1 Slide seven root-beer-coloured glass beads onto the hook shank up against the eye.

2 Tie in the marabou fibres behind the last glass bead for the tail. The tail should extend three times the length of the fly body. Tie off and trim off the excess.

3 Cement the thread.

Masa Araki

Higenaga Dry

The Higenaga is a large caddis fly found in Japan. When the 'usual' approach (greased Muddler Minnows or Stimulators) failed to convince large trout to strike, experimentation led to this successful pattern.

Materials

Hook Maruto i77LS, size 10/0
Thread UNI size 6/0, rusty dun
Abdomen Golden pheasant tail
Thorax Light grey MaXtream High Float Fly Fiber (HFFF)
Veil Light grey HFFF
Main wing Hareline Thick Wing
Antennae Moose mane
Wing and legs Deer hair

Masa Araki owns MaXtream Flies in Yokohama, Japan. His lack of success with the existing methods to get the Tokachi and Shiribetsu rivers' yamame (landlocked cherry salmon) and iwana (Japanese native char) led him to take some of the Higenaga naturals home so that he could study them and work on an imitation.

So successful were his new methods of creating this fly that he has begun adapting his tying methods to tying other patterns as well. Masa reports that the profile created when the deer hair is spread out to represent legs and thorax is a vital aspect of this method.

A natural, drag-free presentation is preferred. Masa also notes that the fly still catches fish, even after it has become covered in slime; his conclusion is the partially submerged fly may look like a pupa or stillborn. Because big fish are the targets, he uses a 0X or 1X tippet, and is able to put pressure on the fish without breaking off.

How to tie

1 Lay down a thread base from the eye of the hook to the bend.

2 Tie in four golden pheasant tail fibres and wrap them forward three-quarters of the way to the eye, making an abdomen. Tie off and trim off the excess. Brush on cement to reinforce the abdomen.

3 Cut a section of HFFF and tie it in over the abdomen. It should be 1.5 times the length of the abdomen.

4 Cut Hareline Thick Wing to imitate caddis wing and attach it over the HFFF. It will be 1.5 times the length of the abdomen.

5 Tie in more HFFF over the wing, the same length as the first section, for the veil. The Thick Wing should be sandwiched between two thin layers of HFFF.

6 Tie in two moose mane hairs the same length as the wing, sticking out over the eye.

7 Make a thorax with dubbed HFFF. Do not trim the fibres.

8 Make a wing from deer hair and tie it in over the thorax. Do not trim the hairs.

9 Leave hairs on both sides and cut only those in the centre on the bottom.

Spread the remaining deer hair on both sides with your fingers. This buggy-looking profile makes this fly special.

10 Make a small thread head and cement.

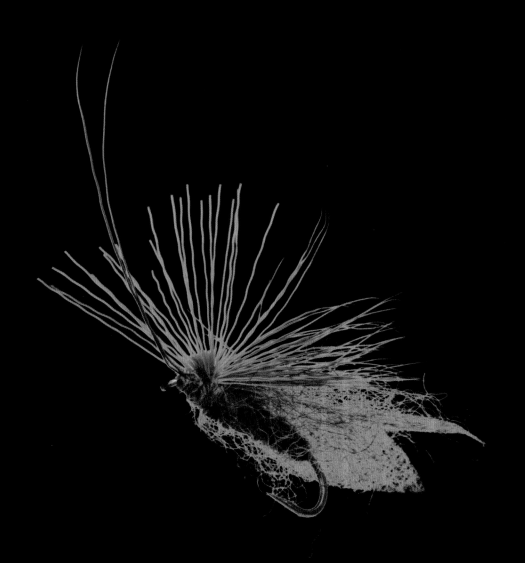

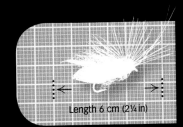

Masa Araki

Mouse

Decades ago, rainbows were introduced into lakes around Hokkaido, Japan. One summer day, Masa Araki watched a 70-cm (28-in) rainbow disgorge a mouse. He decided to design one and this pattern is what he developed.

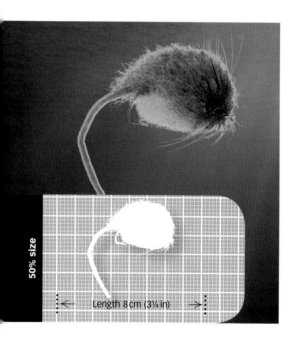

50% size

Length 8 cm (3¼ in)

Masa admits that a mouse pattern is not common in Japan, but after his observation he thought he might be missing out on something important. His technique of adding several consecutive small amounts of High Float Fiber makes a large fly that is easy to cast. Masa has also used this same method to design other kinds of large flies without sacrificing castability.

The attraction of this large dry fly is the water skiing action as the fly is swinging across a river's current. An active retrieve is necessary to give the fly a variable swimming action. The trout are not accustomed to seeing such a large fly and this may explain their interest in striking it. In still waters, a fast retrieve is required to arouse the trout's interest. In either setting, the fly must be well dressed with floatant to keep it riding high.

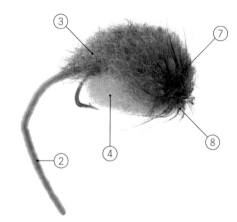

Materials

Hook Daiichi 2050, size 3/0
Thread UNI size 6/0, rusty dun
Tail Tan Hareline Ultra Chenille
Back Dark grey MaXtream High Float Fly Fiber (HFFF)
Belly Light grey MaXtream HFFF
Whiskers Whiting Coq de Leon rooster saddle hackle
Mouth Rust HFFF

How to tie

1 Lay down a thread base from the eye of the hook to the bend.

2 Tie in Ultra Chenille at the bend as a 5-cm (2-in) tail. Burn the end of the tail to give it a taper.

3 Tie in a small piece of dark grey HFFF on top of the hook at the bend. Pull the fibres back to make room for the next batch.

4 Tie in a piece of light grey HFFF below the hook at the bend. Pull the fibres back to make room for the next batch.

5 Repeat steps 3 and 4 until a dark over light body runs the length of the hook shank.

6 Trim the body into a cylinder shape, fat in the middle and thinner at each end.

7 Tie in the saddle hackle and take three turns for whiskers. Tie off and trim off the excess.

8 Tie in rust HFFF for the mouth and trim.

9 Make a small thread head and cement.

Jack Simpson

Cripple Midge

Seventy-five per cent of a stillwater rainbow trout's diet is chironomids. During an emergence, many chironomids become trapped in the surface film, and this makes them easy prey for the rainbow trout that cruise slowly just below the surface.

Jack Simpson owns Sandpiper Fly Fishing in Williams Lake, British Columbia. His Cripple Midge pattern is an imitation of those midges caught in the surface film.

Do yourself a favour: leave your super-fast action fly rod at home and use a moderate-fast, smooth-casting, deep-loading fly rod for the close-in casting to the reed lines. The trout remain unseen by the human eye. The only hint of feeding action is a slight swirl on the water surface.

Let the rod do the work; concentrate on smooth, accurate casting. The hero long-distance casting rods and techniques are for windy days, not for placing flies precisely in the path of cruising fish.

Jack fishes the Cripple Midge on long, fine leaders. The cast is made in an attempt to intercept cruising fish. When the midges are plentiful, this can be difficult because the trout's path is hard to predict. There is but one way to become proficient – get out there and do it.

Actual size

Length 3 cm (1¼ in)

Materials

Hook Mustad R73, size 14
Thread Size 8/0, black
Rib Red metallic thread
Body Clear 2 mm
(¹⁄₁₆ in) Mylar
Wing Tan summer
deer hair
Underbody 4-strand
black floss

How to tie

1 Lay down a thread base from the eye to halfway down the bend of the hook.

2 Tie in the red metallic thread to be used as a rib.

3 Tie in the Mylar strip.

4 Advance the thread three-quarters of the way to the eye.

5 Tie in the deer hair and stand it up at 90-degrees to the hook shank, with the butt ends sticking out over the eye. Trim the butt ends behind the eye.

6 Wrap over the butt ends of the hair and tie in the black floss near the eye.

7 Wrap the floss halfway down the bend and back to the eye. Tie off and trim off the excess.

8 Wrap the Mylar over the floss to the eye and tie off. Trim off the excess.

9 Wrap the red metallic thread in open turns over the Mylar. Tie off and trim off the excess.

10 Fold the deer hair over the top of the body, making a wingcase. Tie in at the eye, being careful to keep the hairs together and not splayed apart.

11 Cement the thread.

Stevie Munn

Munn's Mayfly

Here's a modern fly with its origins in the old gosling style of Irish lough (lake) flies. The traditional way to fish loughs is from a boat as it drifts with the wind. The wind serves to move the fly line so that the flies are kept at a distance from the boat and swimming at or near the surface, imitating escaping insects.

Actual size

Length 3 cm (1¼ inches)

Stevie Munn prefers to fish this pattern as the top fly in a two-fly cast. While the point fly remains under the water, the top fly can be dibbled (worked in small hops) on the water's surface at the boat at the end of the retrieve. Fished in this way, it gives the appearance of a fly attempting to leave the water and goads the trout into striking before the fly can escape. At mayfly time, these flies have taken many fish consistently for many anglers over the years in the British Isles, and they work well on all trout.

Stevie works full time in the angling sector as a guide, writer and qualified game angling instructor, and has appeared in many angling books, DVDs and angling shows all over the world. He has also fished many places in the world, but grew up fishing on the rivers and loughs of Ireland, where he often guides.

As proof of this fly's effectiveness, Stevie reports that he once caught six fish in six casts on Lough Erne — something unheard of in Ireland.

Materials

Hook Pro-Tiers wet fly, sizes 8/0 and 10/10
Thread Size 8/0, grey
Tail Four strands of pheasant tail
Rib Fine silver wire
Body Yellow Lite Brite Dubbing
Body hackle Light blue cock hackle
Wing Chartreuse deer hair
Collar hackle Orange cock with two turns of yellow/olive English partridge in front

How to tie

1 Make a thread base from the hook eye to the bend of the hook.

2 Tie in four strands of pheasant tail as the tail.

3 Tie in the rib at the bend of the hook.

4 Tie in the body hackle.

5 Dub a thin body, wrap it forward to the eye and tie it off.

6 Wrap the body hackle forward in open turns and tie off at the eye.

7 Wrap the wire forward to the eye and tie off.

8 Close to the hook eye, tie in a small pinch of deer hair as the wing.

9 Tie in and wrap the collar hackle. Tie off and trim.

10 Tie in the English partridge, make two turns and tie off.

11 Make a thread head, and cement.

Gudmundur Atli

Rainbow Ghost Streamer

Frustration sends many of us home muttering to ourselves. We can be thankful some tiers think about the cause of those fishless days and go on to develop effective flies that we can all take advantage of.

Gudmundur Atli often fishes for big brown trout in Lake Thingvellir, one hour from his home in Reykjavik, Iceland. The lake's big browns have always intrigued him, but prior to designing his Rainbow Ghost Streamer, his success rate was low. After experimenting, his success rate improved so much that he has also used the fly for Atlantic salmon and rainbow trout.

Gudmundur uses a floating line and long leaders as he tries to spot the fish before he makes his cast – a bit like sight fishing. The cast is made close to the fish, and he strips in slowly, trying to keep the fly alive in the water.

Unlike many fur strips, this wing is only tied in at the front, allowing extra action when the fly is being retrieved.

Gudmundur has had a few fantastic days using this fly. His largest brown trout from Lake Thingvellir was nearly 7.7 kg (17 lb), caught on his last cast in a snowstorm just before dark.

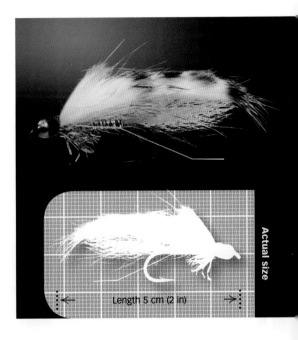

Actual size

Length 5 cm (2 in)

Materials

Hook Tiemco 5236, size 6/0
Thread UNI size 6/0, orange
Bead head Copper or gold
Tail Yellow Icelandic horsehair
Body Axxel silver/black
Beard Rainbow flash
Underwing Silver flash
Overwing White rabbit strip
Marker pen Permanent black

How to tie

1 Slide a bead over the point to the hook eye.

2 Lay down a thread base to the point just above the hook point.

3 Tie in a tail of horsehair equal to the length of the hook shank.

4 Tie in and wind a body of Axxel silver/black from over the hook point to the bead.

5 Behind the bead tie in a beard of rainbow flash equal to one-half the length of the body.

6 At the bead, tie in an underwing of four pieces of silver flash extending to the end of the tail.

7 At the bead, tie in an overwing of white rabbit extending to the end of the tail.

8 Make black vertical marks on the rabbit strip.

Roger Salomonsson

Roger's Damsel Nymph

A stout tippet is recommended for this damselfly nymph because the strikes are always powerful, never gentle. This is because Roger's Damsel Nymph's action, when retrieved, gives confidence to trout wherever trout and damselflies share the water. It is especially effective through the summer months.

Materials

Hook Kamasan B800, size 8/0

Thread UNI size 8/0, black

Eyes Medium Magic Fly Eyes

Tail Olive marabou, olive Krystal Microflash

Rib Olive marabou

Weight Lead wire

Body Flyrite number 3

Thorax Olive ostrich plume

Adhesive Superglue

Roger Salomonsson is a Swedish guide, instructor and tier. He says that, when you use this fly, you use a fast-twist retrieve, because the natural insect is a very fast swimmer. He lets the fly sink for one second between retrieves. Because the weight is concentrated near the front of the fly, the fly tips nose down and begins to sink each time the retrieve is paused. The next retrieve causes the fly to nose upward and therefore appear to be swimming to the surface.

Other fishers have told Roger that they like the fly because its up-and-down action looks very realistic.

The first rainbow trout taken by Roger with this fly was a 3-kg (6½-lb) fish.

How to tie

1 Tie in the eyes right behind the hook eye and secure with a drop of Superglue.

2 Lay down a thread base to the hook bend.

3 Tie in a tail of marabou and four pieces of Microflash. The tail should be 1.5 times as long as the hook shank.

4 At the bend, tie in a rib.

5 At the bend, tie in another marabou feather by the tip.

6 Advance the thread to the eyes.

7 Make five turns of lead wire and secure with thread.

8 Twist the marabou feather and wrap forward as a body. Tie off.

9 Dub the rib with Flyrite, wrap it forward and tie off.

10 Ahead of the body, tie in a small bunch of marabou and trim as a wingcase.

11 Dub some Flyrite and wrap behind, between and in front of the eyes.

12 Whip finish at the head.

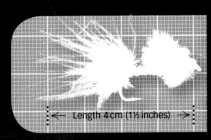

Length 4 cm (1½ inches)

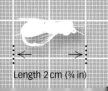

Length 2 cm (¾ in)

Roger Salomonsson

Roger's Wasp

How many tiers would invest five years developing a pattern? Roger Salomonsson would – and did. You can take advantage of his dedication and have a unique pattern that works in both streams and lakes.

Materials

Hook TMC 100, size 10
Body Yellow foam, 3 mm (⅛ in)
Wings Medium grey hackle tips
Legs Medium grey hackle fibres
Antennae 2 horsehairs, natural brown
Marker pen Permanent black
Coating Acrylic varnish
Adhesive Superglue

Roger observed the increase in wasps in the late season, September and October, and began experimenting with different materials to imitate these insects. Although we don't usually think of wasps as trout fodder, they become numerous enough during the late season to get the fish's attention. It makes sense, given the fact that trout are opportunistic feeders that will eat anything that nature offers.

Roger reports that he started by using deer hair, but it became waterlogged too soon to be useful.

Wanting a fly that would stay afloat, he then tried balsa wood, but he noticed that the fish spit the fly as soon as they felt the hard composition of the wood. Roger finally tried foam, and the result was that the fish not only took the fly but, because it was soft, were encouraged to eat it.

Roger's method in streams is to fish it dead drift. In lakes, he casts the fly in front of cruising fish and lets it sit so that the fish can find it on their own. No retrieve is required.

How to tie

1 Run the hook through the middle of a length of the foam.

2 At the bend, tie in the foam under the shank.

3 Advance the thread to the midpoint of the shank.

4 Coat the shank with Superglue.

5 Fold the upper half of the foam over the shank and the lower half under the shank, and tie off at the midpoint of the shank.

6 Apply more Superglue to the shank and advance both pieces of foam halfway to the eye, making a thorax.

7 Repeat the process to the eye, making a head.

8 Use a marker to ring the abdomen, and colour both the thorax and head a solid black.

9 Cover the fly with a coat of acrylic varnish and let dry.

10 Between the head and thorax, tie in several hackle fibres as legs.

11 At the same place, tie in two hackle tips as wings. They should point up at an angle.

12 Between the head and hook eye, tie in two horsehairs as antennae.

13 Tie off and whip finish.

Stevie Munn

Black and Blue Jam

Night fishing is an acquired taste, but it seems only fair that a special fishing situation should have a special fly to do its bidding as the other creatures of the night make their rounds. In Stevie Munn's case, those creatures include Dollaghan brown trout, bats, otters and owls.

Actual size

Length 3 cm (1¼ in)

Stevie owns Irish Angler and lives in County Antrim, Ireland. Although he can take you fishing all over the world, this fly is his favourite for fishing Lough Neagh for Dollaghan brown trout.

Dollaghan achieve growth rates similar to Atlantic salmon while they feed in the lough (lake); on their return to their native rivers, they can weigh up to 8.6 kg (19 lb), and there are stories of bigger ones.

Stevie's biggest was 4.5 kg (10 lb). Holding onto these big fish when you have just hooked them is very difficult. They have hard mouths for a trout, and they shake their heads while falling back. Stevie reports that, to be honest, most of the very big fish are lost, but in a season's fishing, he normally catches quite a few fish over 2.25 kg (5 lb). That's a big trout in anyone's book, and there's always some lucky angler who will get an even larger brute.

Materials

Hook VMC Samurai double or single, sizes 6–12
Thread Size 6/0, black
Rib Silver wire
Body Gold or silver holographic tinsel
Hackle Orange cock
Wing Blue Arctic fox mixed with black squirrel or black bucktail
Flash Two strands of pearl Twinkle

How to tie

1 Lay down a thread base from the eye to just above the hook barb.

2 At the end of the thread base, tie in the silver wire rib and the tinsel.

3 Wrap the tinsel forward towards the eye, making a body. Leave room for the hackle and wing. Tie off.

4 Wrap the wire forward, ribbing the body. Tie off.

5 Tie in and wrap three turns of the hackle. Trim.

6 Tie in the wing material and flash, so that they reach beyond the bend.

7 Make a head, and cement.

Justin Sander

Super Scud

Simple is good – especially when it comes to expendable trout flies. Trout tear up the really effective ones, while streamside trees and rocks eat others. Justin Sander wanted a simple, easy-to-tie pattern that would fool rainbow trout so that he could spend more time fishing and less time at the tying bench.

Justin designs flies for Sandpiper Fly Fishing in British Columbia. His simplified Super Scud takes very little time to tie, is comprised of only two materials, and swims realistically in the water.

He fishes the fly with a full sinking line, either trolling it or slowly retrieving it with a hand-twist method. (By using a sinking line, the depth can be controlled by waiting for the line to sink to the desired depth.) The foam shell back keeps the fly oriented correctly, with the legs down and the shell back up, exactly as the natural scuds swim. Few things frighten trout as quickly as seeing an apparent bug behaving unnaturally.

Justin's most memorable day with the Super Scud happened when he was trolling it behind his pontoon boat as he worked the shoreline. Rainbows were rising all around him: no sooner had he released one trout than the next would strike and be landed. Justin lost count of the number he caught and released that day, but he knew he had a 'keeper' fly.

Actual size

Length 2 cm (¾ in)

Materials

Hook Tiemco 3769, sizes 8 and 10
Thread Size 8/0, olive
Shell back Olive foam
Body Olive hair dubbing
Marker pen Permanent black

How to tie

1 Wrap a thread base from the hook eye to the bend.

2 Cut a 10-cm × 3-mm (4- × ⅛-in) piece of foam.

3 Tie the foam in at the bend of the hook, with the foam hanging out past the bend.

4 Dub and wrap a body made of olive hair.

5 Pick out the dubbing under the hook shank, using a pin.

6 Pull the foam strip over the dubbed body and tie it in at the eye. Trim off the excess.

7 Make a small thread head, and cement.

8 Use the black marker pen to make three lines on the foam.

Marcelo Malventano

Realistic Soft Hackle

Many stream-born insects are translucent. This quality results in a reflected light that triggers a trout's interest. Many patterns try to imitate this reflection by using tinsel or Mylar. Marcelo Malventano discovered a unique, effective alternative that results in a more realistic pattern.

Materials

Hook Daiichi 1270, sizes 12–16
Thread UNI size 8/0, black
Body Mix of natural boar hair dubbing and olive Mohair Dub
Overbody Translucent Fino Skin
Hackle Natural teal duck flank fibres
Head Black ostrich fibre
Marker pens Permanent black and brown

Creating an imitation that mimics this translucent characteristic is difficult. Marcelo's solution is foolproof, and can be mastered by anyone willing to proceed slowly.

Attention to detail is one of Marcelo's hallmarks. In addition to flies for fishing, he also ties full dress salmon patterns and ultrarealistic show flies.

The magic occurs when a brown permanent marker removes some of the black marker applied in the previous step. The solvent of the brown marker liquefies the black and the brown marker picks up some of the black colour, leaving behind a translucent, lightly coloured segment.

How to tie

1 Starting in the middle of the hook shank, wrap a thread base to the bend.

2 At the bend, tie in a 6-mm (¼-in) wide strip of Fino Skin so that it hangs out over the bend.

3 Dub the rearmost segment of the body into a round shape. It should cover one-eighth of the length of the shank.

4 Pull the Fino Skin over the first segment and tie it down in front of the segment.

5 Repeat the process, creating a series of six body segments, each covered by the Fino Skin. The final segment should leave room for the wing and head.

6 Colour the Fino Skin with black marker, being sure to get it down into the space between the segments. Be careful not to colour the dubbing that lies beneath the Fino Skin. Colour one segment at a time, and let the black dry for one minute.

7 Colour one segment at a time with the brown marker. After each stroke, blot the marker pen on paper to remove the black that the marker has picked up. The brown will pick up some of the black. The result will be a graduated colour from dark at the edges to faintly tinted at the centre. The dubbing colour will show through the top centreline of each fibre. Go onto the next segment and repeat until you have five segments.

8 Tie in a teal flank feather next to the body and make five turns. After each turn, stroke the fibres back towards the bend. The individual fibres should extend beyond the bend of the hook. Trim off the excess stem.

9 Tie in the ostrich fibre and wind the ostrich fibre over the thread that secured the wing. Tie off and trim off the excess.

10 Make a small thread head and cement.

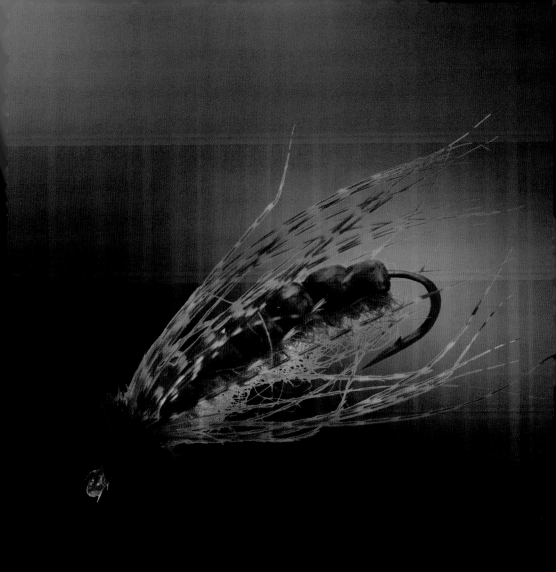

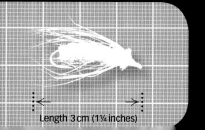

Actual size

Length 3 cm (1¼ inches)

Todd Oishi

Todd's Vampire Leech

As water depth increases, light penetration is reduced and overall visibility is greatly diminished. A fly that can overcome these problems would result in a more effective pattern. Years of competitive fly fishing resulted in a pattern that gives an edge to its designer.

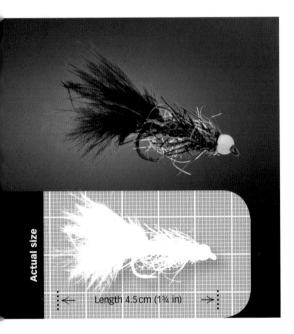

Actual size

Length 4.5 cm (1¾ in)

Todd Oishi is from Maple Ridge, British Columbia. His goal is to stay ahead of the competitive pack. He does this by designing and testing patterns that bring positive results. He knew fluorescent and UV materials help to increase viability at great depths.

Big fish didn't get that way by being reckless. They take advantage of the depths to avoid predators, including fly fishers. The forward-weight design of this pattern, along with its long tail, causes it to dip and dive, while the chenille body material pulsates and pushes the water during the retrieve. The commotion that this pattern creates can be easily detected through the lateral line sensors of any nearby trout. As they advance to investigate, the materials built into the Vampire Leech attract their attention from a greater distance than would other materials. The rest is up to the fly fisher.

Todd fishes this fly on an ultrafast-sinking, Deep-7 fly line. In greater depths, a 2X or 3X tippet is highly advisable, as the takes are often explosive.

Materials

Hook Mustad Signature Hook, 3XL, size 8
Bead Chartreuse or fluorescent orange bead, 1 mm (¹⁄₃₂ in)
Thread Size 6/0, black
Tail Black marabou fibre
Tail flash Polar Flash tinsel
Body Black UV Polar Chenille

How to tie

1 Pinch down the hook's barb, slide the bead up to the hook eye and secure the hook in a vice.

2 Lay down a thread base from the bead to the hook bend.

3 Tie in a marabou fibre tail at the bend. The tail should be as long as the hook shank.

4 Tie three strands of Polar Flash tinsel on each side of the tail.

5 At the bend, tie in the black UV Polar Chenille. Wrap it forward to the bead to make a body.

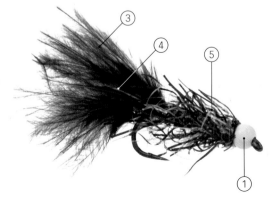

Christian FlyKrouss Belanger

EZ Crayfish

Sometimes a different use for the same material works better than the original. Rabbit fur's movement is limited when it is tied in as a clump. By switching to a rabbit strip, the originator was able to have a much longer and more active waving motion, even when the fly lay upon the streambed.

Christian FlyKrouss Belanger designed this fly in order to take full advantage of the rabbit fur's ease of movement. He prefers to fish the EZ Crayfish for brook trout, using an extra-fast-sinking tip line.

He casts upstream towards the head of deep pools and allows the fly to swim slowly across the bottom. The up-riding hook reduces hang-ups and gets down deep to where the trout are holding. If Christian misses a strike, he immediately begins a series of short, fast strips imitating a crayfish trying to escape.

Christian's most memorable event with the EZ Crayfish almost did not happen. He had gone fishless all day and was heading back to his car when he decided to try one last pool. 'One more cast and then home', he thought. On his proverbial last cast, Christian hooked and landed a 47.5-cm (19-in) brook trout. Christian was so impressed with the beauty of the trout that he released it back to the depths of the pool.

50% size

← Length 7.5 cm (3 in) →

Materials

Hook Mustad 3665A, size 8
Thread Size 6/0, orange
Eyes Small dumbbell eyes
Weight 0.35 mm lead wire
Antennae Root beer Crystal Flash
Claws Orange rabbit strip
Thorax Orange UV Polar Chenille
Rib Copper wire
Body Orange Crystal Chenille
Shell back Thin orange foam
Marker pen Permanent black

How to tie

1 Tie the dumbbell eyes onto the top of the hook shank. This will cause the fly to ride point up when fished.

2 Wrap the shank with lead wire and cover with thread.

3 On each side, at the bend, tie in the antennae and rabbit-strip claws. The hide

on the rabbit strips should face the hook, so that the fibres are free to move in the water.

4 At the bend, tie in the Polar Chenille and the copper wire.

5 Wind the Polar Chenille forward to the eye. Tie off.

6 Tie in the foam shell back at the eye. Push it back and run the hook point through it.

7 Wrap the wire over the foam shell back to hold it in place. Tie the wire off at the eye.

8 Wrap a thread head and cement it.

9 Using the black marker, make eyes, side marks and a top stripe on the shell back.

Todd Oishi

Todd's Czech Nymph

If you find yourself in an international competition, you have to fish, regardless of the conditions. If the fish are deep, you have to get deep to tempt them. Deep trout need deep flies. This pattern is the result of several years' experience on the competitive fly-fishing circuit.

Materials

Hook Snake 200, sizes 8 and 10

Bead Gold 3-mm (⅛-in) tungsten

Thread Size 8/0, fluorescent red

Underbody Self-adhesive lead sheeting or lead wire

Shell back Woven Mylar shell back material

Ribbing Copper wire

Abdomen Fluorescent orange steelhead yarn

Thorax and legs Natural fox squirrel dubbing

Todd Oishi is a member of the Canadian National Fly Fishing Team. He has earned several team and individual awards.

His experience and five years of experimentation led to the creation of Todd's Czech Nymph. Todd describes it as 'heavy as they come, while not compromising its shape and sink rate'.

The 'upside-down' orientation keeps the hook point above the fly and reduces hang-ups on underwater objects. This is important if you need to fish the fly on the bottom where the fish are holding.

Todd reports this pattern shines when combined with the short-line European nymphing techniques used in fast-flowing sections of a river. Yet another benefit is the pattern's durability; it can be bounced along the bottom without ruining its profile.

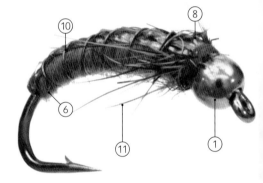

How to tie

1 Pinch down the hook's barb, slide the tungsten bead up to the hook eye, and secure the hook in a vice.

2 From self-adhesive lead sheeting or wire, trim a 2-mm (¹/₁₆-in) wide strip 7.5 cm (3 in) long. Attach the strip halfway down the hook bend and wrap it tightly towards the eye. When you reach the bead, start winding a second layer back towards the bend. Stop three-quarters of the way down the first layer and start wrapping a third layer back towards the bead. Stop just short of the bead to achieve a reasonable taper to the body.

3 Attach thread behind the bead and wrap it towards the bend to provide a solid base for the body materials. Stop where the lead wraps were tied in.

4 Tie on a thin strip of the Mylar shell back material to the top of the hook bend, then tie in the copper wire. Secure with several tight wraps.

5 Tie in a couple of fibres of fluorescent orange steelhead yarn to the bend of the hook, and dub it evenly onto the thread.

6 Wrap the steelhead yarn forward to create a tapered abdomen, stopping just short of the bead.

7 Pinch off a small clump of natural fox squirrel dubbing and dub it onto the thread.

8 Wrap the dubbing forward to the bead to form the thorax and secure the thread behind the bead with a half-hitch knot.

9 Pull the shell back forward to the bead and secure with two wraps and a half-hitch knot.

10 Wind the wire forward with evenly spaced wraps. Secure with several wraps of thread, whip finish and apply a drop of head cement to the knot.

11 With a needle or bodkin, pick loose some of the natural fox squirrel dubbing guard hairs on the underside of the thorax to simulate legs.

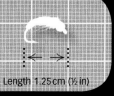

Length 1.25 cm (½ in)

Alessandro Vallerotonda

Blue Wing Olive Cripple

Not every mayfly hatches successfully. Many are not formed correctly, and these 'cripples' get caught in the surface film where they become an easy meal for hungry trout. The Blue Wing Olive Cripple imitates this free lunch, and its profile gives the trout confidence to feed.

Actual size

Length 1.25 cm (½ in)

Alessandro Vallerotonda is a tier from Cassino, Italy. He reports that these small flies often have difficulty hatching and escaping. Their wings get trapped in the water and as they struggle, they wiggle their bodies, legs and wings. This behaviour probably helps trigger the feeding brown trout.

In 2009, on the Rapido River, Alessandro observed trout focusing on the crippled insects and ignoring the healthy ones in the process of preparing to fly away. He took this observation back to his tying bench and created the Blue Wing Olive Cripple. He chose to use soft materials that would move freely, so as to imitate the struggle of the natural insect.

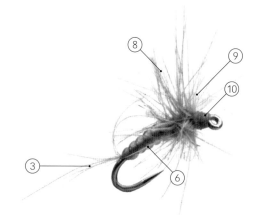

Materials

Hook Daiichi 1190, sizes 16–20

Thread Olive Danville, 70 denier

Tail CDC feather fibres

Abdomen Small olive D-rib

Wing Blue dun Antron fibres and blue dun hen hackle feather tip

Thorax and legs Natural CDC and blue dun hen hackle feather

How to tie

1 Bend the hook shank slightly to the right one-quarter of the way down the hook shank from the eye.

2 Wrap a thread base from the hook eye to the hook bend.

3 At the bend, tie in a tail of six CDC fibres as a tail equal in length to the hook shank.

4 Trim the end of the D-rib to a thin point and tie it in at the bend of the hook.

5 Wrap the thread three-quarters of the way towards the hook eye.

6 Wrap the D-rib to the thread location and tie off. Start with greater pressure and lessen the pressure as you move ahead. This will create a tapered body, thin at the tail and thicker at the forward end.

7 At the forward end of the body, tie in a few Antron fibres at 90 degrees to the hook shank. Trim the right side fibres very short and trim the left side fibres into a wing shape.

8 At the same location, tie a hen hackle tip directly on top of the Antron fibres that stick out on the left side of the hook shank.

9 Ahead of the wing, tie in dubbed CDC, making two wraps. Tie off and trim.

10 Wrap the hen hackle feather twice, ending ahead of the CDC. Tie off and trim. Make a small thread head. Trim and cement the thread head.

Tom Loe

Crystal Tiger Midge

This simple, effective pattern is designed to represent the larval stage of the chironomid. The red ribbing accents the segmentation and provides the red colour found in the haemoglobin that is vital to the insect. Chironomids are found in many areas, so this pattern should serve you well.

Here's a fly designed from the bottom up by Tom Loe from Mammoth Lakes, California. The Crystal Tiger Midge is a chironomid imitation, chironomids being an important food source for trout in alkaline still waters.

Chironomids have no escape mechanism. They just suspend there, hoping to avoid the trout's detection. Now, the trout are no dummies, and when this stage is on, and hundreds of thousands of chironomids are just hanging around, they take advantage of it and swallow them up like whales on krill.

Fishing this stage of the emergence is not too difficult. Simply suspend a Crystal Tiger Midge, or two, or three, and wait for the slightest movement of your strike indicator. Unless the emergence is obvious, hang your fly less than 30 cm (12 in) off the bottom of the lake. But be sure to strike with exuberance, because it may be a long way between the flies and the strike indicator, and you don't want to take a chance on missing what may be the trout of your lifetime.

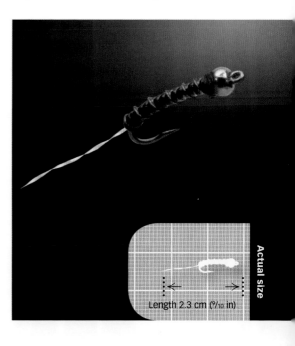

Actual size

Length 2.3 cm (⁹⁄₁₀ in)

Materials

Hook Tiemco 200 RBL, sizes 18–22

Thread Size 8/0, black

Bead 2 mm (¹⁄₁₆ in) black metal, filled with four wraps of 0.25 mm lead wire

Tail Lime Krystal Flash

Body Black latex or micro D-rib

Ribbing Fine, red copper wire

How to tie

1 Slide a bead over the hook point and up against the hook eye.

2 Take four wraps of 0.25 mm lead wire around the hook shank and force it into the bead opening.

3 Lay down a thread base from the bead to the hook bend.

4 At the bend, tie in one Krystal Flash fibre.

5 At the bend, tie in a length of copper wire and a black latex strip.

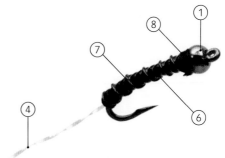

6 Wrap the latex forward to the bead.

7 Wrap the ribbing forward to the bead in fairly close wraps. The rib and body should show in equal amounts.

8 Make a thread head, whip finish and cement.

Mladjen Juskovic

Lim River Yellow Stonefly

There's something about yellow stoneflies that trout love. The Yellow Sally has long been recognized for its importance to fly fishers. British writer Richard Bowlker's 1747 work, *The Art of Angling*, seems to be the first mention of this important fly.

Mladjen Juskovic, from Montenegro, wanted a more realistic yellow stonefly pattern, because the trout in his home waters had become wary of the existing patterns. This area is part of the Adriatic drainage system and includes brown trout, grayling, marble trout, lake trout, char, strun and huchen.

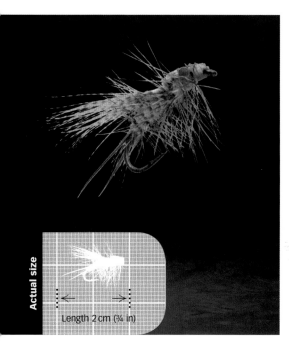

Actual size

Length 2 cm (¾ in)

Materials

Hook Tiemco 2302, size 14
Thread Size 8/0, yellow
Eyes Melted monofilament
Tail Olive goose biots
Rib Silver wire
Abdomen Yellow dubbing
Hackle Yellow hackle feather
Thorax Yellow dubbing
Thorax cover Yellow dyed mallard flank feather
Wing Yellow dyed mallard flank feather
Adhesive Softex

How to tie

1 Melt two ends of mono and tie in at the hook eye.

2 Wrap a thread base from the hook eye to the hook bend.

3 At the bend, tie in two olive goose biots as tails and silver wire for ribbing.

4 At the bend, tie in a yellow hackle feather by its tip.

5 At the bend, make a length of yellow dubbing. Wrap an abdomen forward about halfway to the hook eye.

6 Wrap the wire in open turns over the abdomen. Tie down and trim the excess.

7 Wrap the yellow hackle over the abdomen in open turns. Do not trim.

8 At the front end of the abdomen, tie in a wing of yellow dyed mallard flank feather. It should extend almost to the end of the tails. Do not trim the butt section.

9 At the same location, tie in another hackle feather.

10 Wrap the dubbing forward almost to the hook eye, making a thorax.

11 Wrap the hackle over the thorax. Trim the excess.

12 Pull the butt section of the mallard feather over the thorax, pushing the hackle fibres down. Tie off and trim.

13 Make a small thread head and cement the thread wraps.

14 Coat the thorax cover with Softex.

Bruce Corwin

Wally Wing Peccary Spinner

This trout pattern takes advantage of the natural look of a segmented body through its use of peccary hair. The wings are fashioned in the method made famous by Canadian Wally Lutz. It results in a delicate wing that can trap air bubbles and improve flotation.

Bruce Corwin is a guide, fly tier and watercolour artist from New York. He fishes the streams of New York, New Jersey, Montana and Yellowstone National Park.

The size and colour of the Wally Wing Peccary Spinner can be changed to match spinner imitations for a wide variety of mayfly species.

Materials

Hook TMC 200R, sizes 12–16

Thread Rusty brown UTC 70

Tail Light orange micro-fibbets

Abdomen Long peccary hair taken from the mane area on the peccary skin

Thorax Rust dubbing

Wing Wood duck breast feather

Adhesive CA glue

Marker pen Orange number 317 Staedtler Lumocolor

How to tie

1 Tie on at the hook eye and lay a base to the hook bend, making a small thread bump for splaying the tails.

2 At the bend, tie in two pairs of micro-fibbets, and splay them.

3 Wind the thread towards the hook eye, stopping one-third of the way from the eye.

4 At this point, tie in a peccary hair with the end hanging over the hook bend.

5 Wind the thread over the hair and down to the bend.

6 Cover the hook shank with CA glue.

7 Wrap the hair towards the hook eye, stopping where it was tied in.

8 Taper the abdomen by winding thread over the hair, and colour it with an orange marker pen.

9 Coat the abdomen with CA glue and allow it to dry.

10 Stroke most of the wood duck feather back 'against the grain' and tie it in at the forward end of the abdomen. The tip of the feather should be over the eye of the hook. Trim off the butt ends.

11 Grab three fibres from one side of the tip while holding the rest in your other hand. Split the feather down the centre stem. Repeat with the other side. Trim the stem.

12 Tease the feather segments back into a downwing position and figure-of-eight wrap them in place. Apply CA glue.

13 Dub a thorax over the wing tie-in thread wraps. Whip finish the thread wraps.

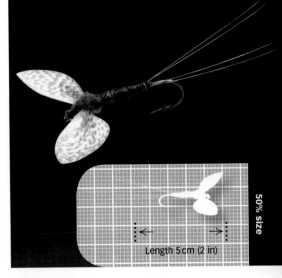

Length 5 cm (2 in)

50% size

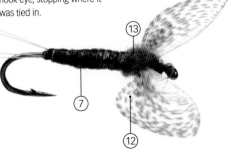

Walter "Wolly" Bayer

Facocchi May Fly

There are two crucial characteristics of this trout fly. First, you are not using a 'standard' vice. Second, the fly is not tied around the hook shank; instead, it's tied 'around' the strings of monofilament line, and the hook hangs freely under the fly. The advantage of this is a substantially thinner fly body.

Actual size

Length 4.5 cm (1¾ in)

Walter 'Wolly' Bayer is from Ireland. His home water includes the River Boyne in Leinster, in County Meath.

Wolly reports this style is effective because the hook is attached underneath the fly in a loop. It acts as a keel, allowing the fly to move freely with the current. The weight of the fly is so low that it lands like a feather. The light weight of a Facocchi fly means that it is easier to cast and the leader will turn over with even the largest flies. Also, the monofilament body does not absorb water – so it continues riding high even after being taken by several trout. Unlike fur-bodied flies, the monofilament easily sheds fish slime and goes back to floating without being treated.

As much as you may be tempted to display this fly, remember – it is intended to be fished.

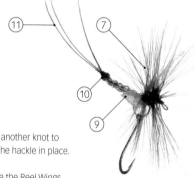

Materials

Hook Kamasan B440, size 16

Hackle Brown dry fly hackle

Wings Joseph Ludkin's Reel Wings – Upwings, medium or small

Body 1.8- to 2.7-kg (4- to 6-lb) Maxima nylon, clear and rust

Tail Pheasant tail fibres

Loom Wood dimensions, monofilament

How to tie

1 Build a loom from wood from which the fly will be suspended while construction takes place (see page 274 for Walter's website).

2 Make a double loop from the clear monofilament and connect it to the loom, maintaining tension with a rubber band and paper clip.

3 Knot the monofilament to create the fly's head.

4 Knot the dry fly hackle behind the head.

5 Make another knot to secure the hackle in place.

6 Secure the Reel Wings behind the hackle with another knot.

7 Wind the hackle in front of the Reel Wings and secure with another knot.

8 Tie in the coloured monofilament, make a loop below the fly and thread the hook on so that the hook point faces the monofilament head. Secure with a knot.

9 Build the body by knotting the clear and coloured monofilament. Stop when the desired length is attained.

10 Make a nail knot, but do not pull it tight.

11 Place three pheasant tail fibres in the nail knot and pull the knot tight, securing the tail fibres.

Günter Feuerstein

Minky Mouse

The advantage of the Minky Mouse over other mouse patterns is that it floats low in the water. In addition, due to the materials used, it is unsinkable. Also, its silhouette looks realistic, which means that it can be used successfully in slow currents where the fish get a good, close look at the fly.

Günter Feuerstein is a Master Flycasting Instructor and a member of the Loop Pro Team. He lives in Austria and fishes around the world.

Günter heard that mouse patterns were effective in Kamchatka, where he was scheduled to fish. On his way to Kamchatka, he made a presentation in Polar Ural, where he tried the Minky Mouse for big grayling. Of all the mouse patterns tried, his was the best for big grayling and big trout. Günter thinks its effectiveness is because nothing but mink fur can be seen from below.

Günter reports that this pattern fishes best during the darkest part of the evening in areas so far north that it never gets completely dark. He observed that when the grayling strikes, it does not close its mouth completely until it lands. As a result, do not strike the fish until it returns to the water, or it will not be hooked.

50% size

Length: 9 cm (3½ in)

Materials

Hook Gamakatsu F16 long shank streamer hook, size 2

Thread Dyneema size 3/0, black

Tail Straight-cut mink fur, 3 mm (⅛ in) wide

Body Cross-cut mink fur, 3 mm (⅛ in) wide

Back Dark brown 2-mm (¹⁄₁₆-in) closed-cell foam, 10 cm × 66 mm (4 × ¼ in)

Adhesive Zap-A-Gap

How to tie

1 Wrap a thread base from the hook eye to the hook bend.

2 At the hook bend, tie in a strip of mink straight-cut fur as a tail. The overall length of the fly should be 9 cm (3½ in).

3 At the hook bend, tie in a length of foam 1.5 times the length of the hook shank, so that the long end hangs out over the hook bend.

4 At the bend, tie in a length of cross-cut fur for the body. It should hang out over the hook bend.

5 Wrap the thread one-quarter of the way towards the hook eye.

6 Apply Zap-A-Gap to the thread wraps.

7 Wrap the fur strip, hide side against the hook shank, forward to where the thread stopped. Tie down the fur strip, but do not trim the excess.

8 Pull the foam strip over the top of the fur body and tie it in at the same point. Do not trim the excess.

9 Wrap the thread another quarter of the way along the hook shank. Repeat steps 5 to 8. This will result in a four-segment body covered by foam.

10 Trim the excess fur.

11 Fold the foam back to the previous segment and tie it in. Trim the excess, leaving a small tab sticking straight up.

12 Apply Zap-A-Gap to the thread wraps.

Aco Popov

New Village

Professional fly tiers spend many hours at the vice, either tying for customers or inventing new creations. This fly's inventor wanted a pattern that would settle on the water very gently. The soft CDC wings act as a parachute and slow the descent of the fly before it hits the water.

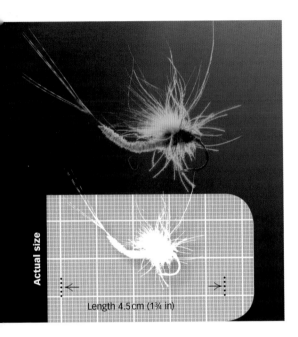

Actual size

Length 4.5 cm (1¾ in)

Aco Popov runs the Big Fisherman in Switzerland, and he has used this fly in many Balkan rivers. Reversing the hook when tying a dry fly is something that not many tiers attempt.

Placing the weight-supporting wings over the heaviest part of the hook allows the fly to ride higher, longer. Also, the 'business end' of the hook is partially hidden by the wings. Tiers will find that this method takes more time to tie, because it requires a finer touch to get the hackle wrapped between the hook point and the shank.

Aco's daily routine requires ten hours at the tying bench. This dedication paid off on numerous trips. In 2007, in three days on the River Unec, the New Village accounted for 30 trout and grayling between 30 and 50 cm (12 and 20 in). The first time he tried the pattern, it accounted for a brown trout of 35 cm (14 in). Over the next two hours the fly accounted for ten fish within a 150-m (500-ft) area. You cannot argue with success.

Materials

Hook TMC 5212, size 10
Thread Size 8/0, brown
Tail Coq de Leon
Body Yellow duck flank feather biot
Wing White CDC and yellow floss
Hackle Rust brown CDC

How to tie

1 Bend the front third of the shank up at a 30 degree angle.

2 Lay down a thread base from the eye to the hook bend.

3 At the eye, tie in four fibres of Coq de Leon.

4 At the bend, tie in a yellow biot. Wrap it forward three-quarters of the way to the hook eye, making a body.

5 At the end of the body, tie in yellow floss.

6 Tie in white CDC feather. Wrap around the shank and

pull the fibres up as a wing. Trim the butts.

7 Tie in a brown CDC feather. Wrap around the shank and pull the fibres down as legs. Trim the excess.

8 Pull the floss forward over the white CDC to separate it into two wings.

9 Make a small thread head and cement the thread wraps.

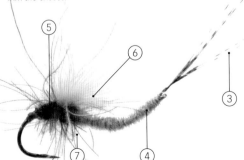

Jarkko Suominen

Olive Shuttlecock

Flies used for international competitions are guarded secrets until they show up in the competition. At that point, they become fair game for all who want to use them. The Olive Shuttlecock was developed for the 2006 World Fly Fishing Competition in Portugal.

International competitor Jarkko Suominen is on the Finnish team. He said he wanted to develop a small olive emerger pattern for easily spooked, educated, selective trout.

Although there are many similar patterns, this one was a good imitation of the naturals that hatch in Portugal during the competition. It can be adapted for size and colour to match the naturals found in your home area.

Jarkko's memory of his best day with the Olive Shuttlecock comes from that 2006 contest. He drew a good beat on the Alva River and spotted a few good trout before the official starting time. They were very easily spooked, so he had to get into position carefully without being seen. He crawled through a side stream and lay face down, awaiting the starting signal. He knew he would have only one attempt at the rising fish. It was a difficult cast of 10 m (30 ft), made from a prone position. The cast went well – and on the first and only drift the fish took the fly.

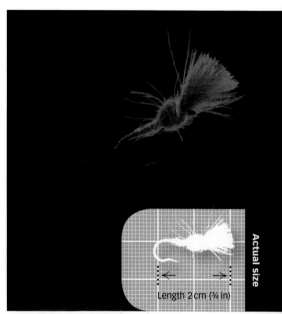

Actual size

Length 2 cm (¾ in)

Materials

Hook Justice 01WB, size 18
Thread Benecchi size 12/0, white
Tail Few fibres of grey polypropylene yarn
Body UNI size 8/0, olive
Thorax Natural CDC, dubbed
Wings Natural CDC

How to tie

1 Depending on their fullness, stack one to three CDC feathers.

2 Lay down a thread base from the hook eye to the bend.

3 Behind the hook eye, tie in the stacked CDC feathers as a wing.

4 Trim the feather butts.

5 Make two turns of thread behind the CDC feather wing to stand it up.

6 At the bend, tie in a few fibres of grey polypropylene yarn as a tail. Trim to the length of the hook shank.

7 At the bend, tie in olive thread and wrap a body almost to the base of the wing.

8 Dub a thorax from CDC fibres and make the last wrap in front of the wing.

9 Tie a small thread head and cement.

Olli Toivonen

Olli's Damsel

Only the best fly fishers are included on a country's national fly-fishing team – so when one of the elite tells me about a go-to pattern, I listen closely. This stillwater damselfly pattern is elegant in its simplicity.

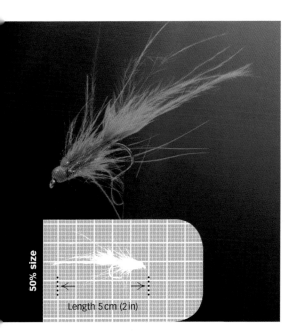

50% size

Length 5 cm (2 in)

Olli Toivonen is a member of the Finnish national team. He has used Olli's Damsel in fly-fishing competitions in Finland, New Zealand, Scotland and Italy for rainbow and brown trout.

Olli's Damsel works best in eutrophic lakes with plenty of weeds but clear water. His advice is to tie lots of variations of this pattern. Try a variety of hues to match the naturals where you fish.

Olli uses this pattern as the point fly in a two-fly rig. A floating or slow intermediate fly line works well. Of course, choosing the fly line depends on how deep the fish are in the water. By varying the weight of the bead, you can make the fly sink very slowly or swim very aggressively, like a jig.

Passive and feeding fish often take this slow-sinking version, while active or recently stocked fish often take a faster-retrieved fly. When you have fished almost to the end of the cast, leave the fly hanging in the water 1–2 m (3–6 ft) deep. Many times, the following fish takes the fly as it hangs.

Materials

Hook Kamasan B170, size 8
Thread Size 8/0, olive green
Bead 3–4 mm (⅛–⅙ in), hot orange brass
Tail Olive marabou
Body Olive marabou
Thorax hackle Olive CDC feather
Thorax Golden brown Hareline Ice Dubbing

How to tie

1 Slide a bead onto the hook and stop against the hook eye. Large beads will sink the fly faster than small beads.

2 Wrap a thread base from behind the bead to the bend.

3 Tie in a tail of olive marabou fibres about three times the length of the hook shank.

4 At the bend, tie in a dubbing loop made with marabou fibres and wrap it forward almost to the eye. After each turn, sweep the fibres to the rear before making the next wrap.

5 Just behind the bead, tie in an olive CDC feather as a thorax and make two turns. Trim the excess.

6 On top of the thorax feather wraps, make a short dubbing loop of golden brown Hareline

Ice Dubbing. Make two wraps. Tie off and trim the excess, leaving several long fibres as flash.

7 Cement the thread wraps.

Bruce Corwin

Organza Softy

The Organza Softy takes advantage of the characteristics of a common material not often included in the fly-tier's arsenal. Organza fibres reflect light in all directions, giving the impression of the trapped gas bubble created when many kinds of insects hatch.

Bruce Corwin had success using organza on other patterns, so he decided to try it with the age-old traditional soft hackle trout patterns.

Use the following method to prepare the ribbon. Organza ribbon can be found at any craft, haberdashery or fabric store. Do not purchase a ribbon with a wire edge – you need one with a soft edge. Take a 7.5-cm (3-in) strip of ribbon and lay it flat. With a straight edge and razor, cut along the length, about 3 mm (⅛ in) from the finished edge. This leaves the rib edge and 3 mm (⅛ in) of the weave. Use a bodkin to remove individual strands of the weave in the long direction. You'll be left with the ribbed edge and the short fibres sticking straight out.

Bruce uses the Organza Softy as a traditional soft hackle and a searching pattern. He fishes the fly across the water and on a swing. At the end of the drift he often uses the Leisenring lift method to imitate an insect rising to the surface in preparation for hatching.

Actual size

Length 1.25 cm (½ in)

Materials

Hook Gaelic Supreme Sylvester Nemes Up-Eyed Soft Hackle, size 13

Thread Pearsall's gossamer silk (chestnut)

Underbody Light rust fur

Overbody Light rust stripped organza ribbon

Thorax Light rust fur

Hackle Ginger hen hackle feather

How to tie

1 Wrap a thread base from the hook eye to the hook bend, stopping above the barb.

2 At the bend, tie in the organza ribbon with the fibres pointing rearward.

3 Dub an underbody of fur and wrap it forward nearly to the hook eye.

4 Palmer the organza ribbon over the underbody, making sure that the fibres lean back and point towards the hook bend. Tie off at the hook eye and trim the excess.

5 Dub fur and wrap a thorax.

6 At the hook eye, tie in the hen hackle feather and make three wraps. Tie off and trim.

Alan Bithell

Little Black Bug

Little black bugs are common on trout rivers. Unfortunately, small flies can be difficult to tie. The Little Black Bug is an exception. It is easy to tie, and the foam body ensures it will float forever – well, at least until it is torn apart by hungry trout.

Actual size

Length 1.25 cm (½ in)

Alan Bithell, owner of Crackaig Flies, reports this isn't a fly tied with the intention of imitating any specific insect. If the fish are taking something small and black on the surface, then the Little Black Bug is what Alan will throw at them.

When using small hooks, it is very easy to fill up the gap with materials and thread. With this pattern, there are only a couple of layers of thread on the underside of the hook. The all-important gap isn't filled up at all. Everything else goes on the top of the hook shank.

Materials

Hook Scud hook, size 18
Thread UNI size 8/0, black
Abdomen Black 2 mm (¹⁄₁₆ in) closed-cell foam
Wings Pearl foil
Legs Grizzly hackle feather
Thorax Black 2 mm (¹⁄₁₆ in)) closed-cell foam

How to tie

1 Wrap a thread base over the middle half of the hook shank. Return the thread to a point directly over the point of the hook.

2 Cut a 2 mm (¹⁄₁₆ in) strip of black foam. Quickly hold it in a flame to soften it without melting it. Roll it between your fingers to change the cross-section from square to round.

3 At the middle of the hook shank, tie in the foam body, securing it with three turns of thread. The abdomen should stick out 6 mm (¼ in) beyond the tie-in point.

4 At the same point, tie in a length of pearl foil at 30 degrees to the hook shank. Fold the forward-pointing section back, and secure the wings with thread wraps. Trim the wings to equal length; they should reach slightly past the abdomen and splay out at 30 degrees to the hook shank and have a flat V-shape.

5 Advance the thread to in front of the foam and tie in a grizzly hackle. Wrap it parachute style around the foam. Tie off to the hook shank. Trim the excess hackle.

6 Advance the thread to the hook eye. Trim off the forward-facing hackle fibres that hang over the hook eye.

7 Gently pull the front end of the foam down over the hook shank and tie it down at the hook eye. This will form the thorax. Do not pull too tightly, otherwise the foam will be compressed and lose its buoyancy.

8 Make a small thread head, cement the thread wraps and whip finish.

Günter Feuerstein

Pin-Ki

As darkness arrives, most colours disappear. One exception is fluorescent pink. The problem was to discover just the right shade of fluorescent pink and then to experiment with its effectiveness for trout. This pattern is the result of all of that experimentation.

Günter Feuerstein's home water is the River Rhine. He reports that this fly is fished best for migrating lake resident rainbows or steelhead. It can also fish well in rivers with local rainbow populations – but as the fly is a visible attractor pattern, they can soon get used to it, especially when the trout are fished on catch-and-release regulations. The fly is fished at times when the UV rays go deepest into the water and in slightly coloured water or overcast conditions. The Pin-Ki, short for Pink Killer, is never fished in bright sunlight in clear water.

Günter was experimenting with UV colours about 15 years ago and tried to find the perfect colour and attractor pattern for migrating rainbows. Finally, he found the right warm pink colour and material combination. This fly is very visible just before sunset, when it gets dark underwater and all other colours disappear. The combination of soft hackle and colour gives the nymph a translucent look. The flashy tail catches and reflects the last of the sunlight.

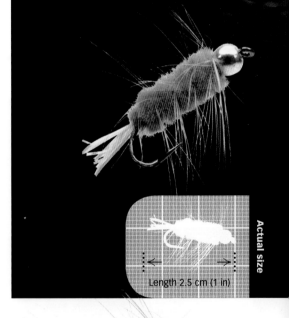

Actual size

Length 2.5 cm (1 in)

Materials

Hook Tiemco TMC 100, sizes 6–10
Thread Dyneema size 8/0, white
Bead Silver steel or tungsten
Weight Lead wire
Tail Pearl Flashabou
Body Fluorescent pink Orvis chenille
Ribs Silver wire and white hen hackle feather
Adhesive Zap-A-Gap

How to tie

1 Slide a silver bead over the hook point up to the hook eye.

2 Wrap a thread base from behind the bead to a point directly above the hook barb.

3 At the same location, tie in a small bundle of pearl Flashabou as a tail. Trim to a length of 6 mm (¼ in).

4 Wrap the hook shank with a layer of lead wire.

5 At the tail, tie in a white hen saddle feather, by the tip, with one side of the fibres removed.

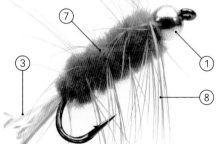

6 At this same location, tie in a length of silver wire and a length of fluorescent pink Orvis chenille.

7 Wrap the chenille forward and secure it behind the bead head.

8 Wrap the saddle feather forward, making five turns, and secure it. Trim the excess.

9 Wrap the silver wire forward in the opposite direction and secure it. Trim the excess.

10 Apply Zap-A-Gap over the thread wraps.

Abel Tripoli

Pajarito Alemàn

Imagine not being able to find hooks large enough to accommodate the local 3.6-kg (8-lb) trout. Abel Tripoli's solution was to extend his pattern with a longer tail. His Pajarito Alemàn translates as Little German Bird, because the cast fly looks like a German flag fluttering in the wind.

Materials

Hook Partridge CS15
  Carrie Stevens, size 2
Thread UNI size 3/0, black
Tail White bucktail
Body Pearl Flashabou
Rib Gold wire
Back wing White bucktail
Mid wing Yellow bucktail
Main wing Orange
  bucktail under
  black bucktail
Topping Peacock herl
Head Black thread
Adhesive 5-minute epoxy

Abel Tripoli uses this fly in the Limay River, in northwest Patagonia, Argentina. There he fishes for brown trout and rainbows.

Abel's goal was to irritate big fish to attack a potential threat. When he tried a regular Bugger or Bunny style, the fish only pursued the fly a few feet without taking it. The idea of using larger patterns brought concerns about the weight of the fly once fully soaked. However, the bucktail shed water during casting, so the fly was aerodynamic.

One spring day, with high, fast, but clear water, Abel hooked a brown trout that took him into his backing. After 20 minutes and a 365-m (400-yd) run, Abel landed the 5-kg (11-lb) brown. That day the Pajarito Alemàn accounted for 14 trout averaging 3.6 kg (8 lb).

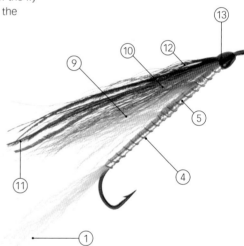

How to tie

1 Wrap a thread base from the hook eye to the hook bend. At the bend, tie in a small bunch of white bucktail equal to 1.5 times the length of the hook shank.

2 To compensate for the increased diameter where the bucktail ends, tie in another bunch of bucktail from the end of the tail, forward to the middle of the hook shank. Build up an even base of thread. Fill any imperfection with thread until you have a nice, even underbody.

3 At the hook bend, tie in a length of gold wire for ribbing.

4 At the hook bend, tie in six pieces of pearl Flashabou and

wrap it as a body three-quarters of the way towards the hook eye. Do not trim.

5 Counter-wrap the ribbing forward to the end of the Flashabou. Do not trim.

6 At the forward point of the body, tie in a back wing of white bucktail. It should reach to the bend of the hook.

7 Wrap the pearl Flashabou forward to within 6 mm (¼ in) of the hook eye.

8 Counter-wrap the gold wire rib to this same point. Trim the Flashabou and the rib.

9 At the front of the body, tie in a bunch of yellow bucktail

that reaches the tip of the white bucktail wing.

10 At this same point, tie in a bunch of orange bucktail that reaches the tip of the white bucktail wing.

11 At this same point, tie in a smaller bunch of black bucktail that reaches the tip of the white bucktail wing.

12 At this same point, tie in six strands of peacock herl that reach the tip of the white bucktail wing.

13 Form a thread head and coat it with 5-minute epoxy.

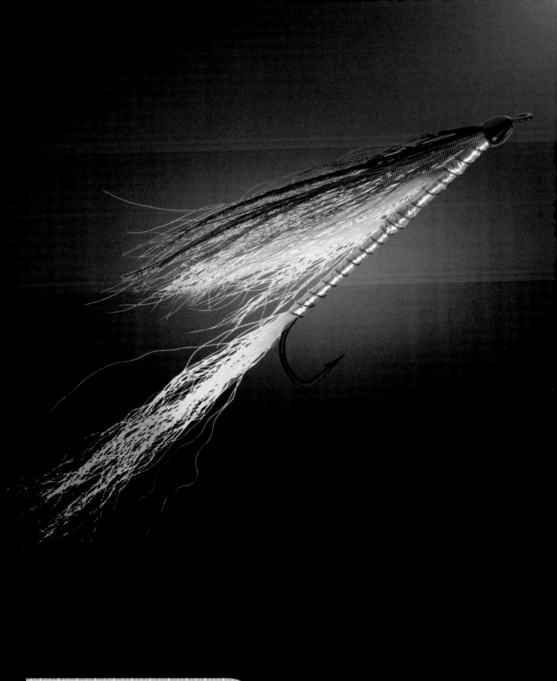

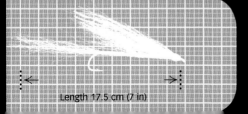

Length 17.5 cm (7 in)

Aco Popov

Popov Gammarus

Although fly tying goes back many years, some tiers are taking advantage of modern materials to make durable flies. UV varnish is one such material. It produces a clear body that allows the colours underneath to show through. This gives the fly an inner glow that fools fish.

Materials

Hook Knapek G, size 12
Thread Size 8/0, brown
Weight 3.3 mm (⅛ in) tungsten bead, copper, and lead wire
Body Rainbow Scud Dubbing
Legs Partridge feather
Antennae Red Senyo's Shaggy Dub
Rib Monofilament
Back UV varnish
Adhesive Superglue
Equipment UV light

Aco Popov, from Macedonia, now lives in Switzerland. His pattern has proven its effectiveness for trout on many Balkan rivers, and the Rhine in Switzerland.

Aco believes that the fly owes its effectiveness to the clear body resulting from the use of UV varnish. The result fools fish and is especially durable, making the time at the vice well spent.

In the winter of 2008, Aco fished the Rhine near Schaffhausen. It was very cold, with temperatures near freezing – not prime fishing weather. In spite of the conditions, Aco landed five fish – all in the 30–40 cm (12–16 in) range.

How to tie

1 Slide a tungsten bead over the point and up to the middle of the hook shank.

2 Cement the bead in place with Superglue.

3 Wrap lead wire on both sides of the bead, covering the shank.

4 Wrap a thread base from the hook eye over the lead to the hook bend.

5 At the bend, tie in two pieces of Senyo's Shaggy Dub so that they stick out past the bend of the hook by 6 mm (¼ in).

6 At the bend, tie in monofilament and a partridge feather.

7 At the bend, start a length of dubbing and wrap it forward to the hook eye, making a body.

8 Coat the dubbed body with UV varnish and treat with a UV lamp for 20 seconds.

9 Pull the partridge feather over the top of the fly, pull the fibres down under the fly and tie it down at the hook eye.

10 Wrap the monofilament over the partridge feather, making segments.

11 Coat the partridge feather with UV varnish and treat with a UV lamp for 20 seconds.

12 At the hook eye, tie in two pieces of Senyo's Shaggy Dub so that they stick out past the hook eye by 6 mm (¼ in).

13 Make a small thread head, whip finish and trim.

14 Coat the top of the fly with UV varnish and treat with a UV lamp for 20 seconds.

Lambert Tripet

Tubestream Orange

Big fish eat big flies. A large fly with sufficient movement in the water will attract fish and entice them to strike. This fly is an attractor, not an imitation of any living organism. It is designed for deep lakes where large trout are lurking in search of dinner.

50% size

Length 5 cm (2 inches)

This pattern by Lambert Tripet has been used successfully in Switzerland, France and Slovenia.

Lambert's preferred technique is to use a sinking line to get the fly deep. The fly is easy to cast, because it is very light. As it sinks, the marabou fibres wave enticingly. He retrieves the fly slowly to give the fibres time to compress and rebound over and over. Although this pattern was originally designed for salmon, it has proven its effectiveness on large trout in deep water.

Lambert hoped this design would reduce the destruction of his flies. A 'normal' streamer will withstand the attack of only one or two fish before the long streamer hackles are torn from the hook.

Materials

Tube Protube System
Hook TMC, size 8
Thread Size 6/0, orange
Head Gold cone,
 size medium
Underbody Cream
 marabou fibres
Body Orange marabou
 fibres
Flash Pearl Flashabou
Adhesive Head cement

How to tie

1 Place the tube on a needle and place the needle in your vice.

2 Wrap a thread base on the rear 3 cm (1¼ in) of the tube. Stop 1 cm (⅜ in) from the end.

3 Cover the thread wraps with head cement and let it dry.

4 Make a dubbing loop with cream marabou fibres and wrap the loop forward to cover the rear half of the thread base. Tie it down and trim the excess marabou.

5 At the forward end of the cream marabou, tie in six pieces of pearl Flashabou evenly around the tube.

6 Make a dubbing loop of orange marabou fibres and wrap the forward half of the thread base. Tie it down and trim the excess orange marabou. Whip finish.

7 Slide a gold cone over the front end of the tube so that

the concave part of the cone overlaps the thread wraps.

8 Cut the tube, leaving 4 cm (1½ in) ahead of the cone. Melt the tube with a flame and push the end of the tube flat, so that it prevents the cone from sliding off the tube. Be sure not to close the tube opening when you flatten the end.

Harri Hytönen

Harri's Sipsipussi

Sipsipussi is Finnish for 'chip bag', and this fly gets its name from the material used for the shiny body. Harri Hytönen noticed the inside of his bag of chips had a highly reflective silver colour. Being the creative sort, he decided to try the material for an early-season fly pattern.

Early season brown trout feed on small baitfish. In Finland, these baitfish are mostly silver-coloured. Harri wanted a streamer with an active wing that could be fished in slow waters yet still be attractive enough to goad the brown trout into feeding in the cold water.

Harri has always preferred black and silver patterns before the water warms. It gives the impression of a swimming baitfish that is easily swimming along. When fished in moving water, it can be weighted with splitshot or by using a sinking line.

Several years ago, during a competition in Finland, Harri was fishing with a friend. The water there is usually very clear, but on that day it was slightly muddy. It was early May and the brown trout were just entering the river from the ocean. Harri caught six fish over 50 cm (20 in) on a day when six fish might not even have been seen, much less caught.

50% size

Length 5 cm (2 in)

Materials

Hook Knapek streamer, size 1
Thread Size 6/0, black
Tail Black squirrel tail hair
Rib Silver tinsel
Body Strip taken from potato chip bag (silver)
Underwing Black squirrel and two strands of Flashabou
Wing Black marabou
Head Black Antron

How to tie

1 Wrap a thread base from the hook eye to the bend.

2 At the bend, tie in a tail made of black squirrel tail hairs equal to the length of the hook shank.

3 At the bend, tie in a length of silver tinsel to be used as ribbing.

4 At the bend, tie in a strip cut from a potato chip bag with the silver side showing. Wrap the body forward almost to the hook eye, leaving room to tie in the wing.

5 Ahead of the body, tie in an underwing of black squirrel tail hair with two strands of Flashabou. The squirrel hair should reach to the end of the fly's tail.

6 Tie in a wing of black marabou over the underwing and reaching the end of the fly's tail.

7 At the hook eye, tie in some black Antron so that it surrounds the fly and reaches as far back as the end of the body.

8 Make a small thread head, and cement.

Ville Vainio

Ville's Peacock Rubber Leg Nymph

Ville Vianio is from Finland and a member of the Finnish National Fly Fishing Team. He needed a third fly to be fished along with two more natural-looking flies. It had to be dark and sink quickly.

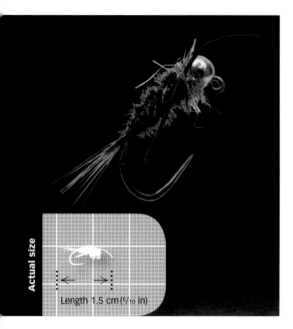

Actual size

Length 1.5 cm (⁶/₁₀ in)

His memorable day with this pattern was in 2005 during the World Competition in Sweden. The Finnish team was in fourth place before the last competition session.

Ville felt that Finland would get a medal, but it would require success from every team member. The judge explained that none of the competitors had waded to the other side of the big, fast river in flood. Wading seemed impossible. Ville fished the 'home bank' side, catching only one rainbow.

He waded across the river, ran to the end of his assigned section and waded like a moose to the other side. With the first cast, he got a grayling and carried it back across to the measuring judge. Sensing the prospect of a medal, he swam back to the same place and another fish took his fly. Again and again he made the round trips. At the end of the session, he was totally exhausted but happy. A total of nine fish gave him the win.

When the final results were announced, the team learned that it had won second place.

Materials

Hook Hanak 400, sizes 10–16
Thread UNI size 8/0, black
Bead 2–4 mm (¹/₁₆–⅛ in) gold, tungsten, or brass
Weighting Lead wire
Tail Black hackle fibres
Body Peacock herl
Legs Black rubber
Collar Red Spectra Dubbing on red UNI size 8/0 thread

How to tie

1 Slide a bead onto the hook so that it is up against the hook eye.

2 Wrap five turns of lead wire onto the hook shank behind and against the bead.

3 Lay down a thread base from bead to hook bend.

4 At the bend, tie in ten black hackle fibres for a tail equal to the length of the hook shank.

5 Tie in peacock herl at the bend and advance the thread almost to the bead.

6 Wrap the herl forward almost to the bead and tie off.

7 At the bead, tie in two pairs of rubber legs equal to the hook shank's length. Let them stick out at 90 degrees to the hook shank.

8 Tie off the black thread, and trim.

9 Use red thread and make a dubbed collar from red Spectra Blend over the wraps holding the rubber legs. Tie off and cement the red thread wraps.

Alan Bithell

BiColoured Nymph

The BiColoured Nymph is a fast, efficient and deadly alternative to woven nymphs. Unlike the woven variety, this pattern requires very little tying time. Because of this, you'll have no concerns about fishing them deeply, and possibly losing them to the rocks.

Alan Bithell, from Scotland, owns Crackaig Flies. To the envy of most fly fishers, he has centred his life around tying, fishing, guiding and instructing.

The effectiveness of woven flies has been proven over time. With two different colours woven together, the flies mimic natural insects that have a dark back over a lighter belly. The downside is that woven bodies take too much time to create. Alan knew that pheasant tail fibres had been used in many nymph patterns for many years. He experimented with a new method for creating the two-colour body without having to weave it. The BiColoured Nymph is the successful result of his experimentation.

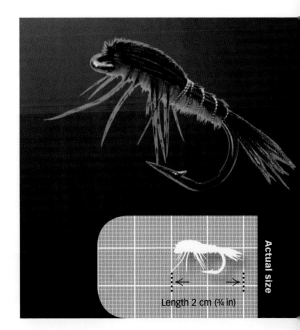

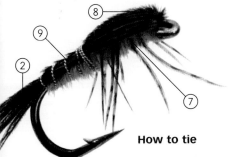

Length 2 cm (¾ in)

Actual size

Materials

Hook Mustad 94840, size 10
Thread Size 6/0, yellow
Tail Pheasant tail fibres
Rib Fine silver wire
Body Yellow dyed pheasant tail fibres

How to tie

1 At the midpoint of the hook shank, tie in 15 pheasant tail fibres forward over the eye. Cover only the forward one-third of the hook shank with the thread wraps. The pheasant tail fibre tips should be three times the length of the hook shank. The butt ends should be hanging over the hook bend.

2 Fold the butt ends forward over the thread wraps and tie them down on top of the pheasant tail tips.

3 Wrap the thread all the way to the hook bend.

4 At the hook bend, tie in a length of silver wire.

5 At the hook bend, tie in ten yellow dyed pheasant tail fibres by their tips.

6 Wrap the thread up to the hook eye, making sure you smooth out any bumps formed by the first bunch of pheasant tail fibres.

7 Wrap the dyed pheasant tail fibres forward to the hook eye. Cement the thread wraps.

8 Pull the tail fibres from over the hook eye back over the top of the dyed pheasant body.

9 Secure the pheasant tail fibres by wrapping them with open turns of the wire. Wrap the wire two-thirds of the way to the hook eye.

10 Secure the wire with a half hitch and 'worry' the wire instead of cutting it off. This will tighten the wire wraps and leave a burr that keeps everything secure.

Joseph Ludkin

Tiger Fly

Seeing a fly that's flush in the surface is often difficult, especially in low light conditions. The Tiger Fly employs a new winging material that catches the light and sparkles. As a bonus, a dropper loop is incorporated into the fly, so additional flies do not have to be tied to the hook's bend. This makes for a more natural drift.

Unsatisfied with other manufactured wings and desiring something more realistic, Joseph Ludkin, from England, invented Reel Wings. They have a cellular finish that catches any available light and twinkles as it dances down the river, allowing for fishing into the evening.

Joseph's home river is the Upper Swale, North Yorkshire – a very colourful free stone river. For this reason, Joseph selected orange dyed peacock herl because it would show up better in the moorland-stained water.

Actual size

Length 2 cm (¾ in)

Materials

Hook Partridge Klinkhammer Extreme, size 18

Thread Brown flat silk, size 8/0

Dropper loop 1.3-kg (3-lb) fluorocarbon

Body Orange Christoph Grzybowski stripped peacock herl/body quill

Thorax Peacock herl dyed orange

Hackle Brown cock hackle feather

Post Joseph Ludkin's Reel Wings – Upwings, L or M

Adhesives Superglue and Sally Hansen Hard As Nails

How to tie

1 Wrap a thread base from the hook eye to the point directly above the hook barb and back halfway to the hook eye.

2 Cut a 2-cm (¾-in) length of fluorocarbon and bend it in half. Tie it in where the thread stopped and wrap over it to the hook eye and back to the starting location. Trim the excess. The dropper loop should extend 3 mm (⅛ in) beyond the thread wraps at the hook point.

3 Wrap a tapered body base, with the thread wrapping

between the loop and the midpoint of the hook shank.

4 At the dropper loop, tie in a stripped peacock herl and wrap it forward to the midpoint of the shank. Trim the excess.

5 Tie in the Reel Wings halfway between the hook eye and the midpoint of the shank, holding the wings flat under the shank at right angles. Fold the wings up and hold the tips of the wings together. Catch the base at the back of the wing with the thread and then repeat at the front in a figure-of-eight lash.

6 At the midpoint of the shank, tie in orange herl and wrap to the back of the wings. Do not trim the excess.

7 Tie in the hackle and wrap around the base of the wings in a parachute style, using the wings as a post. Tie off in front of the wings and trim the excess.

8 Wrap the herl in front of the wings and trim the excess.

9 Make a small thread head and finish.

Silvio Edmund

Pinky

The Pinky is an easy, basic nymph pattern. The important feature of this fly seems to be the pink dubbing. It becomes translucent when wet and looks like a natural nymph.

The Pinky comes from Silvio Edmund of Westport, New Zealand. It would be more exciting if Silvio had some fantastic story to go with this fly's development. However, he reports that he simply got tired of tying the standard nymphs and cobbled this one together just for fun. In fact, he admits to having carried it around for a couple of years before trying it.

The discovery of this fly's effectiveness came much later. Silvio had spotted a 3-kg (6½-lb) brown in very clear water, but the fish would not take his client's offerings. While Silvio scanned his fly box, the client was looking over his shoulder and asked about the pink one. Two casts later, the brown was hooked, landed, photographed and released.

The conversation immediately turned to the name of the fly. Silvio, not thinking especially creatively at that moment, dubbed it 'Pinky'.

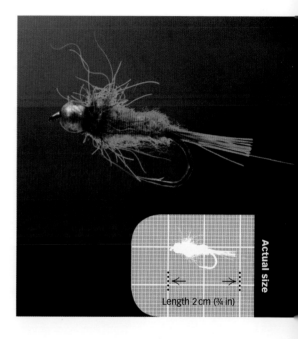

Actual size

Length 2 cm (¾ in)

Materials

Hook Kamasan B 830, sizes 10–16
Thread UNI, brown or olive 6/0
Head Gold or black tungsten bead
Tail Tan or brown hackle feather fibres
Body Pink synthetic craft fur
Legs Spiky hare's ear dubbing

How to tie

1 Slide a bead onto the hook and push it up against the hook eye.

2 Tie in behind the bead to hold it against the eye.

3 Wrap a thread base from behind the bead to the hook bend.

4 At the hook bend, tie in a tail of hackle fibres.

5 Dub a tapered pink body and wrap it forward to the bead.

6 Dub a scraggly collar of hare's ear and pick it out to look like legs.

7 Make a head, whip finish and cement.

Pat O'Keefe

Damsel Nymph

This simple trout fly represents the damselfly that is prolific in the weedy lakes throughout New Zealand. Its effectiveness cannot be disputed. It was the top-performing fly used at Lake Otomangakau during the Oceania Fly Fishing Championships in 1999.

Over the years it has proven to be a top performer. Pat recommends using a floating line and a 3.5–4.5-m (12–15-ft) leader. The preferred retrieve is a series of four short strips followed by a pause.

The Damsel Nymph can be used with different techniques, including stalking the lake edges for cruising fish, stillwater nymphing and drift fishing.

Actual size

Length 3 cm (1¼ inches)

Materials

Hook Black Magic A12
Thread Olive monocord
Tail Olive marabou
Body Synthetic peacock
Head Ruby red bead

How to tie

1 Slide a red bead onto the hook and secure it against the hook eye.

2 Lay down a thread base to the bend of the hook.

3 Tie in a tail of olive marabou. The tail should be twice the length of the hook.

4 Dub a body of synthetic peacock. Wrap it from the bend up to the bead.

5 Whip finish and cement.

6 Pick out dubbing to make it fuzzy.

Jim Kitis

Jimki Marron

Lurking in Western Australia are the largest freshwater crustaceans in the world. The marron can grow to nearly 1.3 kg (3 lb) and the local trout love to dine on them. This pattern, looking like our crayfish, imitates the smaller, more delectable marrons.

Jim Kitis, who owns Australis Fishing, wanted a 'close enough' looking pattern. In fact, the Jimki Marron not only looks like the local crustaceans, it also looks like many of the other resident black organisms, such as leeches, juvenile lamprey eels, nightfish and some galaxias.

In ponds and lakes, Jim fishes the fly on the bottom with an erratic stop-and-go retrieve. In rivers, his retrieve is much slower, allowing the soft materials to move with the current.

50% size

Length 6 cm (2¼ in)

Materials

Hook Black Aberdeen, size 4
Thread Black flat waxed nylon
Eyes Lead dumbbell, painted black
Body Black Sparkle Chenille
Legs Black hackle feathers
Claws Olive rabbit zonker strip
Carapace Plastic sheeting
Paint Black nail polish

How to tie

1 Wrap a thread base from close to the hook eye to above the hook's barb.

2 At the hook bend, build a thread base for the dumbbell eyes. On top of this base, tie in the lead dumbbell eyes, using figure-of-eight wraps.

3 Turn the hook so that the point is above the hook shank.

4 At the hook bend, tie in two 3-mm (⅛-in) wide rabbit zonker strips, one on each side of the dumbbell eyes, with the hide sides facing each other.

5 At the hook bend, tie in a length of Sparkle Chenille and wind it over the lead eyes, almost to the hook eye. Then wrap it back to the hook bend, forming a tapered body that is thicker near the hook bend. Tie off and trim the excess.

6 Behind the lead eyes, tie in a 6-mm (¼-in) wide diamond-shaped strip of clear plastic sheeting.

7 Push the sheeting back over the lead eyes. Tie in two hackle feathers. Wind them over the Sparkle Chenille, in the opposite direction, almost

to the hook eye. Tie in and trim the excess.

8 Pull the plastic sheeting over the body, forcing the hackle feather fibres down. Tie down and cement the thread wraps.

9 Trim the plastic sheeting so that a 6-mm (¼-in) length sticks out at 90 degrees to the hook shank. This represents the marron's tail.

10 Paint the plastic sheeting with black nail polish.

Todd Miller

Credit Card Hell

All these years, I've thrown out those free credit cards they send me. Now I learn I could have used the cards for a good purpose: to make a realistic hellgrammite trout pattern with a wide, flat body.

Materials

Hook Dai-Riki 270, size 6
Thread Size 8/0, brown
Weight 0.80 mm lead wire
Underbody A strip of credit card 1 cm (⅜ in) wide
Tail Brown biots
Rib Brown Larva Lace
Legs Black hackle
Body Brown/olive dubbing
Front legs Black hen hackle
Shell back Black Swiss Straw
Feelers Brown biots
Adhesive Superglue

Todd Miller, who owns Todd Miller Black Flies, Illinois, was tired of having lead wire break into small pieces when he tried to flatten it. He started experimenting and developed this method for making flattened bodies with a wide profile.

Todd needed a pattern for finicky fish in a clear river. The Credit Card Hell is best fished on a dead drift, looking like a natural that's been pulled free by the heavy current. The strikes are very hard and, so far, the fish set the hook themselves on the strike.

How to tie

1 Wrap the entire hook shank with lead wire.

2 Cover the wire with thread wraps and coat with Superglue. Let it dry.

3 Flatten the wire with flat-nose pliers.

4 Coat the flattened lead with Superglue.

5 Lay the credit card strip on, starting near the eye. Start wrapping the thread over the card to the bend of the hook.

6 Remove the hook; replace it in the vice, holding it by the hook eye.

7 Continue wrapping the thread over the credit card all the way to the end. Remember to wrap in the opposite direction when you reverse the hook.

8 Place two biot tails on top of the card and tie them in.

9 At the far end of the credit card strip, tie in a length of ribbing.

10 At the same location, tie in a black hackle.

11 Apply dubbing and wrap a body from the end of the credit card strip to the midpoint of the hook shank.

12 Wrap the black hackle forward over the card and up the hook shank to where the front of the body ends. Tie off.

13 Wrap the rib forward, in the opposite direction, and tie off at the end of the body.

14 Switch the hook back to its original position.

15 At the front of the body, tie in some Swiss Straw and the hen hackle.

16 Add dubbing and wrap the body forward almost to the eye of the hook.

17 Pull the hackle and straw forward over the top of the thorax. Tie them in.

18 Tie in biot feelers.

19 Continue dubbing and pull the straw over to make a large, flat head. Trim the excess.

20 Make a small thread head.

21 Use some Velcro to pull some dubbing fibres out, making a shaggy body.

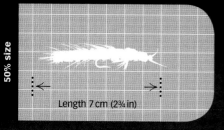

50% size

Length 7 cm (2¾ in)

Length 7.5 cm (3 inches)

Delaware Baby Brown

This pattern accounts for the largest brown trout brought to the net by Ken Tutalo's clients, year after year. It's the placement of the weight on the hook shank and the soft materials that create the illusion of a small fish in distress.

Materials

Hook Size 2, long streamer hook

Thread Size 6/0, red

Weight Lead wire

Head Large gold conehead

Undertail Glissen Glow

Tail Gold zonker strip

Body Rust Ice Dubbing

Wing Gold zonker strip under Glissen Glow

Throat Red Krystal Flash

Big fish eat little fish. Hey, it's a fact of life. However, big browns often eat little browns. This fact of life was something Ken Tutalo took advantage of when he designed this pattern.

Ken, from Roscoe, New York, reports that he has his best success with this fly by fishing it with violent twitches, followed by a pause. Short leaders and heavy tippets are a must. His normal set-up includes 2 m (6 ft) of 5.4-kg (12-lb) fluorocarbon.

Ken says this pattern is his favourite for fishing the east and west branches of the Delaware River – especially during the early season and when there are high water conditions. Each of the Delaware branches is controlled by a dam, so the levels can be affected accordingly. When the levels are up, it's not necessary to avoid them. Instead, Ken launches one of his drift boats and takes advantage of the conditions by showing the local behemoths the Delaware Baby Brown.

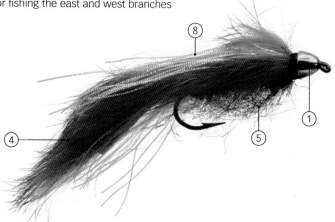

How to tie

1 Slide the conehead onto the hook and up against the hook eye.

2 Wrap several layers of lead wire behind the conehead and extending about 6 mm (¼ in) rearward. It is important to tie the lead in and add a few drops of cement so that the weight will not move.

3 Wrap the thread to the hook bend and tie in a bunch of Glissen Glow.

4 At the same location, tie in a 15-cm (6-in) zonker strip. The tail section of the hide should extend 4 cm (1½ in) beyond the bend. The remainder of the strip will be pulled forward later, so do not trim it off. Secure the thread wraps with a drop of cement.

5 Let the excess zonker strip hang out of the way and dub a generous body with Ice Dub. Wrap the body forward until the body meets the conehead.

6 Tie in a few strands of red Krystal Flash for a throat.

7 Pull the zonker strip forward and tie in behind the head.

8 At the same location, tie in another generous bunch of Glissen Glow directly on top of the zonker strip.

9 Whip finish and cement the thread wraps.

Brad Befus

Glass Bead Ultra Midge

This midge larva pupa can be fished under a small dry fly. It has enough weight to get through the surface film without drowning the fly. Once glass beads became available to fly tiers, it became possible to create a fly that could be cast as a floater/dropper rig.

Actual size

Length 1 cm (⅜ in)

Brad Befus, from Montrose, Colorado, started tying the Glass Bead Ultra Midge during the early 1990s. The glass beads add just enough weight to get through the surface film or to be fished solely as a nymph without any additional weight on the leader when trout are in shallow water. It still performs the delicate job it was designed to do.

Many times during a winter midge hatch on western tail waters, the fish are right on the edges, picking off the emerging midge pupa. A standard gold bead pattern will usually sink too quickly and hang up on the rocks. They usually spook more fish than they end up deceiving.

This pattern can also be fished deep with a tandem nymph set-up and additional weight on the leader with great results. Brad ties this pattern in red, olive, grey, black and cream colours. Larger sizes produce with good consistency in stillwater situations during the chironomid hatches.

Brad has received positive feedback from numerous guides and fly shops across the county.

Materials

Hook TMC 2487, sizes 16–24

Thread Wapsi Ultra, 70 denier, colour to match thorax

Abdomen Turkey or goose biot

Ribbing Fine gold or copper wire

Thorax Muskrat dubbing or Antron dubbing to match abdomen colour

Head Small or extra-small glass bead to match abdomen colour

How to tie

1 Slide a glass bead over the hook point and push it up against the hook eye.

2 Lay down a thread base from behind the bead to halfway down the bend.

3 At the hook bend, tie in a length of wire for ribbing.

4 At the same location, tie in the biot. Advance the thread to the glass bead.

5 Wrap the biot forward to the bead.

6 Wrap the rib forward to the glass bead and tie off.

7 Dub a thorax of muskrat or Antron.

8 Make a small thread wrap behind the glass bead. Whip finish and cement.

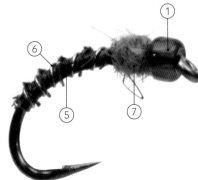

Joseph Ludkin

Reel Daddy

In the bad old days, synthetic fly wings were terrible. They offered so much air resistance that they would helicopter and twist the leader into a useless mess. All that has changed. Reel Wings are super soft and fold out of the way when the cast is made, only to pop back up into position when the fly lands.

The Reel Daddy is a heavy, dry fly and makes a definite splash when it hits the water. The disturbance attracts the fish, and trout always seem interested in things that fall from the overhangs.

After hearing a rumour of a large fish in the Upper Swale in Yorkshire, Joseph found the stretch of water in question. He had been drawn to the stretch by the large splashes he had heard over the commotion of the waterfall. Every time he looked up, there were huge rise rings radiating across the pool's surface. He crawled along the overhanging bank and spent about 30 minutes casting mayflies to a completely disinterested brown trout of about 900 g (2 lb). He left the pool three times out of pure frustration. In a moment guided by anger more than judgement, he tied on the biggest fly in his box, which happened to be the Reel Daddy. A foamy explosion snapped him awake and his fly was gone. Following a noble battle, the fish was caught and released.

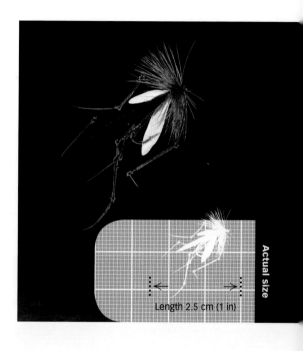

Actual size

Length 2.5 cm (1 in)

Materials

Hook Kamasan long shank B830, size 12

Thread Brown flat silk, size 8/0

Hackle Dark brown cock hackle feather

Body Rainy's X-flies Tube Bodiz micro mayfly (with tail removed)

Legs Knotted pheasant tail fibres

Wings Joseph Ludkin's Reel Wings – Daddies

Cement Sally Hansen Hard As Nails

How to tie

1 Wrap a thread base from the hook eye to the hook bend and then back again, stopping near the eye.

2 At this location, tie in two long hopper legs, then tie in two shorter legs. Do not trim the excess.

3 Take the body and snip a small cut at the large end, so that the body will rest on the hook. Place the body on top of the hook shank just above where you tied in the legs. Tie in only the tip of the body.

4 In front of the legs, tie in a hackle feather. Make four thread wraps, tie down and trim the excess.

5 Part the hackle evenly and pull the fibres down so that they are all below the shank.

6 Ahead of the hackle, tie in the wings above/on top of the parted hackle.

7 Wrap a small thread head. Whip finish and cement the thread wraps.

Saltwater fly directory

Although fly-fishing gear was used in the 1800s for saltwater species, the modern era of fly fishing in saltwater started in the early 1950s. Target fish such as striped bass and bluefish want a mouthful, not a snack. For this reason, most common patterns were imitations of baitfish. As you'll see in this section, this tradition is alive and well around the world today.

Mauro Ginevri

Avalon Bonefish Fly

How about fishing in a place that has not seen sport fishing in 50 years – a place where you can fish 100 miles of flats and not see another fisherman? That's the claim coming from the Cuban Fishing Centers.

Materials

Hook Tiemco 811S, size 4
Body thread UTC Ultra, 140 denier, tan
Head thread UTC Ultra, 140 denier, fluorescent orange
Tail Small pearlescent Mylar tubing
Eyes Medium stainless steel bead chain
Body Pearl Diamond Braid
Wing White craft fur barred with red Prismacolor
Legs Two 5-cm (2-in) medium orange round rubber legs
Flash Pearl Krystal Flash

Mauro Ginevri, who works for the Cuban Fishing Centers, wanted a simple fly for the abundant bonefish found in this area. He is truly a man who does his research before developing a fly.

The Avalon Bonefish Fly is effective over white sand and turtle grass beds. While wade fishing over white sand with a friend, Mauro saw a couple of big bonefish feeding behind a stingrey coming towards them. When the ray was 18 m (60 ft) away, he and his friend cast at the same time and landed their flies close to the ray at the left and right sides. The bonefish moved up to the ray and they hooked them at the same time. The fish weighed 4 and 4.5 kg (9 and 10 lb), respectively.

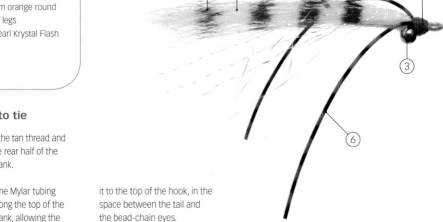

How to tie

1 Tie in the tan thread and wrap the rear half of the hook shank.

2 Lash the Mylar tubing down along the top of the hook shank, allowing the tubing to extend beyond the bend of the hook shank.

3 Hold the eyes directly on top of the hook shank and make a series of diagonal wraps of thread around the hook shank and the centre of the eyes.

4 Cut a 10-cm (4-in) length of pearl Diamond Braid and lash it to the top of the hook, in the space between the tail and the bead-chain eyes.

5 Wrap the braid forward, overlapping each turn slightly. Wrap the braid under and then in between the eyes.

6 Tie in the rubber legs in front of the eyes.

7 Bring the braid under the body just behind the eyes, and then cross over forward in between the eyes. Tie down the braid in front of the eyes. Whip finish and switch to tan thread.

8 Cut a clump of craft fur. Rotate the vice so that the hook point is up. Pinch the base of the craft fur clump into a tight bundle, then tie it in on the top of the hook shank just in front of the bead-chain eyes.

9 Paint the fur with four broad lines of red Prismacolor.

10 Add six strands of pearl Krystal Flash on top of the fur wing.

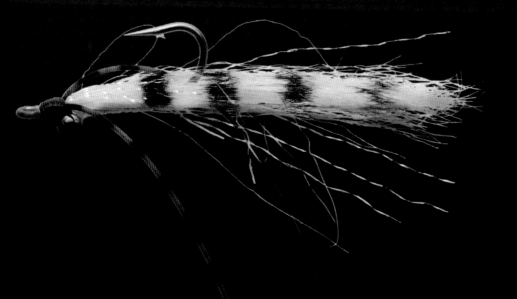

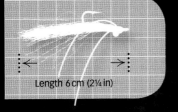

Length 6 cm (2¼ in)

Billy Trimble

Blind Chicken

The ASPCA (American Society for the Prevention of Cruelty to Animals) is sure to be calling about this one! This pattern was designed to solve the problem of Clouser-type flies picking up grass as they are retrieved. It has nothing whatsoever to do with cruelty to chickens.

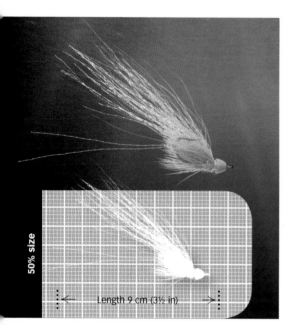

50% size

Length 9 cm (3½ in)

Billy Trimble, from Austin, Texas, doesn't like standard tied Clousers because the eyes tend to pick up grass. This cone-head version allows the fly to slither through grass and remain weed free. Billy has been stalking redfish on the Texas coast and floating Texas hill country rivers with a fly rod for over 20 years.

Though Billy had been tying and fishing this fly for several years, he realized he had been tying it upside down. He had been tying the deer hair in last, but the fly works much better when it is tied in first, because this forces the flash and bucktail to stand like a chicken with its head down pecking, while its tail sticks straight up.

Billy says the name was inspired by the colour pattern on one of his favourite D.O.A. baits, the Electric Chicken.

When finished, the fly should be two to three times longer than the hook shank. The colours can be changed to whatever your favourite colour pattern is. Match the thread colour to the cone colour.

Materials

Hook Tiemco 811S, size 6 or 4
Thread UTC, 210 denier, chartreuse
Wing Chartreuse deer hair
Flash Yellow or salmon Crystal Flash
Body Pink bucktail
Cone Chartreuse, 5 mm (³⁄₁₆ in) size

How to tie

1 Mash the barb down and slide the cone onto the hook point to the eye.

2 Attach the thread at the back of the cone.

3 Invert the hook and tie in a clump of deer hair just behind the cone, with the tips evened. Tie the deer hair so that it completely covers the point and bend of the hook, and trim the butts off.

4 Cut a few strands of Crystal Flash, then fold them around the thread and draw them into the cup of the

cone, on top of the deer hair.

5 Cut a sparse section of pink bucktail and trim the butts to the right length.

Place the bucktail on top of the deer hair/Crystal Flash, and draw the butts into the cup of the cone.

6 Pile a little thread behind the cone, then whip finish.

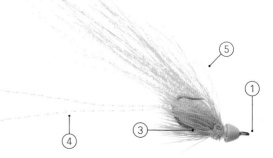

Roan zum Felde

Rz's Mangrove Slider

Captain Roan zumFelde owns Rz's Fishing Extremes. He guides out of Naples, Florida. Roan used to use Dahlberg Divers, but they didn't move the way he wanted. This is the result of his search for a better pattern.

This Mangrove Slider provides just the right amount of wiggle for snook, redfish and small tarpon. Roan accomplished this by shaving behind the crown. As a result, the fly would catch air bubbles and give a better wiggle when stripped through the water.

The Mangrove Slider continues working to this day. If you want it to sit a little higher, add a little silicone. But Roan likes to fish it just under the water's surface. He gets some of his most vicious strikes on this pattern.

His two favourite colour combinations are red and white for fishing outside and red/yellow and rust when fishing on the inside.

As an added bonus, Roan has used this fly for large-mouth bass and released one weighing 6.3 kg (14 lb).

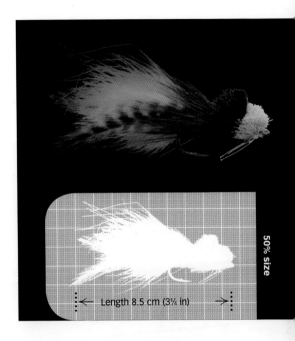

50% size

← Length 8.5 cm (3¼ in) →

Materials

Hook Mustad 3407, size 1/0

Thread Yellow Danville's Flat Waxed, size A

Tail Marabou feather, white or yellow

Flash Silver or gold Flashabou

Hackles Four natural or yellow grizzly

Body White or rust brown deer belly or body hair

Collar Red deer body or belly hair

Head White or yellow deer body hair

Weed guard 14-kg (30-lb) monofilament

How to tie

1 Above the barb of the hook, tie in two clumps of white or yellow marabou feather.

2 Tie in ten strands of silver or gold Flashabou on top of the marabou, extending past the marabou.

3 Tie in two natural or yellow grizzly hackles on each side.

4 Spin two applications of white or rust deer hair in front of the wings.

5 Spin one application of red deer hair in front of the rust hair.

6 Tie in one application of white or yellow deer hair in front of the red hair.

7 Trim the bottom of all the deer hair flat.

8 Trim the coloured deer hair to leave a collar of red deer hair and a yellow head.

9 Add a weed guard of 14-kg (30-lb) monofilament.

Length 11 cm (4½ in)

Mauro Ginevri

Avalon Permit Fly

After getting poor results with existing shrimp patterns in Caribbean waters, Mauro Ginevri decided to design his own. He thought that improving the presentation and the position of the fly in the water would improve chances for hooking up.

Materials

Hook Tiemco 811 S, size 2
Thread for body UTC Ultra 210, tan
Thread for head UTC Ultra 140, orange
Eyes Silver-coloured solid brass eyes, 1.5 mm (5/32-in)
Mouth Arctic fox tail hair dyed yellow-orange
Antennae Black Krystal Flash
Legs Two strands of 5-cm (2-in) grizzly barred medium rubber, orange
Shell back Two strands of pearl Diamond Braid
Body Large tan marabou herl
Claws Two tan, straight-cut zonker strips
Keel 9-kg (20-lb) Rio nylon line with four 1-mm (1/32-in) Spirit River Brite beads

Research in pools and the open water revealed that other flies often fell upside down or took too long to get to the bottom. Some would windmill during retrieves.

In 2009, Mauro finally had a fly that would sink fast, land right side up and track correctly on the retrieve. The addition of four silver eyes stopped the windmilling by acting as a keel. As a bonus, the metal eyes made vibrations that attracted fish.

Within a few months of its development, the Avalon Permit Fly accounted for 53 permit. Observation of the permit revealed the fish's reaction was to attack the fly without hesitation or suspicion.

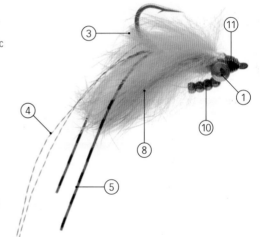

How to tie

1 Tie the dumbbell eyes on top of the shank, about one-fifth of the way back from the eye of the hook.

2 Tie in a 7.5-cm (3-in) length of nylon line behind the dumbbell eyes.

3 Tie in a small bunch of Arctic fox tail hair approximately 3 cm (1¼ in) long. After the fibres are well secured, shorten the tips until about 1 cm (⅜ in) is left.

4 Tie one Krystal Flash fibre on each side of the hook shank. Cut the flash off at a length of 7 cm (2¾ in).

5 Tie in two rubber legs – one on the left side of the hook shank, the other on the right side. Trim each to 5 cm (2 in).

6 Tie in two strands of pearl Diamond Braid over the rubber legs. Trim them to 4.5 cm (1¾ in).

7 Tie in the marabou by its tip. Wrap the marabou feather forward and secure it with your tying thread. Cut off the surplus.

8 Tie in the zonker strips, one on each side. Start from the hook eye and secure the strips well, all the way from the hook eye to just behind the dumbbell eyes. Be sure the insides of the zonker skins are facing towards the body. The claws should be positioned at an angle of 45 degrees away from the body of the fly.

9 Pull the right piece of Diamond Braid over the body to the left side of the hook eye and secure. Pull the left Diamond Braid over the body to the right size of the hook eye and secure both with your thread.

10 Slide four silver beads onto the nylon line. Pull the line forward until your keel has a loop 2 cm (¾ in) long and 1 cm (⅜ in) deep. Tie the nylon line in at the eye, on top of the hook shank, and tie off.

11 Switch to orange thread and make a head.

Mike Rice

Cichetti's Sand Eel

Inventors of flies usually name their creations after themselves. Here's an exception sure to please the inventor and anyone who tries it, as well.

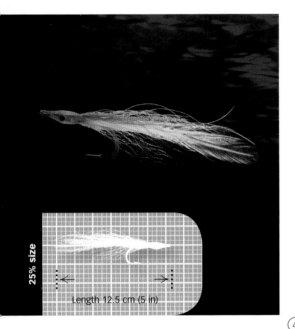

25% size

Length 12.5 cm (5 in)

Mike Rice of Mud Dog Saltwater Flies came by a few flies tied by Rob Cichetti from Cape Cod, Massachusetts. After making a few minor changes and having great success, Mike asked Rob for permission to tie them commercially. Rob said yes and Mike named them after Rob as a tribute.

The sand-eel pattern has a very slim, sparse, translucent profile, allowing you to present the fly to spooky fish. It also looks exactly like a sand eel. Mike thinks the gold holographic flash is what triggers the take.

Mike and his friend Henry Godin were fishing structure off Cohassett, Massachusetts. Mike was convinced the Clouser was the fly of the day. He was wrong. Henry fished the Cichetti's Sand Eel all morning and boasted nearly a dozen striped bass to Mike's zero. Mike clipped the Clouser off and tied on a Cichetti's Sand Eel and evened the score.

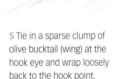

Materials

Hook Mustad 370SD, size 3
Thread Danville fine monofilament
Pillow White rabbit fur
Tail Two skinny white saddle hackles
Flash Gold holographic Flashabou
Wing Olive bucktail
Belly White bucktail
Body 30-minute epoxy adhesive
Eyes 1-mm (1/16-in) stick-on eyes

How to tie

1 Tie in a pinch of white rabbit fur about mid-shank on the hook. This creates a pillow into which to tie the hackle stems.

2 Tie one white saddle hackle into the rabbit pillow, with the curved side down.

3 Tie in another white saddle hackle on top of the first, with the curved side up.

4 Tie in two strands of gold holographic Flashabou on top of the hackles.

5 Tie in a sparse clump of olive bucktail (wing) at the hook eye and wrap loosely back to the hook point.

6 Tie in a sparse clump of white bucktail (belly) at the hook eye and wrap loosely back to the hook point.

7 Squeeze the wing and belly together so that they surround the hook shank and then securely wrap with thread.

8 Coat the wrapped portion of the body with 30-minute epoxy adhesive.

9 After about 20 minutes, the epoxy adhesive should tack up enough to put an eye on either side of the head.

10 Let the epoxy adhesive set for an hour and then apply a second coat over the first and the eye.

Fabrizio Gajardoni

Gaja's Orange Shrimp

Fabrizio Gajardoni, of Gaja's Flies, wanted to improve on existing shrimp patterns for use in the Adriatic Sea. Several American guides in southern waters have since adopted this one.

The key to this pattern, according to Fabrizio, is the stiff tail section. The Bug-Bond coating yields a tail stiff enough to give the Gaja's Orange Shrimp an enticing action as it is retrieved through the water. The tail acts as a rudder and sets up the vibration.

Fabrizio's technique for fishing with this fly is, he says, very simple. Usually he fishes with a Teeny Nymph line of 200, 300 or 400 grains, depending on the depth of the water. The best retrieve is made by stripping the fly back with a medium-to-fast cadence and some occasional short pauses. Striped bass will inhale the fly as it pauses.

50% size

Length 7 cm (2¾ in)

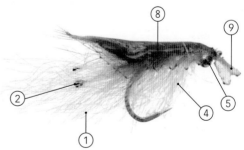

Materials

Hook Gamakatsu SC 15 or SL 12 S, sizes 1–1/0

Thread Danville 210 denier flat nylon, clear

Legs Saltwater yak hair, white; Gaja's Crystal Hackle, clear white

Eyes Burned nylon with black varnish

Scud and tail Small strip of white rabbit fur covered in orange organza (painted with acrylic iridescent orange)

Adhesive Bug-Bond

Weight Lead eyes or steel bead chain

Equipment UV light

How to tie

1 Tie in yak fibres at the bend in the hook, making them as long as the hook.

2 Tie in the eyes. Add more yak hair.

3 Tie in rabbit hair on top of the hook.

4 Tie in two Gaja's Crystal Hackles, double them and wrap around the hook as a hackle. Brush them rearward.

5 Tie in the lead eyes below the hook shank.

6 Trim the painted organza to a shell shape.

7 Make a small hole in the tail end and slide the organza over the hook eye. Tie in with thread. Add a drop of Bug-Bond to the shank behind the organza. Cure with UV light.

8 Fold the organza shell over the top of the body. Add a drop of Bug-Bond and cure with UV light.

9 Add more Bug-Bond to the top of the tail and shell and cure with UV light.

Gary Graham

Baja Wasabi Deepdiver

Wasabi – hot stuff! Any fly named for wasabi had better live up to its name. In this case, it does.

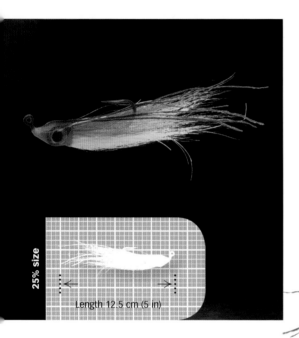

25% size

Length 12.5 cm (5 in)

Captain Gary Graham owns Baja On The Fly. He charters in and around the Sea of Cortez, Baja California Sur, Mexico and the Pacific Ocean. The Baja Wasabi Deepdiver is his medicine for yellowfin tuna, black skipjack and dorado.

Gary noticed that flies with turquoise and grey were successful. However, he wanted a fly that improved on the shape and flash of previous patterns. A broader silhouette and wider body were needed to match up with local bait shapes, so he designed the Baja Wasabi Deepdiver with these characteristics in mind.

This is a user-friendly pattern for beginners as well as experts, because it works with different retrieve styles. It really shines for tuna that are travelling with porpoise or are in a feeding frenzy on the surface.

Materials

Hook Eagle Claw 413, sizes 1/0–4/0
Weight 0.5-mm (0.019-in) lead wire
Thread Flat waxed nylon
Wings Bucktail: white, chartreuse, turquoise and grey
Flash Pearl saltwater Flashabou, pearl Crystal Flash
Topping Peacock herl
Eyes 6-mm (¼-in) moulded gold eyes
Adhesive Softex or 5-Minute Z-Poxy

How to tie

1 Wrap 15 wraps of the lead wire around the hook near the eye.

2 Tie pearl Flashabou on the shank of the hook, extending a hook length beyond the bend of the hook.

3 Tie white bucktail under the hook shank, extending one hook length beyond the bend of the hook.

4 Tie in a small amount of Crystal Flash on top of the white bucktail.

5 Tie in chartreuse bucktail over the Crystal Flash.

6 Tie in another small amount of Crystal Flash on top of the chartreuse bucktail.

7 On top of the Crystal Flash, tie in turquoise bucktail, with the material extending one hook length beyond the end of the hook.

8 Add more Crystal Flash on top of the turquoise bucktail.

9 Add a small amount of grey bucktail.

10 Add a small amount of white bucktail over the grey.

11 Top off with several strands of peacock herl.

12 Tie pearl saltwater Flashabou to the sides and top of the wing.

13 Attach 6-mm (¼-in) moulded gold eyes.

14 Finish by coating the head with Softex or 5-minute Z-Poxy.

Pedro Pablo Yañez Duran

Xtreme Squid

Don't you just hate it when big fish crush your squid pattern and tear it apart? Pedro Duran decided he'd had enough, so he designed a squid imitation that was easy to tie, used a minimum of materials and was durable enough to stand up to many fish.

Pedro originally designed the Xtreme Squid for corbina off the coast of Chile. Since its introduction, it has caught sea bass off Spain at the Delta del Ebro in the Mediterranean, yellowtails off New Zealand and big striped bass off Montauk, Long Island.

The pattern works best in relatively calm surf conditions, with waves no higher than 60 cm (2 ft). During squid hatches, it has also accounted for baby bluefin tuna, bluefish, false albacore and mahi mahi.

Pedro reports that there are a few nice patterns on the market, but in general they are tied on low-quality hooks with weak materials that do not stand up to the strike of predator fish. Other existing patterns are unnatural-looking or have incorrect proportions.

By adjusting the Xtreme Squid's colours and size, it can be made to imitate any kind of squid – and, because squid are eaten by gamefish wherever they are found, it should work around the globe.

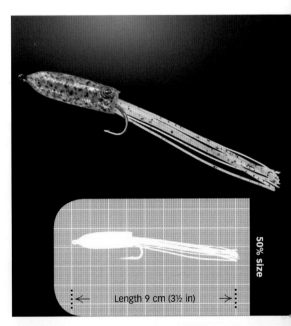

50% size

Length 9 cm (3½ in)

Materials

Hook TMC 777 SP, size 4/0
Thread UNI size 3/0 Mono Thread
Tentacles Sili Legs with sand/orange/black flake
Body Pearl Flashabou Minnow Body, medium
Eyes 1.25-cm (½-in) crystal Gator Eyez
Body cover Clear Cure Goo Tack Free
Marker pens Red, black and orange

How to tie

1 Wrap a thread base from the hook eye towards the hook bend, covering three-quarters of the shank.

2 Ahead of the hook bend, tie in ten pieces of Sili Legs so that the total length of the fly will be 9 cm (3½ in).

3 At the hook eye, tie in a 7.5-cm (3-in) length of Flashabou Minnow Body so that the material sticks out over the hook eye. Cut the thread.

4 Turn the Flashabou Minnow Body inside out, so that the

tie-in point is hidden inside. The rear end of the Minnow Body should form a shroud over the tie-in point for the Sili Legs and reach the hook bend.

5 Make tiny dots over the entire body with the permanent markers. Use good-quality markers so that

the dots will not fade when the Clear Cure Goo Tack Free coat is added.

6 Near the rear of the Minnow Body, apply the adhesive Gator Eyez.

7 Coat the entire body and eyes with Clear Cure Goo Tack Free.

Jeff Priest

Ghost Sardina

How about a pattern that is so realistic it fools the prey fish it imitates? Jeff Priest claims the flatiron herring will school around his Ghost Sardina and even swim with it.

Jeff fishes in the Sea of Cortez for sailfish, dorado, yellowfin tuna, roosterfish and jack crevelle.

In the upper water column above 9 m (30 ft), all colours are visible. Below this depth, silhouettes or nondefinable shades are all that can be seen. Refusals diminished when Jeff created this pattern that matches the size and shape of baitfish, but it is translucent so as to give the predatory fish only a quick glimpse.

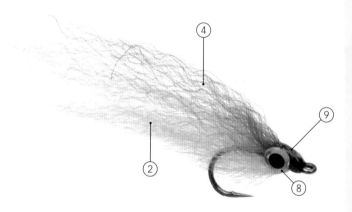

How to tie

1 Lay down a thread base from the eye to above the hook point. Apply head cement after each step.

2 At the bend of the hook, tie in a 6-mm (¼-in) bundle of full-length, light-coloured Slinky Fiber for the body. The tie-in point is at the middle of the 25-cm (10-in) long fibres, so 12.5 cm (5 in) extend to the left and 12.5 cm (5 in) extend to the right. Repeat the process with the dark-coloured Slinky Fiber.

3 Starting on the top of the shank (hook down), secure the first section of Slinky Fiber by wrapping thread up the shank approximately halfway to the eye of the hook, taking care to keep most of the material on top of the shank. You may also mix in the flash of your choice as scale flash as you create the body.

4 Once the material is secured, take the forward-facing section and fold it backward, so that it covers the shank and hides the previous wraps. Secure it by wrapping over only a small portion.

5 Rotate the hook so that the hook faces up. Repeat the previous step and move forward up the shank to the eye of the hook.

6 Rotate the hook again and use a selected colour to create the back of the baitfish. Secure the nose section with about 15 to 20 wraps to even out the nose. Whip finish and coat with head cement. Colour the top of the nose only, using a marker pen that matches the back of the baitfish pattern.

7 To trim excess material and shape the body, hold the hook upside down between your thumb and forefinger. Starting at the throat or the bend of the hook, trim backward at an angle, sloping from the belly to the back or tail.

8 Once you have the desired shape and length, lay the pattern on its side and place the bottom of the eyes in contact with the top portion of the shank. Secure the eyes with gel Zap-A-Gap.

9 Fill the gap between the eyes with a small amount of UV Knot Sense. Coat the nose, eyes and head only with a light coat of UV Knot Sense. Cure with UV light.

Length 11 cm (4½ in)

Chris Reeves

Bluefish Soda

Many saltwater guides are fond of saying, 'If it ain't chartreuse, it ain't no use!' Iconoclast Chris Reeves is of a different opinion: he's convinced root beer is the go-to colour for bluefish.

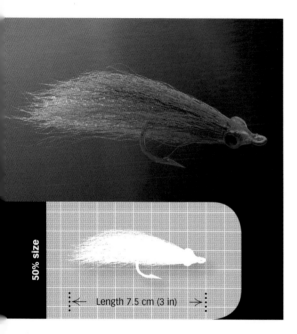

50% size

Length 7.5 cm (3 in)

After witnessing the effectiveness of root beer-coloured jigs and plastic worms, Chris decided to develop a fly of the same hue. He wanted the fly to stay on an even keel when retrieved. He also wanted the fly to rely on a sinking line to get to the desired depth rather than building in too much weight to make casting the fly difficult. His experimentation was proven to be effective when, in 2010, he christened the Bluefish Soda.

Chris found a shoal of bluefish in 3.6 m (12 ft) of water. They were not the double-digit blues of the Northeastern American coast, but weighed 1.3–2.7 kg (3–5 lb). The fish stayed in the area for 90 minutes. In that time Chris, using an 8-weight rod, caught and released 50 fish. In fact, the fly out-fished rubber worms and jigs three to one. The last of his patterns accounted for more than 20 fish before it was reduced to a scrap of orange thread and the lead wire underbody.

Materials

Hook Mustad 34007, size 1

Thread Madeira Neon, hot orange

Underbody Medium lead wire

Tail Hot orange bucktail

Wing Root beer bucktail

Flash Fine pearl Crystal Flash

Collar Fine bucktail, root beer on top, orange underneath

Eyes 2 mm (1/16 in), red with black centre

Adhesive Bug-Bond

Equipment UV light

How to tie

1 Tie in ten turns of lead wire along the hook shank. Secure with Bug-Bond adhesive.

2 Tie on the tail at the hook bend.

3 Ahead of the lead wire, tie in the wing of root beer bucktail with six pieces of Crystal Flash.

4 Spin a collar of bucktail, root beer on top, orange underneath. Trim the butt ends.

5 Make a thread head and build it up with Bug-Bond.

6 Apply the eyes and cover with more Bug-Bond. Cure the Bug-Bond with UV light.

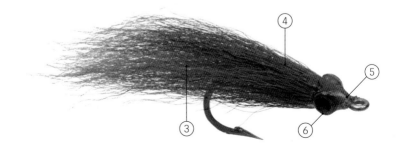

Vic Shirley

Jamaican Salty Shrimp

I had Jamaican salty shrimp one time, along with too many beers. What little I remember of it looked nothing like the pattern sent by Captain Vic Shirley from Montego Bay, Jamaica.

Here's something I didn't know: there are no fly shops in Jamaica, so materials are limited and animal products are difficult to get and very expensive. As a result, synthetics are really a great alternative. Captain Vic reports that he got the polyester thread at a local pharmacy.

Vic reports that this pattern works on snook, tarpon, permit, yellowtail snapper, mahogany snapper and great barracuda. It works well in muddy or clear water, over coral or grass, and it works best on sunlit days to make the fly shimmer.

This Salty Shrimp has come to the rescue when no other fly resulted in bites. One client went through his entire stash of factory flies with no luck. Within ten minutes of tying on this pattern, he reeled in a permit and then a barracuda. At that point, they probably threw some shrimp on the barbie and hoisted a few more. I know that's what I'd do.

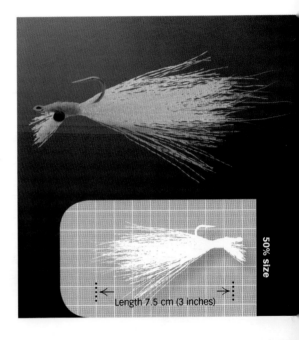

50% size

Length 7.5 cm (3 inches)

Materials

Hook Umpqua TMC 800S, size 4
Thread Polyester, chartreuse
Adhesive Superglue
Eyes Dumbbell or bead chain
Wing Chartreuse bucktail, chartreuse Krystal Flash
Cement Softex or Patex

How to tie

1 Glue the hook shank.

2 While the glue on the thread is still wet, tie in bucktail three-quarters of the way back towards the bend of the hook.

3 Wrap the thread to within 6 mm (¼ in) of the eye.

4 Tie eyes on top of the hook shank, using cross wraps.

5 Add Krystal Flash wrap thread to the bend, and return to just behind the eye.

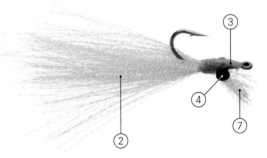

6 Add some Krystal Flash to the bottom of the hook.

7 Tie behind the eyes to make the eyebrows stand up.

8 Whip finish and cement.

Paul Noël

Click-Clack

This fly was years in the making, and Captain Paul Noël, from Chalmette, Louisiana, who runs Lagniappe Charters, LLC, has been improving the pattern. Now that its evolution is complete, he's graciously sent it along. It's his favourite for specs and reds.

50% size

Length 6.5 cm (2½ in)

The construction of this fly gives it its name: the fly sinks nose down, separating the beads. A sharp strip will snap it forward and the beads will collide. On a slack line, the nose falls down and the front bead makes another sound as it hits the eye. It's the click-clack sound that lures the fish. This works really well in turbid water or in low-light conditions.

No need to use a hard strike. Just take up the tension and the circle hook will find its way to the corner of the fish's mouth and do its job. An added bonus is that the circle hook is practically snagless and weedless.

The two beads provide just enough weight to get the fly down quickly in front of a speeding red, yet it is light enough to cast with a 6-weight outfit. This pattern caught a lot of salmon in Alaska. The silvers loved it and the chinook could not spit the hook.

Paul's favourite colour combination is a purple body with chartreuse tail and bright brass beads. Closely followed by a black body with yellow tail and black beads.

Materials

Hook Mustad Circle Streamer, C71s SS, size 2
Thread Size G, black
Beads Orvis 5 mm (³/₁₆ in) brass caddis beads
Tail Chartreuse marabou herl
Body Spirit River Estaz Grandé, purple
Cement Sally Hansen Hard As Nails

How to tie

1 Flatten the barb of the hook and slide two beads up to the eye. Be sure the rear bead has the open end of the tapered hole facing the tail.

2 Start the thread near the bend and tie in a marabou tail.

3 Tie in the Estaz Grandé, and wrap a body. Stop when there is room for at least one bead diameter between the front and rear beads.

4 Whip finish a head that's small enough to fit snugly inside the tapered hole of the rear bead.

5 Coat the head with Hard As Nails and force the rear bead over the head. Let dry.

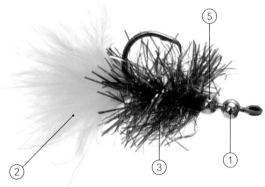

Peter McLeod

Pete's Cheat

Fishing in heavy cover means trouble. Flies get hung up or covered with bottom vegetation. Peter McLeod, from the UK, decided to overcome the problem by constructing a fly for fishing for flighty bonefish in shallow waters at Los Roques in Venezuela.

The pancake flats in Los Roques present a real challenge as, on the push of the tide, large bonefish come up out of the deep water to feed on flats, sometimes with their backs out of the water. Peter needed a fly that would land softly and not spook the fish in the skinny water, yet still present enough of a mouthful worth eating. He needed a fly that blended colour-wise, but did not become lost in the turtle grass.

50% size

Length 7 cm (2¾ in)

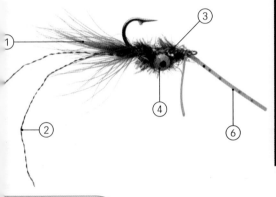

Materials

Hook Gamkatsu SL45, sizes 6 and 8

Thread Clear monofilament

Tail Olive green marabou plus two strands of black Crystal Flash

Body Fine cactus chenille, olive

Eyes Lead dumbbell eyes, painted yellow with a black dot for the pupil

Adhesive Superglue

Legs Two strands Sili Legs, olive

How to tie

1 Tie in a small clump of olive green marabou onto the back of the hook and run the thread forward.

2 Tie in two strands of black Crystal Flash securely on the top of the marabou, so that they extend 12 mm (½ in) behind the marabou tail.

3 Strip the tip of some fine olive cactus chenille and catch the bare thread just where the marabou extends from the thread. Run the thread forward to a point halfway along the shank of the hook.

4 Using a figure-of-eight motion, bind a small lead dumbbell eye to the top of the hook shank, and then run the thread forward to the eye. Secure the dumbbell with a small dab of Superglue to prevent spinning.

5 Using a pair of hackle pliers, run the olive cactus chenille forward around the body, ensuring it is looped over the dumbbell eye on the top and bottom before tying off at the eye.

6 Take two lengths of olive Sili Legs, trim to 2.5 cm (1 in), and then catch in on either side of the eyes.

7 Whip finish and secure with cement.

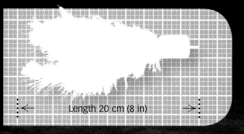

Warren Sellers

Murderous Marshmallow

Every once in a while a fly comes along and everyone says, 'Why didn't I think of that?' Well, Captain Warren Sellers did. For many years he has used this style fly extensively in Costa Rica and Panama for Pacific sailfish.

Materials

Thread Nylon thread, size D, black

Hook shank substitute Hollow plastic coffee stirrer, with an inner diameter of 2 mm (¹⁄₁₆ in)

Wing 15–18-cm (6–7-in) pink and white feathers

Body Foam marshmallow

Eyes Large, reflective self-adhesive eyes

Cement Clear or black nail polish

Equipment Rotary tool with conical sanding stone

Note: You will need a brass rod with an outer diameter of 2 mm (¹⁄₁₆ in) OD to build the fly.

During a typical season, Captain Warren usually goes through nearly 40 of these flies, so he wanted high function and low cost. One fly is usually good for two or three sailfish before it is destroyed.

Warren used about 15 feathers to give the fly some bulk, because the fish needs to be able to see it easily. The marshmallow gives the bubble-chugging effect so the fish may hear it as well. Adhering to IGFA (International Game Fish Association) fly rules, the presentation is made to the fish when the moving boat is out of gear and the trolled teaser is suddenly taken away from the attacking fish as it is coaxed into casting range of the fly angler.

Warren says sailfish behaviour is to chase a flying fish until it takes flight. At that point, they stop and extend their long pelvic fins like an antenna to pick up tiny vibrations to tell them where the prey has landed. A sailfish gets a better look at a conventionally trolled lure, and it may follow the lure and look for several seconds before making a decision to strike or not, so a fly has to stand out and be very eye-catching as soon as it is presented. This pattern was designed to meet that requirement.

How to tie

1 Insert the brass rod into the coffee stirrer so that the ends are even. The excess stirrer will be trimmed later.

2 Tie some white feathers onto the stirrer with several wraps, so that the feather butts are parallel to the rod and the tips splay out.

3 Repeat with some pink feathers.

4 Move 1 cm (³⁄₈ in) up the stirrer and repeat, using shorter feathers.

5 Make a large stop of thread wraps and trim any butts that extend out from under the wraps.

6 Seal the thread wraps with three coats of nail polish, allowing it to dry between applications.

7 Drill the foam marshmallow to accept the rod and stirrer. Use a rotary tool with a conical sanding stone to make a concave surface that will accept the thread wraps.

8 Apply nail polish to the thread and slide the marshmallow on so that it meets the thread wraps, exposing only the feathers.

9 Apply the eyes.

10 Remove the brass rod and trim the exposed end of the stirrer to 12 mm (½ in).

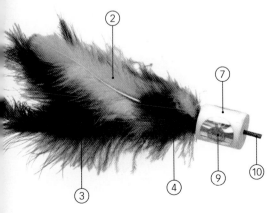

Lance Petersen

Mona Lisa

Lance Petersen wanted a fly for sight casting to roosterfish from shore in Baja California in Mexico. He's been guiding there for over ten years, so he knows what it takes. This fly turned out to be so effective, he has used it for pompano, dorado and any other fish that feed on mullet.

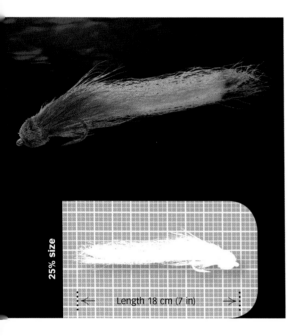

25% size

Length 18 cm (7 in)

The Mona Lisa is the culmination of Lance's experiments with long flies tied to represent the mullet. The addition of the spun head completed a fly that looks big in the water, yet is easy to cast under varied conditions.

This fly lends itself perfectly to sight fishing in shallow water. It sinks slowly and the head provides just enough neutral buoyancy to allow an angler to place the fly ahead of an oncoming roosterfish without it sinking to the bottom and out of the strike zone. The head and collar make the fly track straight at any speed and give the long tail its lifelike action.

One particular and unusual event stays with Lance. He cast to, hooked and landed a dorado from the beach. He says that taking a pelagic fish while standing firmly on the sandy beach is his best memory of success with the Mona Lisa.

Materials

Hook Gamkatsu SC-15 2H, size 4

Thread White Big Fly

Tail Layered combination of Spirit River Super Hair (white, yellow and tan) topped with tan-coloured yak hair

Flash Pearl or root beer Krystal Flash

Head/collar Spun deer hair trimmed to shape

How to tie

1 Begin by creating the tail with layers of Super Hair cut to the desired length. Start with white topped by a sparse layer of yellow. Add a few strands of Krystal Flash and top off with tan Super Hair.

2 Add tan yak hair to provide the bulk of the tail.

3 Tie in the finished tail above the hook point, leaving just enough exposed shank to create a collar and full-bodied head.

4 Using the longest deer hair you can find, spin the deer hair to create the head and collar.

5 Trim the spun deer hair to a bullet shape.

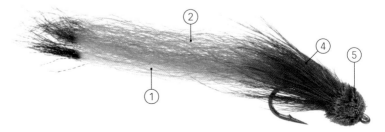

David King

King's Chimera

We should all be so lucky as to have the 'problem' of fish destroying our flies. However, if you're a guide, this destruction can become expensive – not to mention giving you additional time at the tying bench.

David King noticed that, when fishing standard deceivers, Spanish mackerel would destroy a fly each time they hit. By switching to bucktail, he could use the same fly for many fish and so his catch rate improved. The pronounced eyes appear to trigger aggressive strikes from gamefish.

David prefers to fish this pattern on a 3.7-m (12-ft) leader and uses a loop knot to give the fly additional action. He allows the fly to sink and strips back with a long, fast retrieve.

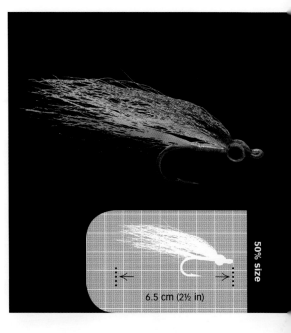

50% size

6.5 cm (2½ in)

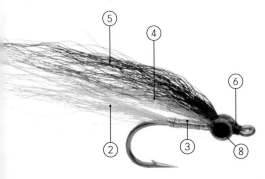

Materials

Hook Varivas 2610 ST-V, size 4
Thread UNI Big Fly, white
Body Veniard flat mirror flash
Wings Bucktail, brown over white
Varnish Hard as Hull head cement
Eyes Veniard Epoxy Eyes, 5 mm (³⁄₁₆ in), silver/black

How to tie

1 Wrap thread along the shaft of the hook, touching turns and stopping just past the point. Repeat twice.

2 Tie in 25 white bucktail hairs, extending past the hook bend by approximately the length of the hook.

3 Tie in a 15-cm (6-in) section of flat mirror flash. This should be wrapped up and down the body two to three times to build a slim body, finally tying off two-thirds of the way along the hook length.

4 Tie in 20 hairs of white bucktail, reaching to the end of the tail.

5 Tie in 20 brown bucktail hairs over the white and the same length.

6 Turning the vice back over, trim off any excess bucktail, front to back, because this helps form the head build-up. Making more turns with the white thread, build up the head to a suitable size, then tie off.

7 Build up a large thread head over this and build up several coats of varnish, allowing it to dry between coats.

8 While the varnish is still tacky, press an eye onto each side.

9 Add more varnish to cover the eyes and secure them to the head.

Length 7 cm (2¾ in)

Mike Cook

Ron's Red Eyed Shrimp

Captain Mike Cook, from Rockport, Texas, reports that this fly was originated by Rockport resident Ron Head for redfish in shallow water.

Materials

Hook Mustad 34007, size 4
Thread UTC 280, olive
Eyes X-small dumbbell eyes, painted red
Antennae Javelina (collared peccary) bristles and Arctic fox tail, olive
Head Brown hackle feather
Legs Brown hackle feather
Body Variegated chenille, medium brown/yellow

Mike guides in the ultrashallow flats and back-bay lakes around Rockport, Aransas Pass, and Port Aransas, Texas. Much of his fishing is done in water less than 30 cm (1 ft) deep and all of it is sight fishing.

Although the fly was designed for redfish, Mike has also caught speckled trout and flounder on it. The small size of the Red Eyed Shrimp allows him to cast the fly very close to the fish without spooking it. He works it with short, quick strips and brings it to the fish's

nose. A short pause is usually all it takes for the fish to eat it.

Mike's first experience with the Red Eyed Shrimp was in the Light House Lakes near Port Aransas. The tide was coming in, filling the lakes. Groups of redfish were coming in with the tide through a narrow inlet. He stood in one spot, casting to reds as they entered the lake, and they ate the fly like it was popcorn. He caught and released seven reds on one fly and it has been his go-to fly ever since.

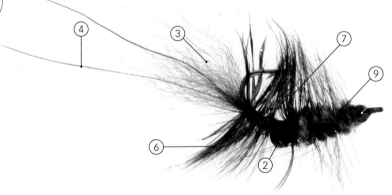

How to tie

1 Place the hook in the vice, tie on and wrap thread to the middle of the hook bend and back to the tie point at the start of hook bend.

2 Tie in the eyes with figure-of-eight wraps at the tie point.

3 Tie in a medium clump of olive Arctic fox tail on the bend side of the hook; bind down to the centre of the hook bend.

4 Tie in two javelina bristles, one on each side, extending 1.5 hook lengths.

5 Tie in the hackle and wrap the thread back to the eyes.

6 Palmer the hackle between the Arctic fox and the lead eyes. Tie down the hackle and move the thread behind the lead eyes.

7 Tie in the hackle for the legs behind the lead eyes; leave it free at this time.

8 Tie in the chenille and wrap the thread to the hook of the eye.

9 Wrap chenille to the lead eyes, then wrap back to the hook eye. Tie off and cut the chenille.

10 Palmer the free hackle around the chenille to the hook eye, then tie off the hackle.

11 Wrap the head and whip finish. Cut the thread.

Jeff Priest
Rock-N-Candy

Jeff Priest is an established guide in the Los Angeles and Sea of Cortez areas. His speciality is fly fishing from the beach. He wanted to improve on unweighted squid patterns that rely on sinking lines to get them moving in the water column.

Materials

Hook Tiemco 911S, 3x or 4x long and x-strong

Thread Danville flat waxed nylon, tan

Weight 0.035 mm lead-free round wire

Mouth Hareline Dubbin cactus chenille, medium pink

Flash Hareline Dubbin Krystal Flash, pearl

Tentacles Chinese rooster neck feathers #1, natural ginger

Body Cross-cut rabbit strips, tan or two-tone peachy pink

Eyes Spirit River 3D moulded eyes, pearl white, 6 mm (¼ in)

Adhesives Head cement, gel Zap-A-Gap, UV Knot Sense

Marker pen Tan to match the body colour

Equipment UV light

His corbina pattern appears more natural because it can be fished along submerged structure without plunging unnaturally to the bottom.

The controlled dive gives the appearance of a squid, dislodged and orienting towards the structure.

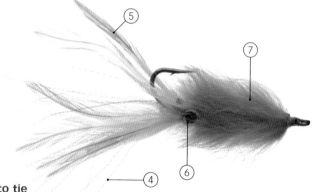

How to tie

1 Wrap ten turns of wire at the bend of the hook.

2 Start thread wrappings at the eye, run them back and completely cover the wire, finish wrapping back to the eye. Coat with head cement.

3 Tie in the cactus chenille at the forward end of the wire and wrap backward and forward to make a small ball. Tie off.

4 Take three or four strands of Krystal Flash and lay them along the side of the shank, extending backward and forward where the chenille was secured. Secure three or four strands at a time in the middle of the material. Once secured, fold back the forward-pointing material so that it is on all sides of the hook, splayed over the chenille.

5 Take two longer Chinese rooster neck feathers and secure one on either side of the hook shank, so that they splay outward. Tie in closest to the forward portion of the chenille, but on the shank. Add three shorter hackles on the top and three on the bottom of the shank, rotate the hook as needed to complete this step, and trim the excess from the hackle butts. Make sure all hackles splay outward, then whip finish and coat with head cement. Trim the Krystal Flash to uneven lengths, but no longer than the hackle.

6 Put a small amount of gel Zap-A-Gap on the back of one eye at a time and press it firmly on the side of the shank, where the hackles were secured on top of the thread. Once the eyes have set, fill the gaps with UV Knot Sense and cure with UV light.

7 Secure the tip of the rabbit strip closest to the squid's eye. Wrap the strip forward, keeping the tips pointing backward and each wrap next to the other, all the way to the hook eye. Secure and whip finish, then colour the thread with a pen to match the body. Coat the thread with UV Knot Sense.

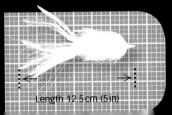

Length 12.5 cm (5 in)

Simon Young

Sparkle Charlie

This fly came about after Simon read an article in an American magazine about anglers spinning for bonefish. It occurred to him that a very bright fly version of the proven Crazy Charlie could be tried.

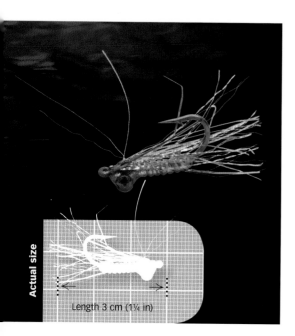

Actual size

Length 3 cm (1¼ in)

Several samples were tied, in silver/pearl and gold/pearl versions, and these were given to friends who were going to the Bahamas for bonefish. They proved a great success, particularly the gold version – so much so that, on two different trips, the guides were asking where the flies came from and if they could have some more.

The effectiveness of this pattern is credited to the fact that bonefish feed on small minnows and find the sparkle/flash attractive. As a result, the Sparkle Charlie should be fished to look like a minnow. Simon recommends fishing it on a floating line, casting well ahead of the cruising bonefish. When the fish gets near, retrieve the fly in short pulls, pausing between each pull.

Thanks to the sparkle and flash, this pattern also fishes well in cloudy or dirty water.

Simon's most memorable day with this fly involved casting to, and catching, one of a pair of big bonefish around 3.6 kg (8 lb) on the flats of Los Roques, in Venezuela.

Materials

Hook Tiemco TMC 811S, sizes 6 or 8
Thread UNI size 6/0, tan
Overbody Clear vinyl ribbing
Underbody One strand of silver holographic tinsel in open turns
Eyes Gold dumbbells
Wings A mix of gold and pearl tinsel
Adhesive Superglue

How to tie

1 At the bend in the hook, tie in the vinyl ribbing overbody material.

2 Tie in the silver holographic tinsel underbody in open turns at the bend.

3 Wind the underbody forward along the hook shank.

4 Wind the overbody material forward and tie off.

5 Tie in the dumbbell eyes on top of the shank.

6 Tie in the wing material.

7 Make a thread head and build it up with Superglue.

Enrique Laviada

Turish

We sometimes make a big deal about the use of natural materials and reference the original patterns of long ago. Here's one that goes back to before the time of the Spanish explorers.

Enrique Laviada is an IGFA-certified Captain. His home port is Progresso on the Yucatan, Mexico, and he owns Mayan Fishing Tours.

From ancient times, the Mayans used the sisal (*henequen*) fibre to manufacture ropes and other kinds of woven threads. They even tried some of them for fishing, using different colours obtained from dyes made from roots and seeds.

Enrique wanted to see if he could use some of the Mayan tactics for bonito along the coast in order to give his clients a unique experience. Not only did he use sisal, he went so far as to do his own dyeing with area plants to get the bright colours that he was sure would have been used by the Mayans. His experimentations yielded a series of sisal flies that have shining colours.

The Turish is a deep minnow pattern. When the fly is being retrieved, the fibres give off vibrations that attract even the most cautious fish.

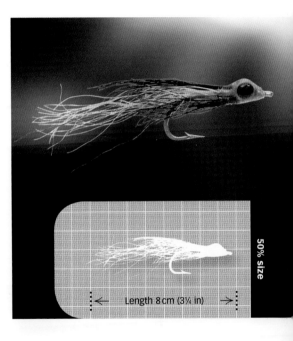

Length 8 cm (3¼ in)

50% size

Materials

Hook Gamakatsu SL11-3H, size 1

Thread Danville flat waxed nylon, yellow

Wing Natural sisal fibres, non-dyed

Body Natural sisal fibres, red and natural

Tail Natural sisal fibres, red

Eyes Red weighted lead eyes, 6 g (⁷⁄₃₂ oz)

How to tie

1 Lay down a short thread from the eye to a quarter of the way towards the bend.

2 Tie in a wing of natural sisal fibres extending twice the hook's length.

3 Tie in a topping of red sisal.

4 Turn the hook over and tie in a throat of red sisal, extending beyond the bend in the hook.

5 Turn the hook over and tie on the eyes, using many wraps of thread, including cross wraps over the eyes.

6 Apply several coats of cement, extending back far enough to hold the sisal fibres in place, close to the hook shank.

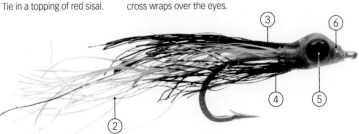

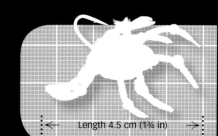

Length 4.5 cm (1¾ in)

Christof Menz

Cuban Crab

Why would a guide from Austria be interested in making a better bonefish/permit fly? Because he guides all over the world, Christof Menz, co-owner of Pro-Guides Fly Fishing, saw the shortcomings of other crab patterns and set about improving the pattern for his clients in the Florida Keys, Cuba and Australia.

Materials

Hook Gamakatsu SL12, size 1

Weight Lead eyes, medium

Silk Dyneema 6/0, black

Eyes Monofilament with two glass beads

Legs Tan chenille

Claws Leather zonker strip with hair sheared off

Underbody Foam tape

Body Sili Skin, belly white

Marker pens Permanent brown and black

Adhesives Superglue, epoxy glue

Above all, the fly had to be realistic enough to fool shy saltwater species such as permit, bonefish and snapper. The Cuban Crab has claws that move like the real deal, and Christof thinks this is what accounts for the fly's success.

The fly's construction also solves a problem shared by many other crab imitations – spinning, if the retrieve is too fast. This fly, with two lead eyes, prevents twisting, giving it more stability than other patterns. Christof prefers to fish it with longer strokes, because it will not twist and give an unrealistic appearance. His favourite retrieve is two short pulls followed by one longer pull. He also makes sure that there is a pause between pulls, and this seems to be the trigger for enticing fish to strike.

The Cuban Crab has worked in many oceans, and the confidence it gives Christof makes it his go-to fly. Recently, several guides from the Florida Keys have been giving the pattern a workout, and now they're back looking for more.

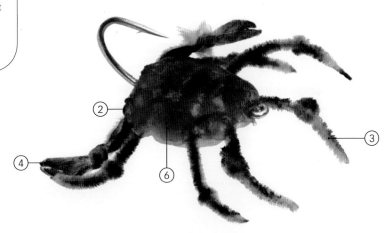

How to tie

1 Tie two pieces of lead eyes in the middle of the hook shank, upside down.

2 At the bend, tie in the two glass bead-and-monofilament eyes.

3 Tie in three pairs of chenille legs. Knot the middle of each leg. Burn the tips of the legs to get a nice taper.

4 Tie in the claws next to the eyes. The claws can be coloured with brown and black permanent markers.

5 Wrap foam tape around the two lead eyes, then wrap a body with the foam.

6 Cut two pieces of Sili Skin into the shape of a crab's body: one will be the upper side and one the bottom. The upper side can be coloured with brown and black permanent markers.

7 Stick the body pieces to the body with Superglue. Fill the edges where the two pieces of Sili Skin come together. Cement and then glue the legs and claws in place with epoxy glue.

Length 18 cm (7 in)

Mike Rice

Yak Hair Deceiver – Herring

Wind can create problems for fly fishers using big, bulky flies. If the materials foul during the cast, the fly will not show the correct profile to the fish and its effectiveness will be diminished.

Materials

Hook Mustad C70SD 3/0 or 34007, size 4

Thread Danville fine monofilament

Tail White yak hair

Body flash Pearl Flashabou and peacock Krystal Flash

Body Yellow bucktail over pink bucktail

Underwing Chartreuse yak hair

Wing Olive yak hair

Topping Extra-long peacock herl

Underbelly White yak hair

Belly White bucktail

Throat Saltwater Krystal Flash, red

Lateral flash Krystal Flash, pearl

Eyes 3D moulded 6-mm (¼-in) eyes

Head 5-minute epoxy adhesive

Mike's pattern is designed so that other materials hold the soft yak hair in place while it is being retrieved. Yak hair allows for a big fly that sheds water quickly, so that it can be easily cast. The pink and yellow bucktail 'shoulder' in the mid-wing helps maintain the bulky profile without adding a lot of weight. Adding the peacock herl topping and the white bucktail on the belly helps to hold the yak hair in place during the cast and maintains the wide body profile in the water.

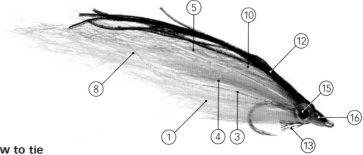

How to tie

1 Tie in a clump of 18-cm (7-in) white yak hair on top of the shank for the tail, just above the hook point, then wrap the thread back to the hook bend.

2 Repeat directly below on the underside of the hook.

3 Tie in four to six strands of pearl Flashabou on top of the first clump of white yak hair for tail flash.

4 Tie in a clump of pink bucktail just in front of the white yak hair tie-in point for a short underwing.

5 Tie in a clump of yellow bucktail directly on top of the pink bucktail.

6 Tie in a 12.5-cm (5-in) clump of white yak hair for the belly on the bottom side of the hook, at the bucktail tie-in point.

7 Tie in six to eight strands of pearl Polar Flash on top of the pink bucktail.

8 Tie in an 18-cm (7-in) clump of chartreuse yak hair in front of the Polar Flash.

9 Tie in six to ten strands of pearl Polar Flash on top of the white yak hair as wing flash.

10 Tie in an 18-cm (7-in) clump of olive yak hair on top at the hook eye.

11 Tie in a good-sized pinch of white bucktail on the bottom of the shank at the hook eye to fill out the belly.

12 Tie in seven to ten strands of peacock herl on top at the hook eye.

13 Tie in six to eight strands of red Flash on the bottom at the hook eye as a throat.

14 Tie in four to six strands of pearl Polar Flash at the hook eye running along the side of the fly for body flash.

15 Attach the eyes using 5-minute epoxy adhesive.

16 Epoxy the head and run a bead of adhesive between the eyes to lock them on.

Coach Duff

Spam and Eggs

Eighteen species of mantis shrimp inhabit the Hawaiian Islands. While it might be possible to imitate each of these species, it is not necessary because the Spam and Eggs pattern can be tied to match the size and colour of each variety.

Materials

Hook Gamakatsu SL11-3H, sizes 8–2/0
Thread Danville monofilament, clear
Tail Tan EP Fibers
Egg sac Orange dyed Finnish raccoon
Palmered hackle Tan neck hackle
Dubbing Tan Hairline Custom Blend
Legs Sand Hareline Loco Legs
Eyes Tungsten Predator medium with red eye
Weed guard 13.6-kg (30-lb) monofilament spike
Marker pen Permanent brown

Coach Duff, owner of Hawaiian Bonefishing With Coach Duff, wanted a fine-tuned mantis pattern with subdued colours and no flash. He made this decision after observing mantis shrimp in their natural habitat and in a fish tank where he kept three. He realized their importance to the diet of the bonefish after getting stomach samples from local biologists who were doing bonefish studies.

Coach reports that the Spam and Eggs works well due to its silhouette, its natural, subdued colouring that matches the surroundings, the egg sac and the action the rubber legs give. Sink rate is paramount to big bonefish, and Coach fishes his flies on the heavy side.

Memorable events for Coach include a client landing a 6.3 and a 4.5 kg (14- and 10-lb) fish with this fly in the same day, and the day another client landed six bonefish over 3.6 kg (8 lb). A 4.5-kg (10-lb) Hawaiian bonefish is over ten years old. Add in 32-km-per-hour (20-mile-per-hour) winds, and you begin to understand how hard it can be to land these large bonefish.

How to tie

1 Tie in a piece of 13.6-kg (30-lb) spike-shaped monofilament in front of the eyes. Wrap the monofilament with thread so that the monofilament stands at 90 degrees to the shank. This will be the weed guard. Trim to a length equal to the hook's gape.

2 Lay down a thread base from the eye of the hook to the bend.

3 At the bend, tie in a 6-mm (¼-in) diameter bundle of tan EP Fibers. They should be three-quarters of the length of the hook shank.

4 Make brown vertical marks on the EP Fibers.

5 Move the thread forward about 3 mm (⅛ in) and tie in a small tuft of the orange Finnish raccoon under the hook shank.

6 In front of the tuft, tie in the tan hackle.

7 Dub a body with the tan Hairline Custom Blend by wrapping the dubbing forward nearly to the weed guard. Tie off and trim the excess.

8 Wrap the hackle over the body to the end. Tie off and trim the excess.

9 In front of the body and under the hook shank, tie in three pieces of sand-coloured Hareline Loco Legs, tying them at their centres so that you have six legs all pointed at 90 degrees to the hook shank. Trim them to three times the hook's gape.

10 In front of the body, tie on tungsten eyes on top of the hook shank.

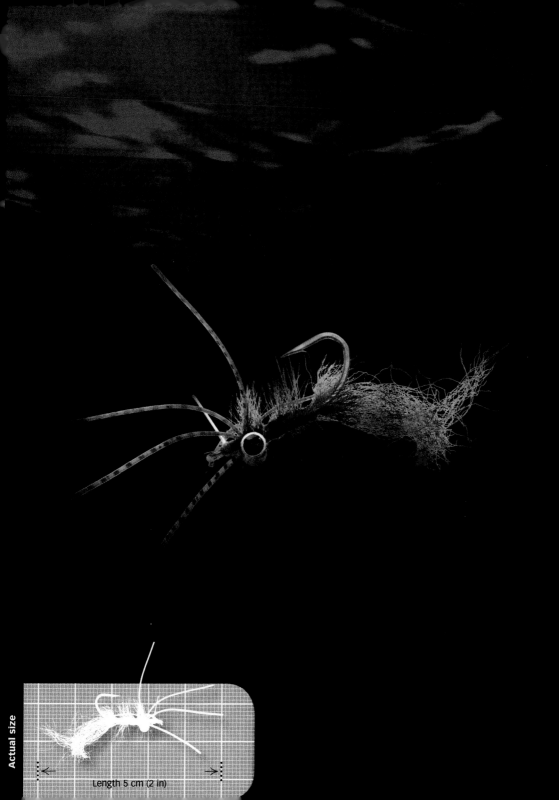

Length 5 cm (2 in)

Audrey Ciurca

AC Diamond Fly

They say that diamonds are a girl's best friend. They could become yours, too, when you try this pattern developed by Audrey Ciurca.

50% size

Length 10 cm (4 in)

Audrey discovered that rhinestones could complement the effectiveness of many patterns. This pattern's colour scheme can be modified to match baitfish in your area.

Frank, Audrey's husband, first tried out this pattern in sizes 2, 1 and 1/0 and had no problem hooking fish throughout the water column. By varying the size of the head, you can create different rates of sink.

It performed very well with a sinking line. Frank used long strips followed by short strips, and the fly swam much like a Clouser but with less sinking.

During experimentation, Frank discovered that the reflection from the rhinestones alone was attracting fish.

The AC Diamond Fly has also accounted for grey and speckled trout, stripers, bluefish, albacore, tuna, dolphin, ladyfish, snook, reds and jacks.

In addition, Frank won the 2005 Chesapeake Bay Striper Fly tournament in Maryland using a chartreuse/white AC Diamond Fly.

Materials

Hook Daiichi X427, size 2
Thread Silver Gudebrod HT, size A
Body Pink, light grey and white bucktail
Head 12 × 6 mm (½ × ⅛ in) marquise-shaped acrylic rhinestones
Flash Silver Krystal Flash and pink Shimmerflash
Eyes Silver Prisma tape eyes
Cement Superglue and 5-minute epoxy mixed with alcohol

How to tie

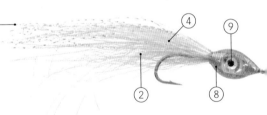

1 Lay down a thread base from the eye of the hook to about two-thirds of the way to the bend.

2 At the rear of the thread base, tie in some 7.5-cm (3-in) lengths of pink bucktail.

3 Top with light grey bucktail.

4 Top the pink and grey bucktail with white bucktail.

5 In front of the white bucktail, tie in ten strands of Silver Krystal Flash and ten strands of pink Shimmerflash.

6 Add some Superglue to the head and attach rhinestones 2 cm (¾ in) back from the hook eye. Do not crowd the head.

7 Mix a couple of drops of alcohol in the 5-minute epoxy to eliminate bubbles and prevent yellowing.

8 Begin adding epoxy, starting where the body

thread wraps end and moving towards the hook eye, creating a double tapered head.

9 Apply Prisma tape eyes to the rhinestones.

10 Mix up more epoxy with alcohol and lay down a finish coat over the eyes and the previous epoxy head. Let it dry in a rotating dryer.

Butch Cooley

911

There's no reason this fly should work on sailfish – at least that's what its designer, Butch Cooley, says. The overall appearance and colour represent nothing that swims where he normally goes after sailfish. In fact, it's the wrong colour by most standards. Sailfish love bright flies. So, why is this the go-to fly for finicky sails?

Every now and again, Butch will tease a sailfish or two to the back of the boat, and when 'normal' colours are presented, the fish simply will not take. When this occurs, the usual wisdom is for the captain or mate to present a live bait on a conventional rod. They put live bait in the water, and almost every time the fish will take it.

This fly was developed for those times when live bait would not work. He tied absolutely the wrong fly for the situation and found it worked 90 per cent of the time that the normal bright flies would not. Surprisingly enough, Butch found it worked all over the world, not just in one area.

The secret of this fly's effectiveness is the same thing that triggers a trout to take a fly it's never seen before: maybe it's the novelty; maybe it's curiosity. It just goes to show you that conventional wisdom might have become the norm simply because no one else was willing to experiment.

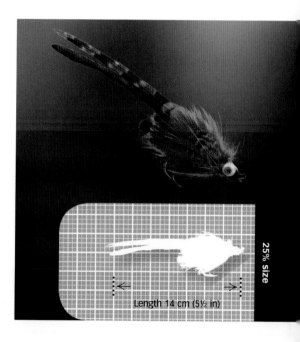

25% size

Length 14 cm (5½ in)

Materials

Hook Mustad, size 6/0
Thread Brown thread or floss
Tail Pheasant tail fibres
Body Thread wraps
Wing Two 25-cm (10-in) lengths of pheasant tail tips
Beard Pheasant tail fibres
Eyes 6-mm (¼-in) 3D eyes
Adhesive Superglue

How to tie

1 At the bend of the hook, tie in a tail made from a bunch of 5-cm (2-in) pheasant tail fibres.

2 Wrap the thread ahead, three-quarters of the way to the eye.

3 Tie in the wing made from two 25-cm (10-in) pheasant tail tips.

4 Cover the thread wraps and wing bases, using three or four pheasant breast feathers on each side.

5 Strip some long pheasant tail fibres and tie in a beard under the fly.

6 Wrap a large thread head and finish with brown enamel.

7 Glue the eyes to the thread head.

David Bitters

Baymen Universal

Captain David Bitters of Baymen Outfitters in Duxbury, Massachusetts, set out to create the perfect fly. Haven't we all? He wanted a pattern to consistently catch striped bass all along the East Coast.

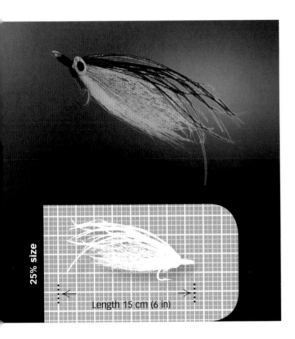

25% size

Length 15 cm (6 in)

His first step was to examine all the bait species of Cape Cod Bay. He found that stripers ate a huge number of species. In fact, the rule of thumb became that, if a striper could fit it in its mouth, it would eat it – so he knew there could never be one fly to do it all.

He decided to go with a medium baitfish pattern with a white belly, a dark back and a slight pink hue in the scales that can be seen at certain angles. In addition, he discovered that fly patterns with eyes will outfish fly patterns without eyes.

You'll notice that this pattern has a long, thick 'neck'. Here's why: David likes to have a 'handle' to grab when he slides his thumb and index finger down the tippet into the fish's mouth. The heavy thread wraps also give some weight to the fly and cause it to dip as it is stripped.

The final result is a very effective, durable pattern. How durable? One local angler claims to have caught and released 150 stripers on a single Baymen Universal.

Materials

Hook Eagle Claw 254 SS, size 2/0
Thread Danville flat waxed nylon, black
Wing Bleached white bucktail; pink dyed bucktail; dyed olive bucktail; pearl Krystal Flash; peacock herl
Throat/gills Red bucktail
Eyes 3D prism eyes in silver, a black pupil
Head Black thread
Adhesive Sportsman's Goop

How to tie

1 Use small, sparse bunches of material and stack them so that the white bucktail shows both above and below the hook shank.

2 Stack pink dyed bucktail. One small bunch above the hook shank and one small bunch below.

3 Next comes pearl Krystal Flash. One small bunch above the hook shank and one small bunch below.

4 Then olive bucktail. One small bunch above the hook shank and one small bunch below.

5 Finally, top the fly with peacock herl.

6 Add a short throat of red bucktail under the hook shank.

7 Use Sportsman's Goop to attach the eyes.

8 Make a long head with black tying thread.

9 Reinforce the entire head with head cement.

Ariel Cabrera

Bullethead

The Bullethead is effective on most Everglades and Gulf Coast species. It is deadly on the flats, especially for snook. As a bonus, it is easy to tie and can be tied in many colours, including gold and pink.

Captain Ariel Cabrera thinks the effectiveness of this pattern is due to the pulsating action of the marabou, the shine and reflection of the EZ Body, and the small wake it creates, caused by the shape of the head. This pattern is very durable once coated with epoxy. It can be adapted to many sizes, but Ariel prefers these flies on 1/0 up to 3/0 hooks, even for large tarpon.

Snook facts: Snook are hermaphrodites and change sex from male to female. Why? No one knows, and the snook are not talking. Snook do not run their prey down: instead, they ambush their prey. Preferred locations include areas where currents bring their lunch to them. Because they are strong fighters, they are favourites with sport fishers. The fact they have a mild, delicate flavour also makes them popular.

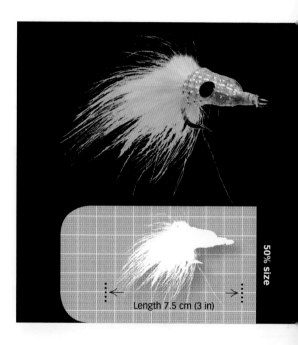

50% size

Length 7.5 cm (3 in)

Materials

Hook Any saltwater hook, sizes 1/0–3/0
Thread Nylon to match the colour of the EZ Body
Tail Marabou
Body/head EZ Body
Eyes Red stick-on eyes
Cement 5-minute epoxy

How to tie

1 Tie in a marabou tail at the shank bend (white is a good colour).

2 Cut a 4-cm (1½-in) piece of pearl EZ Body and place it over the hook, beginning at the eye.

3 Secure the EZ Body from the eye of the hook to halfway to the bend of the hook shank. Secure with a drop of cement.

4 Now turn the EZ Body tube inside out in order to form the head of the fly.

5 Tie and wrap thread near the hook eye. This makes a head that is actually twice the thickness of the EZ Body, 2 cm (¾ in) long.

6 Apply red stick-on eyes.

7 Mix some 5-minute epoxy and coat the stick-on eyes for a durable finish.

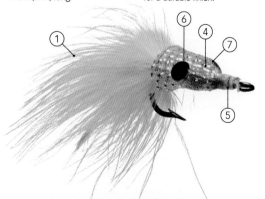

50% size

Length 10 cm (4 in)

Bryan McGowan

Blackbone

Captain Bryan McGowan, from Jacksonville, Florida, says that sight casting to black drum can be a frustrating thing. So, after much trial and error, he created the Blackbone. Because these fish are used to eating large crabs, he needed a fly that had a large profile.

Materials

Hook Gamakatsu B10S, size 1/0

Thread UTC flat waxed nylon, black

Weight Small or extra-small dumbbell lead eyes

Tail Four hot orange barred rubber legs

Wing/Shell Orange cross-cut rabbit strip

Body Black cactus chenille and black strung hackle

Eyes 18-kg (40-lb) hard Mason monofilament

Cement Loon Hard Head Fly Finish

By using wound hackle and rabbit fur, Bryan was able to achieve a large profile fly without making it bulky. He also needed movement like a crab – something that yelled out, 'come and eat me'.

The other thing Bryan wanted was a quick sink rate that would allow him to get in front of the fish but that at the same time was weedless. He used large lead eyes and accented the fly with the mono eyes that also kept it weedless.

Bryan throws to blacks more than 22 kg (up to 50 lb) with this fly, so the hook that he uses is very important. The Gamakatsu B10S hook is his hook of choice because of its superb strength, extremely sharp point and large hook gap.

These attributes result in a fly that has been deadly on blacks. The first black drum that Bryan caught on this fly was 17 kg (38 lb). He was sight casting and watched the fish move 90 degrees and take the fly.

How to tie

1 Begin your thread on the shank just above the hook barb. Take two orange rubber legs, tie in at the bend of the hook, and create four legs by doubling the legs.

2 Tie in the tip of a strip of cross-cut rabbit strip at the bend of the hook and secure by adding a small amount of Loon Hard Head.

3 Wind the rabbit strip forward three wraps. Trim the excess and finish by applying a drop of Loon Hard Head.

4 Tie in black cactus chenille flush to the forward end of the rabbit strip.

5 At same point, tie in a strung hackle, but leave some of the fluff on the hackle to create a webbed effect. Leave the hackle and chenille hanging while you advance your thread to the hook eye.

6 Tie in extra-small or small dumbbell lead eyes to the top of the shank just 3 mm (⅛ in) shy of the hook eye

and secure with Loon Hard Head.

7 Wrap the black cactus chenille forward to the eyes. Make a figure-of-eight wrap around the eyes and tie off just in front of the eyes.

8 Wrap the black strung hackle forward, working it into the cactus chenille and leaving a small gap between wraps. Tie off and trim just in front of the eyes.

9 Turn the fly hook point up and tie in the Mason monofilament eyes, just in front of the dumbbell eyes.

10 Turn the fly back over and trim the hackle tips that are on the bottom, creating a flat bottom.

11 Secure with Loon Hard Head.

Jeff Smith

Buffy the Striper Slayer

There are hundreds of baitfish imitations out there. Captain Jeff Smith says that one major problem he sees in the design is they lack a large profile. Those that do have a large profile require half a chicken to tie. Here's Jeff's solution.

Materials

Hook Mustad SL-12, sizes 2–4/0
Thread Clear monofilament
Wing Baby yak, Polar Flash, pearl Crystal Flash, peacock sword fibres
Spreader EZ Body Tubing
Eyes Stick-on Mylar eyes
Adhesives Goop, head cement and Softex

Buffy the Striper Slayer works well in the outer surf, where a larger fly is more easily seen than a smaller one. Jeff's patterns evolved around a synthetic pearly Mylar tubing called EZ Body Braid. By using a spreader, he designed flies with huge profiles without added bulk.

Most of Jeff's flies are tied with spreaders made from Slinky Hair or natural yak hair. Neither one will retain water, but they can be used to create a very large profile with little material. The flies are easy to tie, fairly foul proof and you can match the colour of your local baitfish.

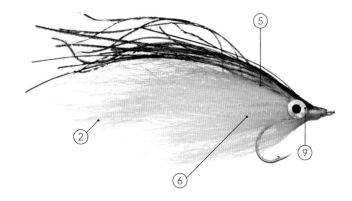

How to tie

1 Lay down a thread base from the eye of the hook to the middle of the shank.

2 Make a tail of baby yak hair, stagger the ends, tie it in at the midpoint and wrap to the bend. Add two strands of Polar Flash.

3 Make a 'spreader'. Cut a 5-cm (2-in) piece of EZ Body Tubing. Slip the tubing over the eye of the hook and tie it down just forward of the midsection. Add a drop of head cement at the tie-down point. Whip finish and cut the thread. Push the tubing back over itself – like turning a sock or trouser leg inside out. With your thumb and index finger, grab both sides of the spreader, pinch and pull up until it stops on the bottom of the shank. Tilt the spreader forward a bit and tie the spreader down 3 mm (⅛ in) or more behind the eye. Add a drop of head cement to hold things tight. You've now made a spreader that will flare all the following materials.

4 Take a small pinch of baby yak, stagger the ends and add one strand of neutral flash. Tie the baby yak on top of the spreader, using the fewest number of wraps possible to avoid thread build-up. Repeat until you have worked the yak hair around the spreader, creating a tapered body.

5 Make a wing of coloured yak hair. Add a strand of matching colour flash. Top the wing with several strands of peacock sword fibres.

6 Tie in several strands of pearl Crystal Flash along the sides.

7 Whip finish.

8 Comb out the fly by cupping the fibres in your hand until the profile is true.

9 Use Goop to secure Mylar stick-on eyes at the middle of the spreader base.

10 Finish with a mixture of Goop and Softex. Coat the fly lightly to just beyond the bend of the hook.

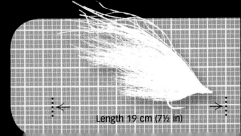

Length 19 cm (7½ in)

Eric Thomas

Cam's Fly

Here's a fly that's been presented to George Bush Sr, Bill Clinton and Mikhail Gorbachev. With these instructions, you can now have your own. It's from Captain Eric Thomas of Newport, Rhode Island. Cam's Fly is an imitation of a juvenile bunker.

Materials

Hook Eagle Claw 245ss, size 1/0
Thread 4.5-kg (10-lb) monofilament
Flash Silver Flashabou
Wing White, purple, yellow and olive bucktail, or synthetics such as Angel Hair
Body Silver Tiewell Sparkle Flash and Bill's Bodi Braid
Eyes Silver stick-on eyes, sized to match the fly

Eric was struck by how prominent the silvery belly was in the juvenile bunker. This got him thinking about how he could create this appearance in an imitation. The fly has gone through several changes and has now been updated to use some of the latest synthetics.

Cam's Fly is made to fish the early season bass in the bay. It was designed to imitate the early season silver sides and small herring. At this time of year, the bass are crashing small baitfish on the surface, so a fairly fast retrieve has worked best. It has also been productive in autumn when fishing for the hard tails, again with a fast retrieve.

Bones and albies have also been known to have a field day with them. Eric usually uses this fly with an intermediate-sinking line.

How to tie

1 Lay down a thread base from the hook eye to above the point of the hook.

2 Tie in ten strands of silver Flashabou. These strands should be 6 cm (2½ in) long.

3 Over this, tie in a small amount of white bucktail long enough to make the total length of the fly 10 cm (4 in).

4 Under the hook shank, tie in a small bunch of silver Tiewell Sparkle Flash as long as the Flashabou.

5 Bill's Bodi Braid is cut into 2.5- and 4-cm (1- and 1½-in) pieces. You will need about eight of these pieces. These will be tied to the bottom of the fly. Tie one piece in at a time. One should go on the belly facing you and the other on the far side of the tier on the belly.

6 Move forward on the hook shank and repeat step 4 to build the belly of the fly.

Repeat this step until you have reached the eye of the hook.

7 On top of the hook, place a small amount of white bucktail. Over this place a smaller amount of purple and yellow bucktail mixed together.

8 Finally, tie in purple Tiewell Flash, as long as the bucktail, on the very top of the fly.

9 Apply small stick-on eyes at the head. The monofilament will disappear when the head cement is applied over the thread and the eyes will show through. This eliminates the need for epoxy and speeds up the drying time.

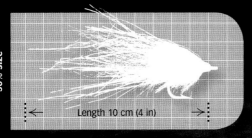

Daniel Beilinson

DB Brown Crab

Do I need a permit for permit? Will they permit me a permit for permit? Daniel Beilinson would know: he's fished everywhere from Florida to Patagonia, so he's seen it all. This is his go-to pattern for permit.

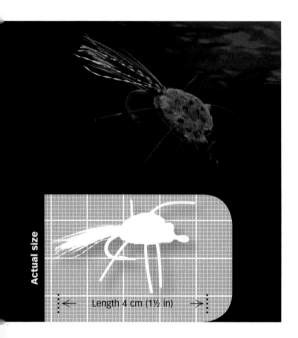

Actual size

Length 4 cm (1½ in)

Daniel tied this fly after trying the patterns offered on the market. Most of them were too heavy and the bead chain eyes were too big, so they were difficult to cast and unnecessarily weighty in shallow waters. The Brown Crab gave Daniel immediate positive results, including the biggest permit he ever caught, 9.5 kg (21-lb), in the north of Isla Blanca, Cancun.

It has proved to be an excellent fly to fish where the bottom is a bit dark. It is light and gives very good results, despite its long legs in shallow waters. It can also be used to fish bonefish in a dark-bottomed or weedy area. For such conditions, Daniel suggests building in a monofilament weed guard.

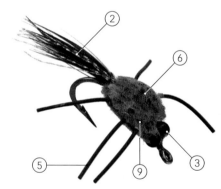

Materials

Hook Mustad 34007, size 6
Thread Black waxed monocord
Tail Olive marabou muddler strip and pearl saltwater Krystal Flash
Eyes Small or medium bead chain eyes
Body Brown wool
Legs Rubber legs
Marker pen Permanent black

How to tie

1 Lay down a thread base from the eye of the hook to the bend.

2 Tie in the marabou muddler tail and eight pieces of pearl saltwater Krystal Flash.

3 Choose the right size of bead chain eyes and tie them firmly, close to the hook eye.

4 Cut six 2.5-cm (1-in) lengths of wool and tie them, one at a time, at 90 degrees to the hook shank, from the marabou tail to the eyes of the crab. Fray both sides.

5 Cut the rubber legs into 5-cm (2-in) pieces. Place them on top of the woollen body in three equal parts and glue them in place.

6 Take a bit of wool and cut it so thin that it almost becomes dust. Apply some fast-drying adhesive to the woollen body and sprinkle on the woollen dust, covering the entire surface on both sides. Secure with your fingers and let it dry.

Once it is dry, trim the borders of the woollen body, being careful not to cut the rubber legs.

7 Trim the rubber legs to length.

8 Cement the head.

9 Once the fly is dry, paint some dots on the body with black permanent marker.

Ralph Poness

Abused Mackerel

Trout fishermen demand that their flies match each stage of a mayfly's life. They have patterns to cover: nymphs, swimming nymphs, emerging adults, crippled emerging adults, drowned adults, etc. Captain Ralph Poness, from Framingham, Massachusetts, has gone one better.

Ralph sent along an unusual pattern designed to look like a mackerel with its internal plumbing hanging out. Don't believe me? Read on.

Although this pattern is for the ardent fly fisher, purists should stop reading here. For the rest, here's an explanation: If you spend first light jigging mackerel, then pack the poor fish in the live well and relocate them 80 km (50 miles) offshore, something untowards happens to them. This fly was designed to imitate what they look like after that ride.

Those of us who grew up trout fishing know that the dropper is indispensable, so Ralph just made it bigger and a bit more – well – gory. Watching 'abused mackerel' make their way in the bait slick inspired this one. Without being too graphic, you can imagine what the 'dropper' imitates.

The gauntlet has been thrown down: trout fishermen – can you top this one?

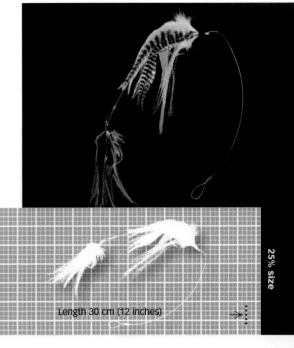

25% size

Length 30 cm (12 inches)

Materials

Hook Two Trey Combs Big Game, size 6/0
Thread Heavy nylon (red and black)
Wing Green, blue and grizzly strung saddle hackle; red and white Crystal Flash
Wire 150# nylon-coated Steelon with a #4 crimp

How to tie

1 Pile green, blue and grizzly hackle and red and white Crystal Flash on the front hook as a wing.

2 Tie the wing in place and fluff it out to get maximum size. Cement the thread.

3 On the rear hook, use the same procedure with primarily red colours. Cement the thread.

4 To connect the two hooks, run the Steelon wire through the rear hook's eye, fold it forward, add a #4 crimp and crimp with pliers.

5 Loop the other end of the wire around the front hook's bend. Lightly crimp with pliers. Adjust the length so that the back edge of the feather wing almost touches the rear hook eye. Close the loop and crimp the connector tightly.

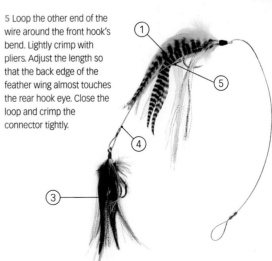

Lynne Heyer

Yak Hair Baitfish

The advantage of yak hair is its long length and low weight-to-volume ratio. As a result, extremely large striped bass flies can be tied that are still light enough to be cast with a fly rod. Yak hair can be dyed any colour, which allows a tier to recreate the colours of the local baitfish.

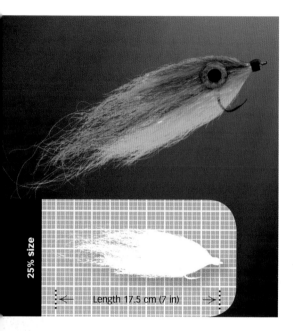

25% size

Length 17.5 cm (7 in)

The Yak Hair Baitfish was designed by Captain Lynne Heyer, from Nantucket, Massachusetts. Lynne says blending yak hair is easy but time-consuming. Start by combing the yak hair to remove snags. The yaks appreciate this immensely. If you blend the yak hair ahead of time, you'll have a big enough bundle for several flies.

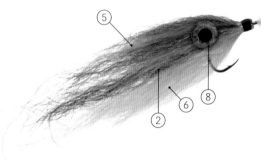

Materials

Hook Tiemco 600SP,
sizes 2/0–8/0
Thread Black Danville flat
waxed nylon, 3/0, black
Lateral line Black
yak hair
Body Light green and grey
blended yak hair with a
trace of black yak hair
Belly Chartreuse yak hair
Eyes Large 3D moulded
eyes with a black pupil
Adhesives Softex
and Goop

How to tie

1 Lay a thread base from the hook eye to the hook bend.

2 At the hook bend, tie in a lateral line of black yak hair. The lateral line should be long enough to almost reach the end of the tail.

3 At the hook bend, tie in a dark back of light green and grey blended yak hair with a trace of black yak hair for the top. The shank should be 15–25 cm (6–10 in) long. Position it so that two-thirds of the length is behind the hook eye and the rest sticks out over the hook eye.

4 At the hook eye, bind in the yak hair with five wraps.

5 Fold the remaining length back over the top and wrap tightly. This should result in a staggered shape, not with all the ends coming together at the same location.

6 Rotate the vice and repeat the steps, using chartreuse yak hair for the belly on the bottom of the hook shank.

7 Take the fly out of the vice and use a bodkin to apply two coats of Softex per side, using just enough to hold the

baitfish shape. This will give the fly stiffness and prevent it from fouling. Work it into the fibres with the point of the bodkin.

8 Use Softex to apply the eyes after the last coat of Softex is dry. The eyes should be positioned just in front of, or over, the bend of the hook. Use a small amount of Goop and position them so that the eyes pinch the hook shank. Use a clothes-peg to hold the eyes in place until the Goop dries.

Tom Carver

Tom's Redfish Magic

Addiction is not always a bad thing. I was once addicted to fly fishing, but too many cold-turkey days helped me get over my dependency. Now I only get the shakes when watching fishing shows on television.

However, consider Tom Carver of Orlando, Florida. He owns Flat Addicted Fishing Charters. When the area visitors aren't chasing Mickey Mouse around the Magic Kingdom, Tom delivers some Redfish Magic of his own and takes them out to chase the redfish.

Tom's favourite area is Mosquito Lagoon. I know it sounds like the location for a horror film, but there's nothing horrific about the way this fly catches redfish. Be certain NOT to leave off the weed guard: it's a necessity in the areas where redfish hang out.

Tom says that, although this pattern can be used all year, it works best in the spring and autumn. The colour combination is a redfish favourite, and this makes it his go-to fly.

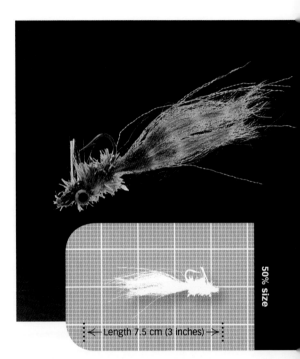

50% size

←— Length 7.5 cm (3 inches) —→

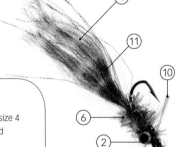

Materials

Hook Mustad SS, size 4
Thread Flat waxed nylon, tan
Loop and weed guard 18-kg (40-lb) monofilament
Tail Tan streamer hair
Eyes Yellow lead dumbbell eyes with black centres
Flash Midge Flash Body
Body Root beer Estaz
Collar Grizzly hackle
Marker pen Permanent brown

How to tie

1 With the hook in an upright position, lay down a thread base from the eye of the hook to the bend.

2 Advance the thread to the eye and tie on lead dumbbell eyes on top of the shank.

3 Wrap the thread back to the bend.

4 Tie in 5 cm (2 in) of tan streamer hair at the bend.

5 Tie in six pieces of Midge Flash on each side of the streamer hair.

6 At the bend, tie in root beer-coloured Estaz and wind a body up to the hook eye.

7 At the hook eye, tie in a grizzly hackle collar and make two turns (staying behind the eyes).

8 Trim the top of the hackle collar to clear the hook gape.

9 Turn the hook over.

10 Between the lead eyes and hook eye, tie in some 18-kg (40-lb) monofilament as a weed guard. The strands should be longer than the hook gape.

11 Draw vertical bars on the tail, using the brown marker.

12 Cement the head thread wraps.

Length 7.5 cm (3 in)

John Ford

Dressed To Kill

How about a fly that started out as a speciality fly and turned out to be a generalist? The Dressed To Kill (DTK) began life as a fly for striped bass, but became good medicine for several more species.

Materials

Hook SS Mustad, sizes 1/0 and 2/0

Thread Danville fine monofilament

Monofilament 18-kg (40-lb)

Wing White or off-white saddle hackles, white bucktail, pink Krystal Flash, pink marabou, grey bucktail, purple fluoro fibre

Belly White bucktail, white Metz polar fibre

Eyes Holographic eyes

The DTK is from John Ford – not the late film producer, but John Ford, owner of the Portland Guide Service from Portland, Maine. His home water is the relatively undiscovered Casco Bay area.

John decided to try this pattern one year during the autumn striper migration. The area was infested with 'peanut' bunker and, after a week or two, the stripers were so gorged on the small bait that they had become very selective and were refusing regular deceivers and Clousers. John took a small, regurgitated bunker home and tried to copy the colours and profile that he saw. It was a hit from the start.

The beauty of the DTK is that it can be fished under almost any conditions at any time. It started out as a killer fly for striped bass and bluefish in the Northeast. John then found it worked well on false albacore when nothing else was working. Since then, he's taken yellowfin and bluefin tuna over 22 kg (up to 50 lb), as well as small tarpon, jacks, and a host of other tropical fish. A guide friend in the Florida Keys has even taken a permit on this fly in deeper water. It has undergone some minor changes over the years, and has become a bit more complex to tie, but it remains a fairly simple offspring of the original.

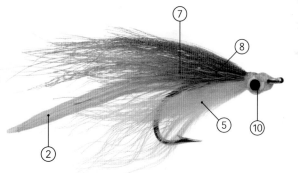

How to tie

1 Start by tying a small monofilament loop (18-kg/40-lb) on the top of the hook, just before the bend; this will help keep any of the hackles from 'fouling' around the hook while fishing.

2 Tie in two small white or off-white saddle hackles on top of the mono loop above the hook bend.

3 Add two small clumps of white bucktail on the underside of the hook, about halfway down the hook shank, to flank each side of the hook bend. Add one small clump of the same on top of the saddle hackles.

4 Tie in six to eight strands of pink Krystal Flash on top of the hook, just above the previous clump of white bucktail.

5 From here, go back to the underside again and add a small amount of white bucktail – just enough to build a small belly and work your way to the head of the fly.

6 To finish the belly, tie in a small clump of white Metz polar fibre on each side of the hook to cover the white bucktail on the underside of the fly.

7 You are now done with the underside of the fly and your thread should be at the head of the fly. Tie in a few strands of pink marabou on each side of the head, just enough to give it colour on the sides.

8 Tie in a good-sized clump of grey bucktail on the top of the fly.

9 Finish it off with a clump of purple fluoro fibre.

10 Apply the holographic eyes.

Greg Morrison

Dorado Delight

Captain Greg Morrison of New Jersey did not always appreciate his father's comments concerning some of his earliest fly-tying efforts. Ed, Greg's dad, commented a little sarcastically that Greg might want to put some glitter on his fly heads to cover up the faults with his thread windings.

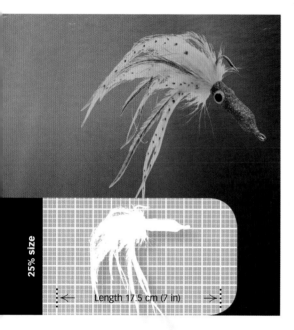

25% size

Length 17.5 cm (7 in)

Greg did just that, and the outcome was so good-looking that his father started using it himself, even though his windings were near perfect. The glitter heads became one of the signatures of Morrison ties, and have been copied by countless fly tiers ever since.

Greg fishes this fly in a chum slick of chopped butterfish, bunker, spearing and squid. The boat is anchored off a 'ball' and the chum mixture is ladled out sparingly to discourage visits from fly-ripping bluefish and sharks. Greg then matches his shooting heads to the drift speed of the day, 350 grains being a good point to start.

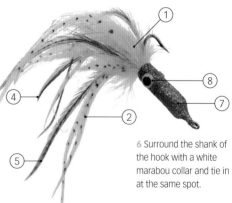

Materials

Hook Mustad 34007, size 4/0

Thread Danville monothread, white

Flash Pearl Angel Hair and Polar Fiber

Tentacles Good-quality white saltwater hackle and contrasting pink, purple or chartreuse

Collar White marabou

Head Clear Corsair Tubing

Body flash Glitter

Eyes Doll's eyes

Marker pen Permanent black

Adhesive 5-minute epoxy

How to tie

1 At the bend of the hook, tie in Polar Fiber and some pearl Angel Hair. They should stick out about 12.5 cm (5 in) beyond the bend.

2 Select a pair of wide, white, 12.5-cm (5-in) hackles with good sheen and tie them in at the bend.

3 Use a black permanent marker and make spots on the white hackles.

4 Select another hackle colour for contrast and tie in a 12.5-cm (5-in) pair at the same spot.

5 Repeat step 4, using colour hackles 7.5 cm (3 in) and then 5 cm (2 in) in length, which gives the profile of different-sized tentacles and also adds to the swimming motion of the fly.

6 Surround the shank of the hook with a white marabou collar and tie in at the same spot.

7 Cut a piece of clear Corsair Tubing to fit from where you tied the materials to the eye of the hook. Tie off the Corsair behind the eye of the hook.

8 Apply 5-minute epoxy over the Corsair and add glitter and doll's eyes in front of where you tied in your materials.

Gary Dubiel

Dubiel's Lil'haden

Lots of anglers feel they need to run 50 km (30 miles) offshore to get good fishing. Truth is, there's lots of action close by in bays and estuaries. Here's a pattern to boost your luck within sight of land.

Gary Dubiel from Oriental, North Carolina, owns Spec Fever Guide Service. He was also the South Atlantic Regional Editor for *Shallow Water Angler* magazine, so you know he has to keep his exaggerations to a minimum, lest he be beset by angry mariners wielding marlin priests.

The Lil'haden is an original Gary developed for fishing the Pamlico Sound Estuary. There are millions of juvenile menhaden that live here, and that makes this the right fly for predators. Initially, he tied the fly with bucktail, but it has evolved with synthetics, particularly select craft fur because of its ability to appear bulky.

Menhaden and countless other oval baitfish are all over this area. This fly has the necessary oval profile, and it has proven itself up and down the East and Gulf coasts. The Lil'haden fishes well on both intermediate sinking and floating lines. Stripping the line with pauses allows the weighted nose to fall, triggering more strikes. The craft fur also breathes very well.

50% size

Length 10 cm (4 in)

Materials

Hook Varivas 990S, size 1/0
Thread UNI monofilament
Weight Ten wraps of 0.6-mm (0.025-in) lead wire
Body Silver Bill's Bodi Braid
Wing and underwing Polar white Craft Fur Plus
Flash Ten strands of silver Kreinik's Flash
Overwing Insect green Craft Fur Plus
Eyes 3-mm (⅛-in) 3D moulded eyes in pearl, silver or chartreuse
Head Superglue and 5-minute epoxy

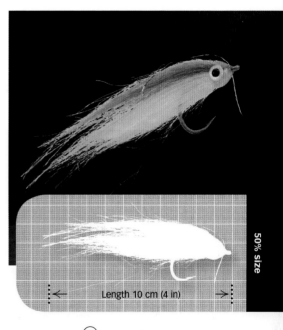

How to tie

1 Wrap lead wire from the hook eye back ten turns and then cover with Bill's Bodi Braid.

2 Tie wings directly onto the Bodi Braid in three equal amounts – one on each side and one under the body.

3 Tie in silver flash over the shank.

4 Add an overwing of insect green Craft Fur Plus.

5 Glue the eyes in place. Let them dry.

6 Shape the head with 5-minute epoxy and rotate until dry.

Mike Corblies

E-Z Eel

'This fly is unquestionably the easiest pattern I know of to duplicate', says Captain Mike Corblies, from Island Heights, New Jersey. Mike owns Coastal Guide Service. He is also the Director of the American Fly Fishing Schools and the inventor of the 'Simul-Cast Pond' show that tours nationwide.

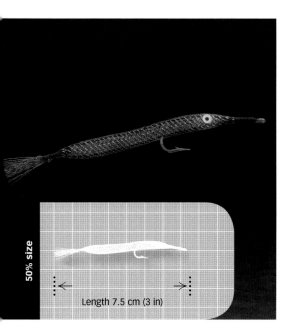

50% size

Length 7.5 cm (3 in)

The E-Z Eel is the saltwater equivalent of a Woolly Bugger for ease of tying. Mike always recommends it for beginners, to increase their satisfaction with their first efforts with bobbin and thread. But, more importantly, it catches a lot of fish.

The E-Z Eel has its origins with master tier Jack Gartside. Jack discovered a tubing material and began using it to imitate sand eels or sand launce, a primary forage species for stripers and bluefish. After watching Jack, Mike came up with a similar but somewhat simpler form of tubing through a craft-store supplier.

Mike learned an important lesson from a 'novice' several years ago. He suggested that Mike should retrieve his fly with two hands instead of one, because the local bass preferred a steady retrieve. It took only three casts to put him tight with his first bass of the night. The point is that you need to experiment with your retrieve techniques and not get locked into just one or two methods with this or any other fly.

Materials

Hook SS 2/0
Thread Monothread, black
Body Captain Mike's Body Parts, pearl Corsair, or similar mesh tubing
Tail Synthetic duster, Krystal Flash or peacock herl
Eyes Prismatic stick-on or glue-on doll's eyes
Marker pen Red fine-line

How to tie

1 Cut a 7.5-cm (3-in) length of tubing. Place the hook in the end of the tubing and push the point out just before the bend of the hook.

2 Tie off the tubing behind the eye of the hook.

3 Cut a 2.5-cm (1-in) piece of tail material, place 6 mm (¼ in) of it in the back of the tube, and tie it in place.

4 Apply the eyes.

5 Add some gills with a fine-line red marker.

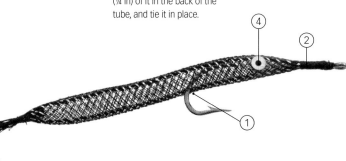

Charles Crue

Epoxy Sand Eel

You wouldn't feed a rabbit a hamburger, so why feed striped bass anything but what's abundant? In the Merrimack River estuary, that means sand eels. Captain Charles Crue, from West Newbury, Massachussetts, owns Channel Edge Charters and he designed this fly to do just that.

The Merrimack River is home to millions of sand eels during the striped-bass fishing season. They are an important food source for stripers, and are probably one of the reasons that the bass come into the estuary area each season. Sometimes schools of sand eels are so thick that they get snagged by a fly being fished with quick strips.

There are dozens, if not hundreds, of fly patterns to imitate sand eels. The one that Charles presents here is one that he found works very well in this area. He's caught both schoolies and large stripers with it. Because of its streamlined shape (similar to that of the sand eel), it casts easily and sinks quickly. This last feature allows the fly to get down where the larger stripers are often waiting under a school of sand eels being attacked by the smaller stripers. Charles usually retrieves the fly with short, quick strips, giving the fly a darting action.

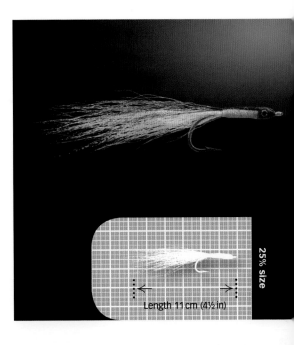

Length 11 cm (4½ in)

25% size

Materials

Hook Mustad 3407, size 2/0
Thread Danville flat waxed nylon, olive
Wing White bucktail and olive bucktail
Flash Pearl Krystal Flash
Body Pearl Sparkle Braid
Eyes WPT 2-mm (¹⁄₁₆-in) pearl/black stick-on eyes
Adhesive 30-minute Z-Poxy

How to tie

1 Cover the hook shank from the eye to the bend with olive thread. Return the thread to the hook eye.

2 Tie a small clump of 10-cm (4-in) white bucktail just behind the hook eye and distribute it around the shank before tying it from that point to the point where the hook shank begins to bend. The thread wraps do not need to be close together because body braid will be wrapped over them.

3 Tie in four pieces of pearl Krystal Flash on each side near the end of the thread wraps, so that they extend back to the ends of the white bucktail.

4 Tie the end of a 12.5-cm (5-in) piece of pearl Sparkle Braid at the bend of the hook, wrap it tightly up to the hook eye and tie it in.

5 Use the thread to form a smooth, tapered olive head.

6 Tie a small clump of 10-cm (4-in) olive bucktail at the top of the head. Holding the bucktail clump by the end, so that it stays on top of the fly,

make four wraps of thread back to the bend and then back to the eye. This will serve to hold it in place before epoxy is applied.

7 Put a stick-on eye on each side of the head.

8 Coat the body of the fly, from behind the eye to the start of the bend, with 30-minute Z-Poxy.

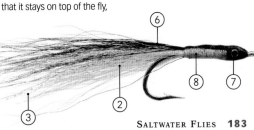

Edward Michaels

Michaels' Big Cake

Bonefish have a hair trigger that will scare them off at the slightest unnatural movement. Such movements include a fly line overhead or a sinking fly imitation that should be found on the bottom. Michaels' Big Cake is intended to stay on the bottom and slowly undulate.

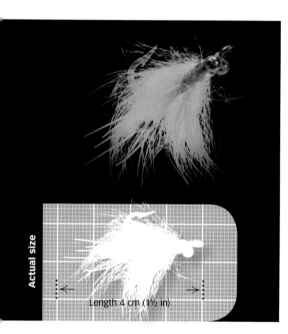

Actual size

Length 4 cm (1½ in)

Captain Edward Michaels is from Sugarloaf Key, Florida. He guides from Marathon to Key West, and, over the past 25 years, this has been his most productive fly for tailing bonefish.

Ed says this pattern is effective because of its flat profile and irresistible action. It lands softly, and that's important when stalking tailing bonefish.

Ed's friend, Bill Danaher of Marathon, stalks fish in his kayak and then wades until he's in casting range. Bill says that when bones get spooky and finicky, no other fly is as effective.

For those times when the fish are especially difficult, Bill doesn't strip the fly at all. He simply casts it and waits for the bones to find it and eat it. The Big Cake settles slowly and undulates when it comes to rest on a blade of turtle grass or other bottom structure.

Materials

Hook Partridge CS52 Sea Prince, sizes 4 and 6
Thread Danville Flymaster, colour to match body
Weight Small to medium stainless steel bead chain
Tail 12 strands of pearl Flashabou
Eyes Epoxy over a clear bead, over 4.5-kg (10-lb) hard Mason mono
Body Cross-cut rabbit strips (white, tan, pink or olive/chartreuse)
Adhesive 5-minute epoxy

How to tie

1 At the hook eye, attach two stainless steel bead chain eyes on top of the hook shank and wrap the thread to just above the hook point.

2 At the bend, wrap 12 strands of pearl Flashabou, extending about 2.5 cm (1 in) beyond the bend.

3 Each eye is made from 5-cm (2-in) of 4.5-kg (10-lb) Mason hard mono. Melt one end near a flame and immediately touch it to a cool, hard surface. This forms a flat end; slide a small plastic bead against the flat end. Dip the bead and mono end in 5-minute epoxy and hang to dry. Tie both eyes on together and wrap with figure-of-eights to separate. The eyes should extend 3 mm (⅛ in) beyond the bend of the hook.

4 At the bend, using figure-of-eight wraps, tie in three narrow cross-cut rabbit strips, 1.25 cm (½ in) long, with the fur streaming backward.

5 After all materials have been tied on, trim the rabbit hide strips to about 3 mm (⅛ in) beyond each side.

6 Apply head cement.

Jim Dussias

Duke's Diver

Sometimes a successful freshwater pattern will find a new life after being revamped for saltwater applications. That's the basis for this fly, sent by Jim Dussias from Miami, Florida, who owns Oasis Angling Adventures. He guides walk-waders and kayak fly fishers for snook, baby tarpon, bass and peacock bass.

Jim fishes Duke's Diver for baby tarpon and snook around mangroves and in strong tidal current areas and creeks. It can be fished on a floating line with the fly treated with floatant to stay high so that it will create a wake. Strip it upstream to create a wake that drives baby tarpon crazy. On a recent trip, Jim had a client walking and trailing this fly behind when a 7-kg (15-lb) baby tarpon launched clear out of the water trying to eat it! The fish took the very next 'legitimate' cast.

For snook, Jim generally fishes the Duke's Diver around mangroves on a slow-sinking intermediate line. Here's Jim's hint for making this pattern sink better: after soaking it, hold the fly underwater and squeeze the air bubbles out.

When fishing around mangroves, he uses a Duke's Diver with a mono V-style weed guard. It's important to use this fly with a loop knot to get a great side-to-side action. Tying a clinch knot kills the action.

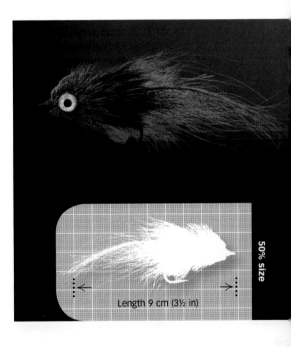

50% size

Length 9 cm (3½ in)

Materials

Hook Gamakatsu B-10S, size 1
Thread Flat waxed nylon, olive
Tail Olive bucktail
Flash Olive Wing-n-Flash and holographic tinsel
Body Cross-cut olive rabbit strips (palmered three times around hook shank)
Head Olive deer body hair
Eyes Silver holographic dome eyes
Adhesive Fletch-tite

How to tie

1 Tie in olive bucktail at the bend of the hook. The tail should be about 1.5 times the length of the shank.

2 Tie both the Wing-n-Flash and the holographic tinsel on top of the tail.

3 Wrap cross-cut olive rabbit strips two-thirds of the way up the hook shank, making three wraps; be sure to leave enough room for the deer hair.

4 Tie in six strands of olive Wing-n-Flash.

5 Spin a deer-hair head.

6 Whip finish.

7 Trim the deer-hair head close to the hook shank on the bottom to expose the hook point gap.

8 Glue the eyes in place with Fletch-tite (archery fletching adhesive).

Length 12.5 cm (5 in)

Jeff Priest

Flatiron Herring

How about a pattern that's so effective it even attracts the baitfish it's intended to represent? How good is this pattern at fooling fish? When retrieving this fly, the sardina (flatiron herring) themselves swim or school with it: now that's got to be a good sign!

Materials

Hook Mustad C68S SS tarpon, sizes 1–3/0

Thread White Danville flat waxed nylon

Body Slinky Fiber – smoked grey or tan (shrimp)

Back Slinky Fiber – smoked grey or tan (shrimp), olive, black or brown

Flash Pearl blue or pearl gold Angel Hair

Eyes 3D moulded pearl or red eyes

Black dot Black hot glue

Adhesives Zap-A-Gap, head cement and Loons UV Knot Sense

The Flatiron Herring is from Captain Jeff Priest of Los Angeles. He owns EE-FISH-ENT Fly Fishing Service and covers both southern California and Baja.

The Flatiron Herring has accounted for numerous species in Baja such as sailfish, roosterfish, yellowfin tuna, dorado, black skipjack, bonito, cabrio, and many more.

Throughout Baja, anything that swims eats the sardina, so this explains why the Flatiron Herring is such a productive pattern. This fly can be fished on either a floating line or a sink tip/shooting head, depending on the targeted species and depth of water.

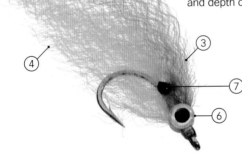

How to tie

1 Lay down a thread base from the eye of the hook to the bend. Coat the thread with cement after each section or step.

2 Take one full-length section of grey Slinky Fiber about 25 cm (10 in) long and 6 mm (¼ in) wide (not compressed). Lay it on a flat surface and lay 12 strands of Angel Hair along the Slinky Fiber. Place the fibre along the shank of the hook at the bend and keep an even amount extending forward and backward.

3 Tie the fibre in and wrap the thread half the distance towards the eye of the hook and cement. Fold the forward portion backward, allowing the fibres to wrap the shank, covering the previous wraps. Wrap the thread back over about 3 mm (⅛ in) to secure the fibres.

4 Turn the hook upside down and repeat steps 2 and 3. Start in the middle of the hook, allowing the fibre to slightly wrap the shank and cover the previous wraps. Work forward to the eye of

the hook and end with an 3-mm (⅛-in) wrap to secure the thread.

5 Turn the fly right side up and repeat steps 2 and 3.

6 Choose a size of eye that is proportionate to the hook size. Apply a very small amount of Zap-A-Gap to the back of the eye, then press it on just behind the nose portion so that the bottom section of the eye meets the shank of the hook. Apply a small amount of UV Knot Sense between the eyes to fill the gap.

7 Using black hot glue, place a small dot just behind and upward of the eye (above the gill plate). This is the defining mark of the flatiron herring.

8 Trim the belly, starting just behind the bend of the hook and trimming the fibres at an angle towards the tail.

Keith Clover

Flipper

Flipper? I always wondered what happened to that old TV animal star. Now, is this pattern designed to catch him or is it made of his hide? Neither: this is designed to catch river snapper and kingfish from the beach in Mozambique, Africa.

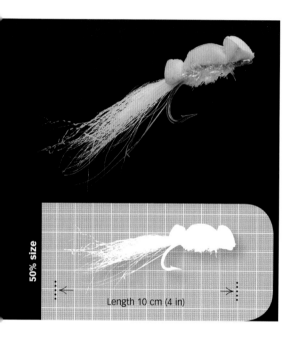

50% size

Length 10 cm (4 in)

Keith Clover, from Kwazulu-Natal, South Africa, owner of Tourette Fishing, sent this fly along. A similar pattern, the Gurgler, uses the same concept. However, the older Gurgler left something to be desired, so this is what Keith developed.

The Flipper differs from a popper in that it skips, sprays water and makes a wonderful gurgling sound rather than popping. It is far easier than a popper to cast in big sizes. It also leaves a long trail of bubbles, giving the impression of a larger prey. In large sizes, the Flipper can be used confidently when targeting big kingfish and pickhandle barracuda. In smaller sizes, queenfish, torpedo scad, perch, rock salmon, springer and shad have all fallen to this fly.

Saltwater species are not the only targets in Africa. Keith has been guiding throughout southern and eastern Africa since the age of 18. He is a Level III FGASA (Field Guides Association of Southern Africa) guide and has guided in all the major National Parks around southern Africa.

Materials

Hook Trey Combs
Gamakatsu, sizes
1/0–6/0
Thread White 3/0
Tail Pink bucktail and
Krystal Flash
Underbody Pearl
crystal chenille
Body Plaztazote Foam,
Etha Foam or closed-
cell foam

How to tie

1 Lay down a thread base from the eye of the hook to the bend.

2 Tie in the tail of bucktail and Krystal Flash three times the length of the shank.

3 Tie in a length of crystal chenille and wind a body forward to the eye.

4 Cut a rectangle of foam for the body. For a 6/0 hook, it should be about 6 mm (¼ in) wide and long enough to reach from the eye to the back of the bend. Cut a wedge in the underside of

the foam, so that the tail will not be forced down.

5 Tie in the foam, both at the head and at the bend ends,

making sure that the head end flares above the hook eye; this makes for a greater gurgling sound, which is the pattern's strong point.

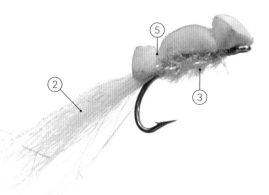

David Blinken

Jellyfish

Captain David Blinken is the first fly-fishing guide I've met who lives in New York City. David's claim to fame is his 30 years' experience in the saltwater of nearby Long Island. He owns North Flats Guiding and he has adapted the Florida Keys technique of sight fishing to his home area.

The Jellyfish was developed because David wanted a fly for bonito. However, it had to be simple to build and not involve the extra steps that epoxy would require. This is what he created.

He had been observing many fly-makers' patterns while watching the fish feed. Everyone was saying that, to catch bonito and albies, you needed a tiny epoxy pattern tied on a size 4 hook. However, the bait that the fish were eating was much larger. David wanted to develop an all-purpose fly that would cross over.

He started with an old style of tying, using the high-tie method like the Platinum Blond. Next, he tried a sparsely tied Deceiver and, finally, a white Cockroach. Soon the fly morphed into the Jellyfish.

David varies the colours depending on the water conditions and forage fish he's imitating. He's caught bluefin tuna, tarpon, snook, striped bass, bluefish, weakfish, jacks, bonito and albies.

25% size

Length 11 cm (4½ in)

How to tie

Materials

Hook Any saltwater fly hook, sizes 2–3/0, depending on the target species

Thread Clear mono

Wing Four splayed white hackles

Flash Gold flash

Body Pearl Mylar braid

Collar White Kinky Fiber with a little silver flash

Adhesive Krazy Glue

1 At the bend in the hook, make a tail of four splayed white hackles, 7.5–10 cm (3–4 in) long. Add some gold flash of equal length.

2 Tie in a length of pearl Mylar braid and wrap a body forward.

3 Make a double-layered collar of white Kinky Fiber mixed with a small amount of silver flash. The bottom of the collar should extend to the bend, while the top of the collar should be slightly longer.

4 Top the collar with gold flash.

5 Make a thread head and coat with Krazy Glue.

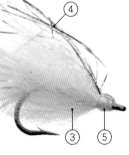

James Klug

Klug's Ranger Burrito

When a man who can (and does) fish anywhere in the world is willing to tell you about his favourite patterns, it's time to listen up. Captain James Klug, from Bozeman, Montana, founder of Yellow Dog Fly Fishing, can book you a fishing adventure anywhere in the world.

50% size

Length 10 cm (4 in)

Jim uses this pattern in deep-water flats fishing situations. It's especially effective for schools of permit and bones found cruising in deeper water. In larger sizes, it can also be tied and fished as a very effective baby tarpon fly.

This pattern is the result of many years, and many variations, of trying to create an imitation that cruising fish in deep water will eat. At certain times of the year, permit will actively and aggressively chase down a shrimp-type pattern and attack it with reckless abandon.

Generally, Jim fishes this fly as a fleeing crab or mantis shrimp imitation. Klug's Ranger Burrito should be cast and stripped – from a moderately slow retrieve to a very fast retrieve. He has had a great deal of success with this fly in Belize and the waters of the Yucatan.

Materials

Hook Owner AKI, sizes 1/0 and 2/0
Thread Size 3/0, pink or light orange
Eyes Spirit River Dazl-Eyes or I-Balz
Tag/Butt section Pink or orange Cactus Chenille or Estaz
Tail Tan extra-long Rainy's Kraft Fur
Legs Spirit River legs with hot orange tips
Body Thin cross-cut rabbit strips, colour to match tail
Head Pink or faded orange dubbing

How to tie

1 Lay down a thread base from the eye of the hook to the bend.

2 Attach Dazl-Eyes to the top of the hook using figure-of-eight wraps, being sure to leave enough room for the dubbed head section.

3 At the bend, tie in a butt section of Estaz or Cactus Chenille. Take three wraps of the material.

4 Tie in a long clump of Kraft Fur over the top of the Estaz or Cactus Chenille. This tail section of the fly should extend approximately twice the length of the hook shank.

5 Tie in rubber leg material on each side of the hook. The legs should be just slightly shorter than the end of the Kraft Fur.

6 Tie in a strip of cross-cut rabbit strip at the rear of the hook (over the tied-in clump of Estaz and Kraft Fur tail material). Tightly wrap the rabbit strip forward towards the eye. This should be accomplished in three or four wraps, depending on the hook size. Tie off and trim the excess.

7 Wrap pink or faded orange dubbing fairly sparsely over the eyes, as well as behind and in front of the eyes, to form a small head.

8 Whip finish and cement the thread head.

Jeff Priest

Baby Mole Crab

Pity the poor mole crab: everything that swims sees it as lunch. This pattern is from **Jeff Priest** of Los Angeles. Jeff says, 'This is a very simple but productive pattern for the surf. Everything that swims along our beaches feeds on the mole crab.'

This pattern is best fished on a long leader for wary fish in shallow water, with short strips and a long pause. It can be fished on either a full sink or intermediate line, depending on the tidal flow, wave size and currents.

This is a must for all surf fly boxes. There are many mole crab patterns on the market today; the beauty of this one is that it is consistent with the natural in size, shape and colour.

One morning, Jeff saw a pod of 12 or more corbina in a large trough. He made his first cast onto almost dry sand. He made a cast to the same area and waited as the water surged again – and out of the hole they came. This time there were five or six fish. He gave the fly a couple of twitches and watched in amazement as two fish broke off and raced towards the fly. A few minutes later, a beautiful corbina came to hand.

Actual size

Length 2.5 cm (1 in)

Materials

Hook Mustad 34007, sizes 6 and 8
Thread Danville size 6/0, hot orange
Eyes Black Dazl-Eyes
Legs Sili Legs, clear with orange and black speckle
Back Grey Furry Foam
Body Orange, pearl or pink ice chenille
Adhesive Head cement, Zap-A-Gap and Loons UV Knot Sense
Equipment UV light

How to tie

1 Place the hook in the vice with the shank on top. Tie on the eyes in a Clouser

fashion, 2 mm (1/16 in) back from the hook eye. Apply a small amount of Zap-A-Gap to help secure the eyes, and continue to wrap the thread along the shank to the hook bend.

2 Take one Sili Leg, 1.25 cm (½ in) in length, lay it along the shank so that half of it extends beyond the bend of the hook and secure; then fold the forward portion backward and secure. Coat with head cement.

3 Cut a 6- × 3-mm (¼- × ⅛-in) piece of Furry Foam. Trim the corners of the front and back edges so

that they are tapered. Wrap one side of the foam at the base of the legs and dab with Zap-A-Gap to secure.

4 Take a 2.5-cm (1-in) piece of orange ice chenille and secure one end to the shank. Wrap the thread forward to the eye and coat with head cement.

5 Wrap one side of the foam at the base of the legs and dab with Zap-A-Gap to secure. Wrap the chenille forward on the shank to the eye of the hook and secure with a few wraps of thread.

6 Fold the Furry Foam over the chenille and secure it just behind the eye of the hook. Coat the thread with a small amount of UV Knot Sense.

Captain Joe Mattiolo

Magnum Minnow

Magnum Minnow? Is that a contradiction in terms – like jumbo shrimp or mild hot sauce? I don't know, but Captain Joe Mattiolo from Staten Island, New York, who owns On The Bite Charters, wanted a go-to fly for striped bass. This is what he developed.

Materials

Hook Mustad 3007, size 3/0
Thread Fine monofilament
Eyes Large nickel-plated dumbbell eyes
Pupils Prismatic dots
Tail Three pieces of 17.5–20-cm (7–8-in) white saddle hackles, full and straight
Collar White bucktail, 7.5 cm (3 in) long
Sides Half a clump of silver Polar Flash, 15 cm (6 in) long
Top wing Chartreuse bucktail
Adhesive Epoxy

Joe reports this is his number-one go-to fly. First, the chartreuse over white is his favourite colour combination, one that works well in all water conditions, including deep, shallow, murky, cold, clear and warm. It also delivers in all daytime weather conditions – sunny, overcast or rainy.

This big pattern should be used with 9- to11-weight outfits, using 400–500-grain full sinking lines. Because of its weight, it can be used to work the entire water column from the bottom to the top in waters as deep as 10.5 m (35 ft).

Striped bass like to bunch up at the bottom, and when Joe marks them on the fish finder, he has to get the fly down to their depth quickly. There is no faster way than to use the line he recommends. Once the line is down to the bottom, Joe retrieves with fast strips. This causes the pattern to jig up and down along the bottom. This motion makes the tail feathers flutter while the bucktail collar pulsates, making for an irresistible meal.

Strikes can occur anywhere in the water column – sometimes on the first few strips at the bottom or even during the last few strips, right at the boat. That's why it should be worked all the way back to the boat.

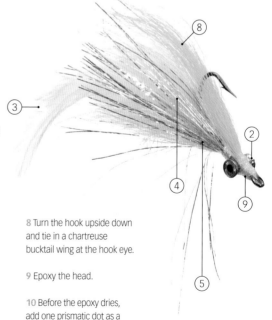

How to tie

1 Wrap a base of monofilament from the eye of the hook to the bend.

2 Tie in the dumbbell eyes on top of the shank, one-third of the way behind the hook eye.

3 Make a tail by tying in three hackle feathers on top at the bend.

4 Make a collar by tying in two matchstick-sized clumps of white bucktail around the hook shank, behind the dumbbell eyes. Trim the excess butts.

5 Tie in an 8-cm (3¼-in) clump of bucktail on top of the shank at the eye of the hook, with the ends pointing out over the hook eye. Fold it over the dumbbell eyes and tie down behind the hook eye.

6 Take one clump of 15-cm (6-in) silver Polar Flash and tie in a 7.5-cm (3-in) length on one side of the hook behind the dumbbell eye. Fold the flash back over on itself.

7 Repeat step 6 on the opposite side of the fly.

8 Turn the hook upside down and tie in a chartreuse bucktail wing at the hook eye.

9 Epoxy the head.

10 Before the epoxy dries, add one prismatic dot as a pupil to each side of the eyes.

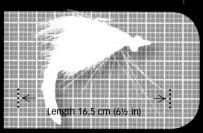

Length 16.5 cm (6½ in)

Length 22.5 cm (9 in)

Jeff Smith

Meatball

Meatball! Just hearing that brings back fond high-school memories – not from lunch, but from my nickname. I'm sure that's not what Captain Jeff Smith from Wellfleet, Massachusetts, owner of Fin Addiction Charters, had in mind. This Meatball is named for the spun deer-hair head.

Materials

Hook Gamakatsu SL-12, sizes 2 to 4/0

Thread Olive Danville Flymaster Plus

Tail Olive bucktail

Body/Wing Bucktail and long olive saddle hackles

Head Deer belly hair for spinning

Eyes 3-D Mylar eyes

Adhesive Goop

The Meatball fly gets its name from the spun deer-hair head. It is a very effective pattern for striped bass around Cape Cod. Jeff fishes this fly with a floating or intermediate sinking line in the brackish estuary waters or on open grass beds.

He ties it in many colour combinations: all white, red/white, yellow/white, pink, black, black/red, olive/white and olive. Some days, the bass want it slow, some days fast – but, for the most part, Jeff never leaves home without it.

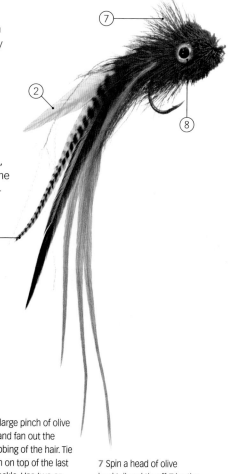

How to tie

1 Place the hook in your vice, start the thread in the middle of the shank and work back to the bend. Do not cover the front half of the shank with thread, since this will impede spinning the deer hair. At the bend, tie in a small pinch of olive bucktail for the tail of the fly.

2 Find a short, stocky olive feather saddle hackle and tie it in, curved side up, right on top of the pinch of bucktail. Keep all the marabou fuzz on the hackle. Besides creating a body, the stiff stem keeps the feathers in place and reduces fouling.

3 Take a long, slender olive hackle and tie it, curved side down, in on top of the first hackle. You want to put this and all the remaining hackles curved side down.

4 Move the thread forward just a bit and add a small pinch of olive bucktail. Add another long slender olive hackle on top of this clump of hair.

5 Repeat step 4 until you have made up five or six long, slender bucktail bunches and have 1.25 cm (½ in) free space behind the hook eye.

6 Take a large pinch of olive bucktail and fan out the underdubbing of the hair. Tie this down on top of the last saddle hackle. Use two or three loose wraps and then work the hair around the hook, so that the natural tips of the deer hair flow over the body material. Once you are satisfied, bring the thread tight and work the thread through the hair to the front.

7 Spin a head of olive bucktail and tie it off. Trim the head to a meatball or bullet shape, leaving the natural collar that you first put in.

8 Apply Goop liberally behind the eyes and add the 3D Mylar eyes, pressing them together.

John Mendelson

Mud Dog Bunny Bunker

The problem of off-coloured water is a common one. When it happens, a captain can turn for port and complain about how you (the client) should have been here yesterday – or can insist you try this pattern. Striped bass, bluefish and school-sized bluefin tuna have all been taken on it.

Materials

Hook Mustad 34007, sizes 2/0 or 4/0
Thread Danville fine monofilament (clear)
Tail White rabbit strip
Belly White bucktail
Wing White bucktail
Wing flash Pearl Flashabou and Crystal Flash
Belly flash Pearl DNA Holographic Chromosome Flash
Back Silver holographic Flashabou
Throat Red pearl Crystal Flash
Eyes 6-mm (¼-in) 3D moulded holographic eyes
Head 5-minute epoxy
Adhesive Goop

Note: A small drop of Krazy Glue or Zap-A-Gap should be applied at each phase of building the body.

This fly works especially well due to its shape, reflective quality and seductive movement. It represents a general baitfish impression that stands in for small herring, juvenile menhaden and other small baitfish found in the waters of Boston Harbor, Cape Cod Bay and Massachusetts Bay.

John says this is a great all-purpose fly with lots of action that works well in many conditions when other, more static flies won't produce. The pattern stands out well in the murky water, and the rabbit strip gives it great movement, whether stripped quickly across an eelgrass flat or dead-drifted through a rip.

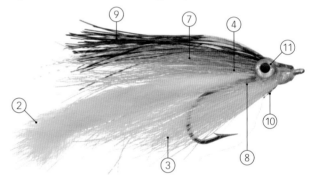

How to tie

1 Wrap the shank of the hook with monofilament from the eye to the bend.

2 At the bend, tie in a strip of 3-mm (⅛-in) white rabbit strip above the hook for the tail.

3 At the bend, tie in a clump of white bucktail about the thickness of a matchstick on the bottom of the shank to start the belly.

4 In front of the fur strip, tie in a clump of white bucktail to begin the wing, followed by four strands of pearl Flashabou and Crystal Flash, leaving about 1.25 cm (½ in) of rabbit strip extending past the bucktail.

5 Add another clump of white bucktail half the thickness of the previous one to the top of the hook shank.

6 Now add another clump of white bucktail to the bottom, tied just in front of the hook eye, to complete the belly.

7 Tie in five strands of pearl Flashabou on the top of the shank. Add a sparse clump of bucktail to finish the wing.

8 At the hook eye, tie in six strands of pearl DNA Holographic Chromosome Flash on one side of the fly. Slightly feather the material as you tie it down to spread

it out along the belly. Repeat this step on the other side.

9 Tie in 12 strands of silver holographic Flashabou on top to create the back.

10 On the bottom of the shank, tie in three pieces of red pearl Crystal Flash to simulate gills.

11 Apply Goop to the moulded holographic eyes and stick in place. Epoxy the head.

12 Trim the belly to create the desired profile.

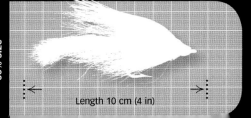

Length 10 cm (4 in)

Josh Mullet Dickinson

Mullet's Fry

Captain Josh Mullet Dickinson, from Silverton, Oregon, guides in Honduras for Baja On The Fly. Josh watched big fish dining on their smaller cousins, so he developed this fly to ring the dinner bell. The finished product should be slim and translucent, like the naturals.

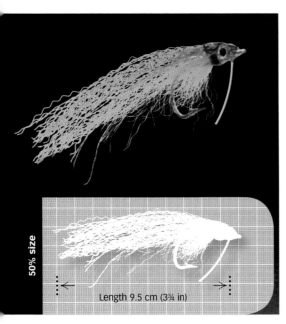

50% size

Length 9.5 cm (3¾ in)

Josh was somewhat surprised the first time he witnessed good-sized tarpon, up to 22.5 kg (50 lb), crashing the tiny bait that the Mullet's Fry represents.

He's since grown accustomed to the almost nightly occurrence of tarpon worked into a feeding frenzy by millions of fry. Josh also reports that he's got used to the fact that, despite their tiny size, the sheer mass of these fry makes them an important food source for virtually all of the 'gamers' associated with Honduras' lagoons and flats.

Josh fishes the Bay Islands in winter and early spring, where the Mullet's Fry gets eaten regularly by snook, tarpon, bonefish, permit, jacks, snapper and barracudas. He first began throwing this pattern at fish that he clearly saw busting thick clouds of guppy-sized fry. As his confidence grew in the pattern, it became a go-to fly on the turtle grass flats, since it casts well and lands softly.

Materials

Hook Mustad 3407DT, sizes 2/0 and 4/0

Thread White 3/0 and monofilament; weed guard 13.6-kg (30-lb) monofilament

Belly White calf tail and Pearl Angel Hair

Gills Red Crystal Braid

Head Pearl Crystal Braid

Wing Olive Super Hair, over olive Krystal Flash, over white Super Hair

Eyes Holographic eyes

Adhesive Epoxy

How to tie

1 Lay down a short thread base of white 3/0 from the eye of the hook, then switch to fine mono.

2 At the hook eye, tie in a length of 13.6 kg (30-lb) monofilament.

3 Tie in white calf tail three-quarters of the way up the shank from the bend of the hook on the bottom side.

4 Ahead of the calf tail, tie in a small amount of pearl Angel Hair slightly longer than the calf tail belly.

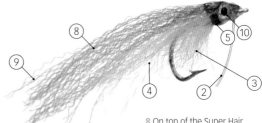

5 Tie in and wrap three turns of red Crystal Braid in front of the calf tail to form gills.

6 Tie in and wrap pearl Crystal Braid the rest of the way to the eye of the hook.

7 Tie in white Super Hair on top of the Crystal Braid, tapered slightly longer than the Angel Hair.

8 On top of the Super Hair, tie in olive Krystal Flash, slightly longer than the Super Hair.

9 On top of the Krystal Flash, tie in olive Super Hair, slightly longer than the Krystal Flash.

10 Glue on holographic eyes.

11 Epoxy the head. The finished product should be slim and translucent, like the naturals.

Jeremy Loercher

Nine Mile Shrimp

A bonefish fly is a bonefish fly is a bonefish fly – right? Captain Jeremy Loercher from the Little Cayman Fishing Club knows better. A guide with many years' experience showed him a similar shrimp pattern and Jeremy made his own version. Now it's his go-to fly.

Jeremy thinks the Nine Mile Shrimp works well there because of the abundance of small natural baits. They don't have many big shrimp or crabs, and the ones they do have seem to have some orange colour on them. Olive is his favourite colour for almost any fly on Little Cayman.

Clients come expecting big weighted flies, like in the Keys and Bahamas, but without sandy flats here, they are not needed, unless you are fishing the mud flats on the south shore.

Jeremy uses this fly while wading on the 14.5-km (9-mile) stretch of flats on the northern shore. The flats are mostly covered with turtle grass and that can be tough on normal bonefish flies.

He uses flies with little to no weight. The water depth is usually between 15 and 60 cm (6 in and 2 ft), so you don't need a heavy fly. The pattern is deadly on cruising bonefish and gets its share of permit. But almost every species of fish in the shallows of Little Cayman has tasted this fly.

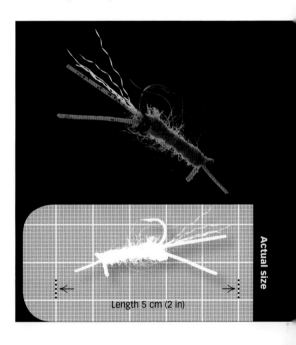

Actual size

Length 5 cm (2 in)

Materials

Hook Mustad 9671, sizes 6 and 8
Thread Olive flat waxed thread, size 6/0
Eyes Monofilament, painted black
Feelers White Crystal Flash
Legs Orange Sili Legs
Body Olive spun wool

How to tie

1 Melt the ends of the monofilament eyes and paint them black.

2 Smash the barb of the hook down.

3 Lay down a thread base from the eye of the hook to the bend.

4 At the bend, tie in six strands of Krystal Flash and two Sili Legs extending 2.5 cm (1 in) past the bend.

5 At the bend, tie in the monofilament eyes on top with figure-of-eight wraps.

Use a drop of head cement to secure the wraps.

6 At the bend, tie on the spun wool and leave it for later.

7 Wrap the thread back to the hook eye and tie on two Sili Legs facing forward over the hook eye.

8 Wrap the spun wool up the shank and over the Sili Legs to the eye.

9 Whip finish. Cement the thread wraps.

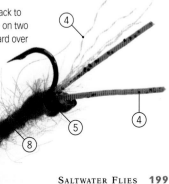

Basil Yelverton

Original Pompano Rocket

Need a substitute for a sand flea? If you do, read on. If you're not sure, you'd better read on. I wasn't sure I wanted anything to do with any kind of fleas until I saw this pattern from Captain Basil Yelverton from Gulf Breeze, Florida, owner of Gulf Breeze Guide Service.

Baz never considered targeting the elusive pompano with a fly rod until about ten years ago. Florida's 'Net Ban' amendment in the mid-90s enabled the pompano population to flourish.

Sand fleas are crustaceans about half the size of your thumb that have greyish-white shells and orange egg sacs underneath. Baz tried everything imaginable to make a 'sand flea' fly, but nothing worked.

He recalled catching pompano as a kid on a yellow Mr Champ lure. The Mr Champ is a spoon with a yellow bucktail and red thread. Baz also recalled catching pompano on jigs with gold heads and yellow nylon tails. The Pompano Rocket was the result. Pompano love it, and so do redfish. It's his number-one fly for fishing the Gulf of Mexico surf.

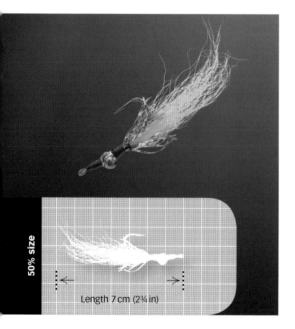

50% size

Length 7 cm (2¾ in)

Materials

Hooks Tiemco 811S, size 1 for larger rocket; size 2 for smaller
Head and body Danville flat waxed nylon (red)
Eyes Spirit River Dazl-Eyes, gold, 6-mm (¼-in) for larger rocket, 4-mm (⅙-in) for smaller
Tail Yellow bucktail
Collar Gold Mylar tubing
Adhesive Zap-A-Gap Ca+

How to tie

1 Lay down a thread base from the eye of the hook to the bend.

2 Tie in the Dazl-Eyes just forward of the middle of the hook shank.

3 Tie in the yellow bucktail over the Dazl-Eyes to the hook eye, feathering the bucktail between the eyes and the hook eye so that you're left with a nice, cone-shaped nose. When finishing the nose, wrap back up to the eyes and just beyond. Your last wrap should be just behind the eyes. The overall

length of the fly should be about 7 cm (2¾ in).

4 Cut the gold Mylar tubing to about 5 cm (2 in), remove the centre coil, flatten the tubing and poke a hole in the centre of it using your dubbing needle.

5 Insert the hook eye in the hole and pull the Mylar tubing back to and over the eyes. Squeeze it down tight to the hook shank and wrap down the shank 3 mm (⅛ in) or so and back up to the eyes. Tie it off.

6 Restart your thread behind the Dazl-Eyes and wrap over the Mylar tubing for 3 mm (⅛ in). Trim the thread.

7 Cut off the Mylar tubing at about the bend of the hook. 'Comb' out the Mylar fibres using your dubbing needle.

8 Coat all the threads with Zap-A-Gap Ca+ to make the fly more durable.

Kennet Damm Petersen

Pink Godbid

Often the same kind of material, made by two different manufacturers, will yield different appearances when in the water. One will only be occasionally successful while the other will be a clear winner. Experimentation will enable you to select the one that works best.

Kennet Damm Petersen is from Denmark and owns Damm's Fly Design. He attributes the success of his Pink Godbid to experimentation with ice dubbing by the same manufacturer.

Kennet and a friend tried two versions of the same fly. Each was made with a different batch of the same material. One gave off a green shadow (glow) when in full sunlight. The second gave off a blue shadow. When all was said and done, 16 sea trout were taken by the blue shadow and only six by the other version. His advice is to observe the ice dubbing in full sunlight before purchasing.

Kennet fishes this pattern year round. Whether a floating or intermediate sinking line, he retrieves the fly with a slow strip. He believes the pink colour is very provocative. When combined with the blue shadow, the fly is very successful.

His most memorable fish was a sea trout of more than 5 kg (11 lb). More recently he caught more than 60 sea trout, each one longer than 40 cm (16 in).

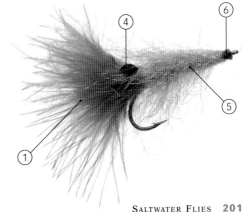

50% size

Length 6 cm (2¼ in)

Materials

Hook Partridge FlashPoint Saltwater CS54 Shrimp, size 6
Thread UNI size 6/0, red
Tail Pink marabou
Flash Pearl Crystal Flash Ice
Body Hot pink Ice Dubbing
Eyes Black FlyEyes

How to tie

1 Make a tail of pink marabou at the hook bend. It should be 1.5 times as long as the hook shank.

2 At the same point, tie in six pieces of pearl Crystal Flash Ice, making them the same length as the tail.

3 Ahead of the marabou, dub a length of Ice Dubbing, make four wraps and hold. Sweep the fibres back towards the tail.

4 Tie in the eyes up against the Ice Dubbing.

5 Continue wrapping the Ice Dubbing forward to the hook eye, sweeping the fibres back after each wrap.

6 Make a small thread head, whip finish and cement the thread.

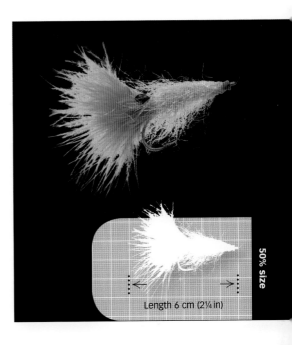

Laurenz van Mook

Pos Chiquito Shrimp

Tarpon can be finicky. Often they will not change their depth to chase a fly, so an effective pattern must be capable of being fished at a specific depth. A fly that sinks at a slow enough rate to be retrieved at the desired depth is ideal.

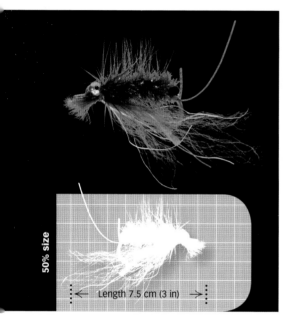

50% size

← Length 7.5 cm (3 in) →

Laurenz van Mook owns Fly Fishing Aruba and finds lots of tarpon around the Aruban mangrove islands. He teamed up with Mike Kucsma and developed the Pos Chiquito Shrimp.

The preferred method is to cast close to a sighted fish and let the fly sink for a few seconds. Then strip and pause at two-second intervals. If your guess as to the tarpon's holding depth is correct, hang on, because it's going to be a bumpy ride.

The Pos Chiquito Shrimp got Laurenz his tarpon for the first ever Aruban Grand Slam on May 22, 2011. He admits he lucked into his permit and that good fortune put him back on track for the Grand Slam.

Materials

Hook Mustad Big Game C70 SD, sizes 1/0–3/0
Thread Danville Flymaster Plus, 210 denier, olive
Eyes Medium black monofilament and large bead chain eyes
Antennae Barred olive Sili Legs
Body Olive Crystal Cactus Chenille and olive saddle hackle
Carapace Olive flash and Slinky Fiber

How to tie

1 Tie in the bead chain eyes at the hook eye and on top of the shank, so that the hook will ride with the point above the body.

2 Lay down a thread base from the chain eyes to the hook bend.

3 Tie in the monofilament eyes at the bend and on top of the hook shank.

4 Tie in the olive Sili Legs behind the monofilament eyes to make antennae, so that they stick out over the mono eyes. Trim the Sili Legs to the length of the hook shank.

5 Tie in a saddle hackle behind the monofilament eyes.

6 Tie in a length of chenille at the same point.

7 Wrap the chenille forward to the bead chain eyes.

8 Palmer the hackle over the chenille to the bead chain eyes and tie off.

9 Gather a 7-mm (³/₁₀-in) diameter combination of flash and Slinky Fiber. Pull several fibres forward over the hook eye. Tie it in behind the bead chain eyes. They should reach the bend of the hook. Trim the forward section of fibres to 6 mm (¼ in) as a tail.

10 Whip finish the fly and cement the threads.

John Kelsey

Ray's Fly Flatwing

Salt is salt, fresh is fresh, and ne'er the twain shall meet – right? Well, maybe! Among John Kelsey's clients is Captain Ken Abrames, owner of Striper Moon, who charters along the Rhode Island coast.

Ken adapted many freshwater techniques, such as using drift to create correct presentation, matching bait and wet fly swings, to his striper hunting. Here's a fly John designed for just such techniques. This is a variation of Ray Bondrow's great Ray's Fly. It can be tied to imitate a variety of baitfish, depending on the profile you create.

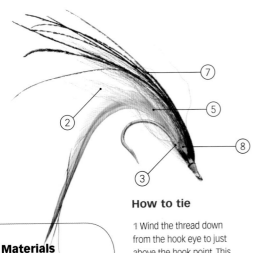

25% size

Length 14 cm (5½ in)

Materials

Hook Eagle Claw 253, size 2/0
Thread Flat waxed nylon, white
Platform White bucktail
Body Gold, silver or pearl Bodi Braid
Pillow White hackle fuzz
Tail One olive saddle hackle
Wing Two strips of pearl flash
Topping Peacock herl
Eyes Jungle cock nails

How to tie

1 Wind the thread down from the hook eye to just above the hook point. This foundation prevents the materials from spinning on the shank while being fished.

2 Just behind the hook eye tie in a bucktail platform (about 30 hairs of bucktail works best) to support and suspend the saddle hackle, so that it swims with every touch of current. Flare the bucktail horizontally with your fingers to create a wide fan to support the hackles that are still to be tied in as the tail. Wrap the thread down to the middle of the hook shank.

3 At the middle of the hook shank, tie in some gold Bodi Braid and wrap it forward, making a body.

4 Strip some soft fuzzy fibres from the base of the white saddle feather and dub 2.5 cm (1 in) of it on the thread. Just ahead of the body, wind this dubbing on the hook shank in a little ball to create a pillow into which you'll seat the stem of your first hackle.

5 Lay an olive neck saddle hackle curved side up on top of the pillow and take two loose turns of thread around the stem. The strong spine in

the hackle will lift the hackles. This support enables the hackles to move from side to side. Hold the tip of the feather with one hand and the butt with the other, and move the feather slightly forward to seat the stem into the soft, dubbed pillow.

6 Tie in a wing of pearl flash and white bucktail, both as long as the olive saddle hackle.

7 Top the wing with peacock herl.

8 Tie in eyes made of jungle cock nails.

Mike Algar

Flashy Floozy

Even fly-fishing guides have been known to take a busman's holiday. No matter where they roam, fishing guides prefer to use their own go-to flies, because they have confidence in them.

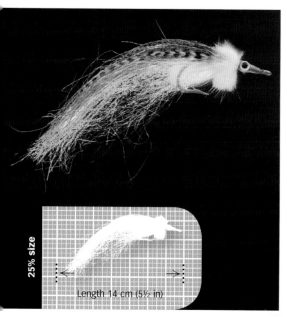

25% size

Length 14 cm (5½ in)

Mike Algar owns Freestone Fly Fishers in Calgary, Alberta. Being miles away from the ocean did not deter him from designing a fly that takes extra-large predators that think they're in for an easy mouthful.

Mike's best day to date with the Flashy Floozy accounted for two barracuda and a triggerfish. It was a couple of years ago during a tour of the Bahamas, so Mike was primarily fishing for bonefish, but the Flashy Floozy was on his back-up rod so he used it for barracuda and sharks on the flats.

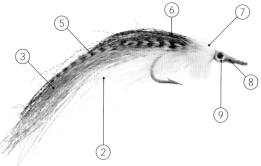

Materials

Hook Tiemco 811S, sizes 1/0 and 4/0

Thread Grey Danville flat waxed nylon, 210 denier

Overbody Pearl EP Flash, under rainbow EP Flash

Underbody Pearl Flashabou

Wing Two 10-cm (4-in) natural grizzly hackles

Flash Black and pearl Krystal Flash

Collar White mink fur strip

Eyes Super Fly chartreuse moulded eyes

Adhesive 5-minute epoxy

How to tie

1 Lay down a thread base almost far enough to line up with the barb of the hook.

2 Turn the hook upside down and tie in a healthy clump of pearl EP Flash, extending for a total of 11.5 cm (4½ in).

3 Turn the hook right side up and tie in an equally long clump of rainbow EP Flash.

4 Repeat these last two steps three or four times until you have built up the body, leaving at least 2 cm (¾ in) of space between the thread and the hook eye.

5 At the same point, tie in one grizzly hackle feather on each side of the body. They should also be 11.5 cm (4½ in) long.

6 At the same point, tie in a mixture of black and pearl Krystal Flash to the top to give some contrast to the back of the fly.

7 Ahead of the wing, tie the mink strip in at a 45-degree angle, going towards the rear of the fly and away from you. Make four wraps of the mink strip and tie off.

8 Build up an evenly tapering head that is approximately 1.25 cm (½ in) long, and tie off using a couple of whip finishes.

9 Tie in two large chartreuse moulded eyes.

10 Apply 5-minute epoxy over the eyes and the thread head to hold it all solidly together.

Mike Corblies

Simple Shrimp

I still read about the 'new' sport of saltwater fly fishing. Here's a pattern that goes back to 1970. Simple Shrimp is an adaptation of Bub Church's pattern, which first appeared in Ken Bey's book – at the time, the only all-saltwater pattern book.

The Simple Shrimp is from Captain Mike Corblies of Island Heights, New Jersey. The Simple Shrimp can be fished with either floating or sinking lines. When stripers or weakfish are slurping from the surface film, a quiet upstream or uptide cast is made. Just allow the fly to drift along naturally. It's also used when anchored up, chumming with live grass shrimp or cracked crabs. You may need some lead wire around the body of the fly to get it to drift in the chum and not above it.

The difference between the Simple Shrimp and other patterns is that it is an impressionistic pattern and is much more brightly coloured. This can make a lot of difference in the amount of strikes you receive in dark or cedar-stained waters. The fish have to see the fly to eat the fly.

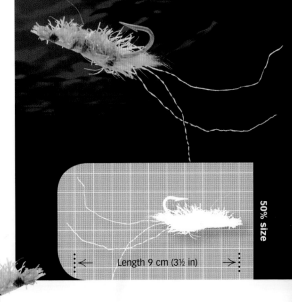

50% size

Length 9 cm (3½ in)

Materials

Hook Any size 2 or 3 stainless steel
Thread Monofilament and red decorative thread
Mouth White marabou
Body Cactus Chenille (pink, pearl, olive or tan) and thin lead wire (optional)
Eyes Hairbrush (plastic teeth), monofilament leader material (burnt ends) or glass eyes on wire
Carapace Plastic film (sandwich bag plastic will work)
Antennae Crystal Flash
Adhesive Loctite or epoxy

How to tie

1 Tie a small piece of white marabou at the bend for the mouth. It should be three-quarters of the length of the hook shank.

2 Wrap wire around the hook shank for a quick-sinking fly (optional).

3 At the hook bend, tie on the eyes.

4 At the hook bend, tie in four pieces of Crystal Flash as antennae extending twice the length of the hook shank.

5 Also at the bend, tie in a piece of Cactus Chenille (pearl, pink, etc.). Select the colour that best matches the shrimp in your area. Wrap it down almost to the hook eye. Then wrap it back up towards the mouth and build it up behind the head.

6 For the carapace, cut a rectangle of plastic film about 4 cm (1½ in) long and 1.25 cm (½ in) wide. Cut it to a point on one short end and lay the piece over the top of the shrimp's eyes, with the

point headed towards the hook eye. Tie it down with monofilament. Pull the plastic over the fly and tie off at the hook eye. Trim the excess.

7 At the bend, tie in some red decorative thread, wrap the body with a criss-cross pattern and tie off the thread at the hook eye. Take a few more turns over the tie-off point with the mono. Seal the end with Loctite or epoxy.

Eric Thomas

Rhody Flatwing

How about a one-pattern-fits-all fly? Here's a do-it-all, fish-it-anywhere, catch-anything pattern from Captain Eric Thomas of Newport, Rhode Island, who owns Teezer Fishing Charters.

Materials

Hook Eagleclaw 254SS, sizes 1/0–5/0
Thread Monofilament, sized to the hook
Wing Bucktail in white, light blue, yellow and olive, plus one straight olive saddle hackle
Flash Gold Flashabou, pearl and olive Crystal Flash
Body Pearl body braid
Topping Peacock herl

The Rhody Flatwing is Eric's go-to fly. It can be tied in various colours and sizes. It will imitate pogies, sand eels and many other baitfishes, depending on how thick you tie it. He uses the Rhody Flatwing for bass, blues and weakfish.

This fly must be fished with lots of action. It needs to be stripped in, using a varied retrieve. Eric uses it on any type of line, depending on the water depth and where the fish are feeding. He has used it on the flats, around rocks, in white water and over underwater humps. It is productive all season long. That says it all.

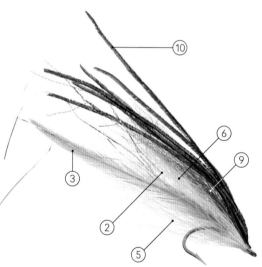

How to tie

1 Tie in a small amount of short white bucktail halfway between the hook point and the barb of the hook, and surround the hook shank, forming a skirt.

2 In front of the bucktail, tie in a sparse amount of long white bucktail on the top of the hook. Then add four strands of gold Flashabou, which should extend past the white bucktail.

3 Ahead of the bucktail, tie in one olive saddle hackle, shiny side down. The feather should be straight and tied in flat along the hook shank, positioning it over the gold Flashabou at the tail of the fly.

4 Tie in pearl body braid and wrap it up the hook shank to the eye of the hook, making sure there is enough room to form the head.

5 Tie in white bucktail ahead of the body, under the hook shank, to form the belly of the fly. This white bucktail should extend slightly beyond the bend of the hook and cover the bottom half of the hook shank.

6 On top of the hook shank, at this same point, tie in a very small bunch of long white bucktail. This should extend to just short of the tail. Be sure to spread this bunch out to connect with the bottom white bucktail to form a collar.

7 Mix together ten to twelve strands of yellow bucktail and six to eight strands of blue bucktail and tie in on top of the hook. This bucktail should extend three-quarters of the length of the tail.

8 Tie in the pearl and olive Crystal Flash, five strands per side, ahead of the coloured bucktail.

9 In the same location, tie in a small amount of long olive bucktail, crushing it over the top of the fly with your thumb to spread it out.

10 On the very top of the fly, tie in six strands of peacock herl, extending the length of the fly.

11 Taper the head to the hook eye with thread and lacquer.

Length 16.5 cm (6½ in)

Bryan McGowan

Silhouette Shrimp

When conditions change, successful captains get their clients into fish by making adaptations. Captain Bryan McGowan, from Florida, charters for The Salty Feather. He is also their fly tier for tying custom patterns and has developed over 30 different local patterns.

During the winter in northeast Florida, the water temperatures drop and the water gets much clearer. By December, these changes become most prominent.

With the clearer water, Bryan found the redfish were being spooked more than normal. He needed a fly that was light, but still created a good-sized profile of the shrimp. So Bryan spent time developing a fly that would make a delicate entry, but could mimic a food source in a 'silhouette' kind of way.

With this pattern you can add more lead wire in the body to get a deeper presentation or to get the fly quickly in front of the fish. Bryan likes to tie it sparsely. It gives the silhouette of a good-sized shrimp, but does so with the bulk of a larger fly.

50% size

Length 7 cm (2²/₃ in)

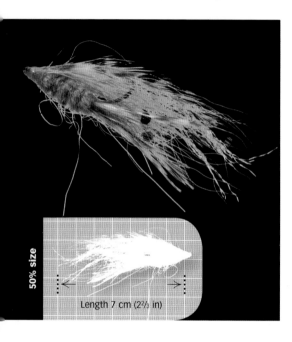

Materials

Hook Gamakatsu B10S, size 4

Thread Brown UTC flat waxed nylon

Tail Tan calf tail, two brown grizzly hackle tips

Eyes 11.3-kg (25-lb) hard Mason monofilament

Body Lead wire, tan Polar Chenille and brown rayon chenille

Wing/Shell Tan bucktail, gold Krystal Flash and brown/tan grizzly hackle feathers

Adhesive Backcountry Laboratories Hard as Hull

How to tie

1 Tie in on the shank just above the hook barb and tie in a small clump of calf tail, allowing it to extend about half the length of the hook.

2 Tie in monofilament eyes the same length as the calf tail. Secure with a light coat of Hard as Hull and leave to dry.

3 Tie in a brown grizzly hackle tip on each side of the monofilament eyes, slightly longer than the eyes and splayed outward.

4 Make ten wraps of lead wire behind the eyes and secure by wrapping the lead with thread.

5 At the tail, tie in Polar Chenille and rayon chenille. Wrap the rayon chenille forward, just shy of the hook eye. Follow by making spaced wraps of Polar Chenille and secure just shy of the hook eye.

6 Now tie in a small clump of tan bucktail at the hook eye, extending to the end of the tail.

7 Take four strands of gold Krystal Flash, double them and tie them in on top of the bucktail.

8 At the hook eye, tie in a hackle feather on each side, also extending to the end of the tail.

9 Secure the thread with half hitches and coat with head cement.

Mike McCoy

Sound Advice

Nowadays, I see high-energy foods for sale all over the place. How about an imitation high-energy food source for sea-run cutthroat? The Sound Advice comes from Captain Mike McCoy of Eugene, Oregon. This is a favourite of his for sea-run cutthroats in Washington's Puget Sound.

The pattern imitates salmon fry and juveniles that end up in the Sound after spawning takes place in the multitude of rivers emptying into this huge estuary. Numerous salmon species spawn in the area's rivers, and these fry and juveniles often have distinctive colour schemes – so be prepared with a few versions in pink and a light green colour as well. The sea-run cutthroat love to eat this high-energy food source.

Sparse is good! Use less of each material than you think necessary, and it will turn out sleek and will sparkle like the real thing. Substituting materials for what you have on hand will work, and they will be appropriate for imitating bait in your area.

Loose wraps of the Fish Hair will help keep it from flaring. This provides a stiff bed to support the more flimsy materials tied on top and helps prevent the wing from wrapping around the hook during casting.

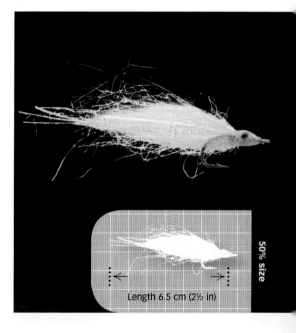

50% size

Length 6.5 cm (2½ in)

Materials

Hook TMC 811S, size 8
Thread Monofilament, 4 mm (⅛ in)
Tail White Fish Hair
Throat Pearl Angel Hair
Overwing pearl Mirage Accent pearl DNA Holo Chromosome flash, pearl Doug's Bugs Electric Scale, pearl Angel Hair
Head EZ Shape Sparkle Body
Eyes 2-mm (¹⁄₁₆-in) silver prism tape eyes
Cement Epoxy

How to tie

1 Tie in five strands of white Fish Hair at the front of the hook and back-wrap over with thread to the bend. They should extend 5 cm (2 in) beyond the bend of the hook.

2 Under the hook, tie in a throat of pearl Angel Hair fatter and shorter than the Fish Hair.

3 At the hook eye, make the wing by tying on these materials in this order: four strands of pearl Mirage Accent; a small bunch of pearl DNA Holo Chromosome flash; pearl Doug's Bugs Electric Scale, two to each side; and pearl Angel Hair. Each layer should be a bit longer than the one underneath to help with the overall silhouette.

4 At the hook eye, tie in EZ Shape Sparkle Body to form the head.

5 Apply the eyes to the Sparkle Body and epoxy over.

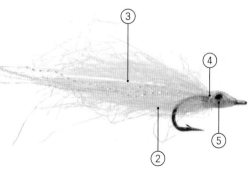

Ralph Poness

Thatcher's Island Zonker

Ralph Poness created this pattern to solve his offshore problems with fly size and durability. This fly fishes deep, with the collar-over-throat material imitating gill flares, and serves as a crossover style for striped bass, tuna and bluefish.

25% size

Length 12.5 cm (5 in)

Thatcher's Island is 1.2 km (¾ mile) offshore. It has the distinction of being one of the first lighthouses to be built to mark a dangerous spot rather than a harbour entrance. Actually, the island has twin lighthouses. Captain Ralph Poness of Framingham, Massachusetts, charters for On-Line Fishing Charters. He needed a durable fly for this area. To develop his pattern, he studied the freshwater zonker-style fly, known for its durability and lifelike movement in even the calmest waters.

The offshore waters offer an excellent opportunity to catch huge bluefish for a few weeks at the beginning of the summer. These waters are so productive that ESPN sent a film crew to document this incredible fishery.

Materials

Hook Gamagatsu SC15, size 6/0
Thread Flat waxed nylon, chartreuse
Body Easy Body Braid
Wing Fluorescent chartreuse zonker strip
Collar White saddle hackle
Tail Fluorescent chartreuse zonker strip
Throat Red Crystal Flash
Eyes Extra-large gold prismatic eyes
Adhesive Epoxy

How to tie

1 Insert the hook eye through the centre of the Body Braid.

2 Press the hook point through the bottom of the Body Braid, leaving enough to extend 5 cm (2 in) past the hook bend.

3 At the hook eye, secure the Body Braid to the hook shank.

4 Insert a fluorescent chartreuse zonker strip into the tail end of the Body Braid. Secure it with thread and epoxy.

5 Tie in a zonker strip at the eye of the hook. It should extend beyond the Body Braid.

6 Reattach the thread at the hook eye.

7 At the hook eye, tie in red Crystal Flash as a throat, allowing the material to wrap up the sides of the body.

8 Tie in a white hackle and make two wraps over the shank.

9 Form a thread head.

10 Epoxy the eyes in place and cover the thread wraps with epoxy.

Ezio Celeschi

Ezio's Needlefish

Quiet nights with dead-flat seas may lull us into quiet contemplation, but the denizens of the deep are on the prowl, as always. It's how they survive – and sometimes we cross paths with them unexpectedly.

Ezio Celeschi of Italy needed a bluefish fly to imitate needlefish in the Mediterranean Sea.

This pattern was designed for fishing estuaries when the sea is calm and needlefish are active. It is best used in the late evening and in the dark. Ezio fishes it with an alternating slow and fast retrieve on floating lines, and uses a steel shock leader to protect from the bluefish's teeth. It is effective fished close to the banks of incoming rivers during hot summer nights when schools of bluefish are on the feed.

Ezio agreed to guide a friend for night fishing. It was the end of the summer, with the night both warm and quiet. The sea was perfectly calm. The fishing was very slow and nothing happened for a while. Ezio's friend was fishing with Ezio's tackle and his new creation, the Needlefish. The silence was broken by his friend's shouts, 'My fly has been attacked by a predator fish, but I was not even retrieving it'. Under the light of their flashlight, they saw a beautiful bluefish.

25% size

Length 15 cm (6 in)

Materials

Hook Mustad S71S, size 2/0
Thread Danville size 6/0, white
Tail Gaja's Krystal Hackle
Body Gaja's Krystal Hackle
Head Green holographic tinsel
Marker pens Black and olive green
Eyes Glue-backed holographic eyes
Adhesive UV glue
Equipment UV light

How to tie

1 Take a length of Gaja's Krystal Hackle and trim to the desired length.

2 Colour the tail section with black permanent marker.

3 Tie in the Krystal Hackle near the hook bend.

4 At the bend, tie in holographic tinsel and wind a tapered thread cone head.

5 Apply the eyes and cover the eyes and thread head cone with UV glue.

6 Mark the sides with olive-green marker and the top with black marker.

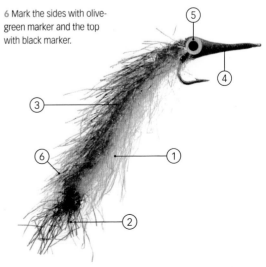

Gordon Churchill

Scrab

Captain Gordon Churchill, from Beaufort, North Carolina, needed a crab pattern for casting to tailing redfish on shallow grass flats. Don't we all?

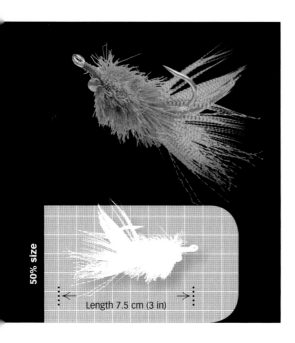

50% size

Length 7.5 cm (3 in)

One of Captain Gordon's friends thought the Scrab looked like a shrimp when he first saw it. (He might have been out too late the night before.) In fact, if you fish it in a certain way, it really does look like a shrimp. Hence the name – Scrab (crab + shrimp).

Gordon throws a weightless version, with weed guard, to reds in the grass. The weighted version, without a weed guard, is used for reds working over a sandy bottom. In the grass, when the reds are tailing, the slightest twitch is all that's necessary to get their attention. Over a sandy bottom, Gordon strips it so that it bumps the bottom. He's watched reds rush in from 12 m (40 ft) to reach the free lunch.

Gordon ties this pattern in sizes ranging from a 20-pence to 10-pence coin to imitate both immature blue crabs and fiddlers. Because there are thousands of them around, the reds make it a point to eat them all. Gordon has also heard from people who've caught stripers on the Scrab. They're probably still smiling, too.

Materials

Hook Mustad 3407,
 size 1/0
Thread Tan Monocord
Weed guard 18-kg (40-lb)
 monofilament
Weight (optional)
 Dumbbell eyes
Tail Gold Krystal Flash
Claws Wood duck flank
 feathers
Body Deer body hair

How to tie

1 Tie in a mono loop at the bend in the hook.

2 Tie in dumbbell eyes (optional) at the hook eye.

3 At the bend, make a tail of gold Krystal Flash.

4 Tie in a wood duck flank feather at each side of the bend for claws.

5 Tie in and spin four bunches of deer body hair.

6 Trim the deer hair with a razor blade so that it is flat on the bottom. Also, leave some untrimmed hair next to the claws.

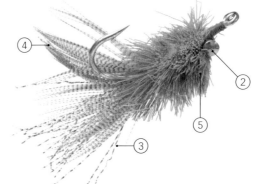

Gene Dickson

Spoon Fly

When the original Spoon Flies started showing up, they had a couple of problems: they were too light to sink quickly enough on the flooded grass flats, and they could not be fished through the heavy cover. Gene Dickson, from Georgetown, South Carolina, owns the Delta Guide Service. He developed a solution.

Spoon flies are used during higher-than-normal tides. The extra 30 cm (1 ft) of water on the flats opens up new feeding areas for the reds.

One of Gene's first experiences with the spoon fly happened when he poled the boat up to a fish that was feeding and tailing in about 40 cm (16 in) of clear water. The client made a perfect cast, the fish gulped the spoon and the hook was set. The fish made a hard run parallel to the boat, the hook tore out of its mouth and, because the rod was bent double, the lure came out of the water and shot up over their heads. As the caster was cursing his luck, he got control of the line as it went behind and he just threw it back into the water. As luck would have it, it landed about 1 m (3 ft) in front of the escaping fish. The fish saw it and grabbed it again! This time, luck held, and they got the photo and released the fish.

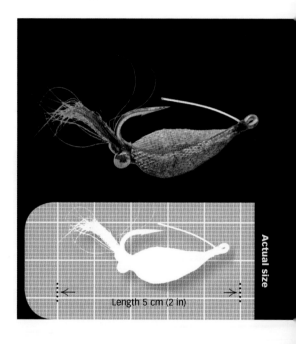

Actual size

Length 5 cm (2 in)

Materials

Hook Gamakatsu SC 15, sizes 1/0 and 2/0
Thread UNI size 4/0, tan
Tail Red fox tail
Eyes Small dumbbell eyes
Weed guard 13.6-kg (30-lb) monofilament
Blade material Gold Offray, 5-cm (2-in) long woven craft ribbon
Adhesives Aerosol spray and two-part epoxy

How to tie

1 Lay down a thread base from the eye of the hook to halfway down the bend.

2 Tie in a tail of fox tail halfway down the bend. The tail should be the same length as the hook shank.

3 Directly over the tail wraps, tie in the eyes.

4 Turn the hook over, wrap the thread forward and tie in the monofilament weed guard loop.

5 Whip finish and cut the thread.

6 Spray adhesive on the back of the ribbon and let it dry.

7 Place the ribbon under the hook shank and then fold it in half to cover both sides of the shank.

8 Trim the ribbon to a teardrop shape.

9 Apply a thin layer of two-part epoxy over the ribbon and also over the thread wraps at each end of the fly.

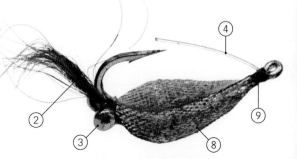

Length 10 cm (4 in)

George Harris

Super Fly Gurglebug

This pattern shines in crystal-clear eelgrass flats, rockweed-covered ledges and along sod banks – lots of places where other patterns get fouled. Fish it for stripers on a floating line with a slow, skittering retrieve.

Materials

Hook Gamakatsu SC-15, size 1

Thread Danville 0.15 mm (.006-in) monofilament, clear

Tail Chartreuse Doug's Bug's Extra Select craft fur

Body Chartreuse Estaz

Rattle Metz 3 mm (⅛ in)

Foam White 3-mm (⅛-in) sheet foam

Flash Pearl Crystal Flash

Legs Tan with red dots Sili Legs

Marker pen Chartreuse

Captain George Harris is from Warren, Maine, and owns Super Fly Charters. He designed this variation of Jack Gartside's Gurgler to ride hook point up, therefore making it virtually weedless.

George mostly fishes this fly for stripers, but has caught numerous snook around lighted docks in Florida. The rattle serves as both a noisemaker and a keel to make the fly ride hook point up.

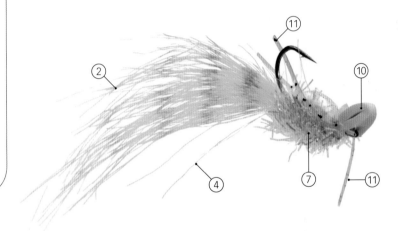

How to tie

1 Lay down a thread base to just before the hook bend.

2 Take 7.5 cm × 6 mm (3 × ¼ in) craft fur and tie it in on top of the hook shank.

3 Tie in a 10-cm (4-in) length of Estaz at the same place.

4 Tie in eight strands of Crystal Flash at the same point.

5 Cut a 10-cm × 6-mm (4- × ¼-in) piece of sheet foam. Trim one short end to a blunt point. Turn the hook over and tie the pointed end of the foam to the hook

shank, just under the hook point. Make several tight thread wraps back over the foam up to the barb of the hook, being sure to tightly compress the foam with the thread wraps. Push the foam aside. All materials should be tied in from the point of the hook to the bend.

6 Turn the hook over. Attach the rattle to the top of the fly with several wraps of thread. Apply head cement to the thread wraps covering the rattle.

7 Wind the Estaz forward over the rattle, making five turns. Tie it off in front of the rattle, leaving some room behind the hook eye. Trim the excess.

8 Turn the hook over, with the point up. Grasp the foam sheet and pull it forward over the Estaz. Make three tight wraps over the foam 3 mm (⅛ in) behind the eye.

9 Pull the Crystal Flash forward and tie down. Clip the excess.

10 Double the excess foam over on itself, creating a

6-mm (¼-in) lip. Bind this down tightly over the other wraps. Trim the excess.

11 At the hook eye, on the left side of the fly, tie in a 7.5-cm (3-in) piece of Sili Legs at its centre, creating a set of V-shaped legs. Repeat the process on the other side of the fly.

12 Move the thread forward of the lip and whip finish just behind the hook eye.

13 Add some subtle barring on the tail with a chartreuse permanent marker.

Chuck Kashner

Kashner Striper Bunny

Seems to me stripers are unusual fish. Near the Esopus Lighthouse in New York's Hudson River, where I used to fish for them, many bait fishermen would soak their sand worms in WD-40, claiming it increased the number hooked. I've seen it work.

50% size

Length 10 cm (4 in)

For Chuck Kashner, however, a fly is still the preferred medicine. Chuck, from Pawlett, Vermont, owns Vermont Fishing Trips and usually guides in freshwater. However, this pattern has been successful in both fresh- and saltwater. This one is fast, easy to tie, durable and effective.

Chuck says the materials are responsible for this pattern's effectiveness. The rabbit fur comes alive in the water, and it will sink very fast with large dumbbell eyes. This durable fly works on blues, stripers, reds and tarpon.

Chuck often uses this fly in a moving tide where he can get a cast-and-swing method. He targets the last two hours of an outgoing tide. At such times, the fish are concentrated in holes but are still actively feeding.

But what about that WD-40? Couldn't you tie a marabou worm and soak it in WD-40? Would it still be considered a fly or would it be considered bait? Enquiring minds want to know.

Materials

Hook Mustad 34007, sizes 1/0–4/0
Thread Flat waxed nylon, white
Eyes Silver or gold prismatic dumbbell eyes
Flash Silver Flashabou
Tail White saddle hackles
Body White cross-cut rabbit strip
Adhesive 5-minute epoxy

How to tie

1 Tie in the thread 1.25 cm (½ in) behind the eye.

2 Tie on dumbbell eyes, wrapping with figure-of-eights and also in front of and behind the eyes.

3 Tie in six pieces of Flashabou near the bend of the hook.

4 Ahead of the Flashabou, tie in two white saddle hackles as a tail.

5 Tie in a cross-cut rabbit strip at the hook bend.

6 Form a body by wrapping the rabbit strip forward, making sure to stroke the hairs back, out of the way, with each turn.

7 Tie off and trim the excess.

8 Epoxy the head, especially the wraps over the eyes.

Ezio Celeschi

Ezio's Mullet

Big bass are ambushers. They prefer to hide among structure so that they can intercept baitfish while conserving their energy. This pattern is especially effective at those times when mullet are on the menu.

Ezio Celeschi, from Italy, needed a bass fly to imitate small mullet found around the rocky shores of the Mediterranean Sea. He fishes this pattern in river mouths, where baitfish get buffeted around and are taken by bass that lay in wait.

The Fish Skull used for the head is tied in 'reversed', so that the weight hangs from the bottom of the fly. This results in a pattern with the hook above the shank, making the fly less likely to get hung up on the rocks used by the bass for cover.

Ezio's Mullet can be fished any time of day over reefs with a medium-slow retrieve. Ezio has had especially good fishing using this pattern with floating lines in the fall.

Ezio recalls the first test of his Mullet pattern. Knowing where a mullet school was located, he made his cast and let the fly settle in its midst. He made only one strip before he was fast to a bass and the question of the fly's effectiveness had been settled.

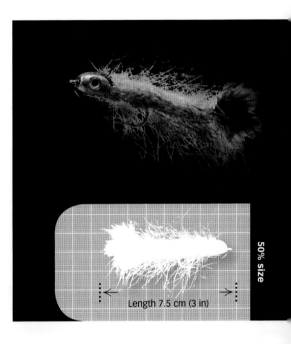

50% size

Length 7.5 cm (3 in)

Materials

Hook Mustad S71S, size 1
Thread Danville size 6/0, white
Tail Brown marabou
Body Gaja's Krystal Hackle
Gills Red flash
Head Flyman Fish Skull, medium silver baitfish
Adhesive Cyanoacrylate glue
Marker pens Permanent black and green

How to tie

1 Take a piece of Gaja's Krystal Hackle and cut it to the desired length.

2 Tie a marabou tail 2 cm (¾ in) long into the end of the Krystal Hackle.

3 Slide the hook inside the Krystal Hackle and tie it in place near the hook eye.

4 Near the hook eye, tie in some red flash for gills.

5 Slide the Fish Skull over the hook eye. Fix it in place with cyanoacrylate glue.

6 Trim the red flash so that only a small amount shows as gills.

7 Colour the side of the Krystal Hackle with a green marker pen.

8 Colour the dorsal side of the Krystal Hackle with a black marker pen.

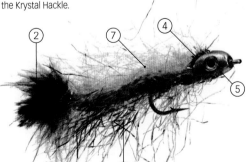

Justin Duggan

Duggan's Suspender Shrimp

The neatest aspect of this fly is not the materials, but the technique. It is designed to be tied quickly using just a few materials. You can tie it in a colour to match the shrimp in your area. It can be tied to suspend or to sink slowly.

Materials

Hook Mustad C70S D, size 6 or 8
Thread Monocord or monofilament, 3/0, colour to match the body
Head/body 6-mm (¼-in) foam 'booby eyes' or white cicada body foam
Legs and antennae DNA Holo Fusion, pearl
Eyes Black-centred stick-on eyes
Adhesive Epoxy

It's a great pattern for Justin Duggan's home waters of Sydney, Australia – and, no doubt, for shrimp feeders worldwide. Justin owns Sydney Fly Fishing Tours.

Justin fishes this pattern on sinking lines in 3–3.5 m (10–12 ft) of water, using more foam on a lighter hook so it floats. The sinking line and floating fly create a seductive motion. He has caught several dusky flathead on them as well, using this technique.

Bream are the main target. The fly works best if it suspends or sinks slowly. The bream get among the oyster racks, and at high tide Justin can throw these suspending shrimps and literally 'hover' them over the racks. Bream love a pause in the retrieve, when they will quite often sit behind the fly and almost put their nose on it, deciding whether or not to eat it.

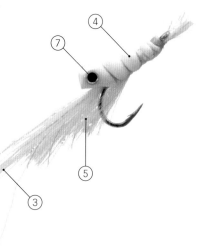

How to tie

1 Thread the hook through the centre of the foam body form and in the foam up past the eye of the hook. Make sure that the hook point comes out of the foam so as to allow one-quarter of the foam to hang past the bend.

2 Tie in thread over the shank at the bend of the hook, being sure to push the foam away gently towards the hook eye.

3 At the bend, tie in a small bunch of DNA Holo Fusion, with several longer lengths on top to make the antennae and front feelers.

4 Make two light wraps of thread over the foam to make a distinct head. Continue wrapping segments towards the hook eye, getting progressively tighter; this will create a tapered body. Tighter wraps will result in a sinking fly, while looser wraps will yield a floating or suspending fly.

5 Now return the thread to the centre of the body and wrap in a length of DNA Holo Fusion to create the front legs and tail.

6 Whip finish at the hook eye and place some head cement on the threads.

7 Add some small eyes to the head with epoxy and trim the fly.

Length 7.5 cm (3 in)

Eric Weissman

Eric's Ugly Coho Killer

Handsome is as handsome does? That may be what they say – but it's not always true. This pattern is from Eric Weissman, from Toronto. He fishes the Ugly Coho Killer along the beaches of Vancouver Island, often casting from a pontoon boat.

50% size

Length 7.5 cm (3 inches)

This particular colour scheme is for a northwestern British Columbia glass minnow. Be sure not to overdress this pattern. It should be kept sparse.

This little fly should be fished just under the surface, with floating lines. Cast to pods of coho and begin stripping even before it hits the water. Strip it fast and continuously, without interruption. Eric reports that cohos up to 9 kg (20 lb) have eaten this simple, if ugly, pattern.

If the cohos turn off, Eric will stop the high-speed retrieve and twitch the fly. After the pods of cohos are done killing and thrashing the bait schools, they begin picking off the dead bait that's floating. Casting and letting the fly simply float down, giving it an occasional twitch, is enough to trigger a strike.

They say beauty is only skin-deep, but ugly goes all the way to the bone. Maybe – but Eric's Ugly Coho Killer has proven its worth: it should go right into your fly box.

Materials

Hook Mustad 3407, sizes 4–8
Thread Grey 6/0
Tail Fluorescent green polar bear hair, dark green flash
Body/wing Fluorescent green polar bear hair
Veiling Red squirrel or badger hair
Head Grey thread, painted red

How to tie

1 Lay down a thread base from the eye of the hook to the bend.

2 At the bend, tie in a tail of fluorescent green polar bear hair extending 2.5 cm (1 in) beyond the bend.

3 Top the tail with green flash, the same length as the polar bear hair.

4 Advance the thread halfway to the eye and tie in more polar bear hair.

5 Wrap a body from the thread, ending 6 mm (¼ in) from the hook eye.

6 Tie in a veil of red squirrel or badger hair.

7 Tie in more wing topping of fluorescent green polar bear hair.

8 Build a prominent thread head and cover it with red cement or paint.

Dexter Simmons

Sandy Merkin

The Sandy Merkin has been designed by Captain Dexter Simmons from Key West, Florida, who owns Key West Fly Fishing.

This is a classic crab pattern, based on a variation of the Del's Merkin Crab Fly. It's an excellent pattern for permit on windy days. You can select the most effective size and weight, depending on the depth of sand flat and wind conditions.

The rabbit fur gives this fly added life that the traditional merkin lacked. It can also be tied with tan marabou, but Dexter prefers the bunny.

Cast the Sandy Merkin close to and in front of the permit. Stay tight to the fly by controlling your slack. If the fish flashes on the fly or if you feel a take, strip long and slow until you come tight to the fish. Hesitate striking the fish until it begins its run. If you strike too soon, you may pull the fly from the fish's mouth – and you will utter words that your mother would not be proud to hear you say.

50% size

Length 7.5 cm (3 in)

Materials

Hook Mustad 34007, size 1/0
Thread Danville flat waxed nylon, chartreuse
Eyes Medium painted dumbbell lead eyes, gold with black eyeballs
Flash Tan Midge Flash
Tail Grey cross-cut rabbit fur and tan barred strung neck hackle
Body Sand-coloured Aunt Lydia's Rug Yarn
Legs White Sili Legs
Marker pen Red
Adhesive Superglue

How to tie

1 Tie in dumbbell eyes next to the eye of the hook.

2 Tie in 15 pieces of flash onto the tail end of the hook near the bend, extending about 2.5 cm (1 in) past the bend.

3 At the bend, tie in rabbit fur, the same length as the flash.

4 Ahead of the rabbit fur, tie in and splay out two hackles on each side of the hook.

5 Ahead of the hackles, tie in six or seven 1.25-cm (½-in) strands of Aunt Lydia's rug yarn. Wrap it until you reach the dumbbell eye.

6 Make a thread head and whip finish.

7 Using overhand knots, tie in four Sili Legs that extend 2.5 cm (1 in) past the body on each side. Colour the tips red with the marker.

8 Finish with a very small amount of Superglue on each leg knot.

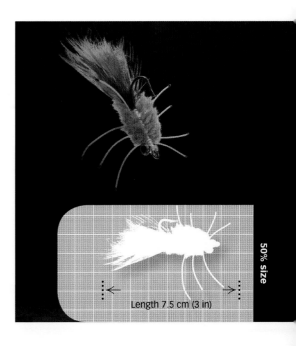

Kenji Sekiguchi

Kenji's Devil May Cry

Some flies are named for the designer, some for what they imitate and some for famous waters where they are fished. This is the first one I've encountered that is named for a video game.

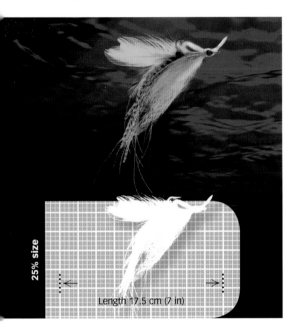

25% size

Length 17.5 cm (7 in)

Kenji Sekiguchi, from Indonesia, created this fly for fishing offshore, although it can also be used to fish from jetties and on the shore. Kenji targets yellowfin tuna, billfish, bonito, mackerel, barracuda, rainbow runner and queenfish – in short, predators.

His favourite waters include the Bali Straight and Menjangan Island. He also fishes offshore oil rigs in Sapolo Madura, where bluefin trevally and bigeye trevally are found, in addition to the other fish mentioned above.

Materials

Hook Maguro mackerel, size 2/0
Thread Fine monofilament
Weight Wapsi large lead eyes
Wing Chartreuse neck hackles
Body Grizzly Whiting Eurohackle
Legs Red rubber
Back White Slinky Fiber
Belly Pink Slinky Fiber, green Slinky Fiber
Flash Krystal Flash
Eyes Stick-on 3D eyes
Tongue Plastic book cover
Adhesive 5-minute epoxy

How to tie

1 Attach the lead eyes on top of the hook shank and slightly below the hook bend. Use criss-crossing thread wraps and cement the wraps when done.

2 Tie in six chartreuse neck hackles, one at a time, just below the lead eyes – three on each side of the eyes.

3 In front of the chartreuse neck hackles, tie in eight grizzly hackles on top of the hook shank, making the overall length of the fly 17.5 cm (7 in).

4 In front of the grizzly hackles, tie on six strands of red rubber legs. They should be the same length as the grizzly hackles.

5 Advance the thread towards the hook eye and tie in a bunch of white Slinky Fiber at the midpoint of its length, so that it sticks out both towards the tail and over the hook eye. Do not trim the Slinky Fiber.

6 Immediately behind the white Slinky Fiber, tie in some pink Slinky Fiber three times the length of the hook shank.

7 At this same location, tie in 12 strands of Krystal Flash long enough to reach the ends of the grizzly hackles.

8 Fold the white Slinky Fiber rearward to create the underbody of the fly. It should reach beyond the hook bend.

9 Above the white Slinky Fiber, tie in a bunch of green Slinky Fiber nearly as long as the

grizzly hackle. Whip finish the thread, but do not cut it.

10 Cut the plastic book cover into a lip shape. Tie it onto the front of the fly and whip finish.

11 Apply the stick-on 3D eyes and coat the entire head area with 5-minute epoxy. Let it dry completely.

12 Trim the hair and fibres as necessary, to obtain a fish shape.

Edward Michaels

Michaels' Permit Pro Choice

Many crab flies turn upside down when they land, or track on an angle when retrieved. This is unnatural and will cause permit or bonefish to spook. Michaels' Permit Pro Choice works well whether fished on the drop or stripped in, because it acts just like a natural.

Captain Edward Michaels from Sugarloaf Key, Florida, wanted to improve his clients' success on permit from Marathon to Key West. Now, instead of starting each day simply hoping to entice a permit to look at his fly, he expects every permit to eat it. Pretty confident even for a professional captain. Judge for yourself.

His first prototype accounted for two permit landed and two more that chased the fly in, only to be spooked by sight of the boat.

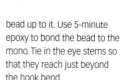

Actual size

Length 5 cm (2 in)

Materials

Hook Gamakatsu SC-15, size 1/0
Thread Danville Flymaster, beige
Weight Nickel-plated lead dumbbell, 0.45–0.85 g (1/60–1/30 OZ)
Egg sac Orange marabou
Claws Rubber bands
Eyes Mason hard monofilament (melted) and a small orange bead
Legs Amber/blue flake Sili Legs
Body Light brown mottled unborn calfskin
Adhesives 5-minute epoxy and Softex
Marker pens Red and blue

How to tie

1 Attach a nickel-plated lead dumbbell to top of the shank, behind the hook eye.

2 Wrap a thread base from behind the lead dumbbell to the hook bend.

3 Turn the hook over and make a tail with a small tuft of orange marabou. It should be equal to the length of the hook shank and stick out beyond the hook bend.

4 Cut claws from a rubber band. Colour with markers and dip in Softex to prevent cracking. When dry, tie the claws in at the hook bend.

5 Melt the end of the mono to form stops, then slide a small

bead up to it. Use 5-minute epoxy to bond the bead to the mono. Tie in the eye stems so that they reach just beyond the hook bend.

6 Make three pairs of amber/blue flake Sili Legs.

7 Make 90-degree joints on the rear pair of legs by tying double overhand knots and tightening slowly.

8 Make the body from mottled, unborn calfskin with the hair pointing towards the back of the fly. Tie two sections in between the orange marabou and the lead dumbbell.

9 Tie in the legs and body parts, alternating between them.

10 Trim the legs to twice the hook gape.

11 Trim the body to a tapered angle, narrow in front, wide in back.

12 Wrap a body of beige thread, being careful to keep the legs and the calfskin sections on the same plane as the hook shank.

13 Add a drop of head cement to each thread wrap.

Lynne Heyer

Yak Hair Squid

Squid are a popular forage for gamefish wherever the squid are found. They are not especially fast, so predators have no trouble catching them. Imitating squid requires a fly that will hold its shape and still reflect the long profile presented by the natural.

Yak hair?! This has all the markings of a shaggy dog story. However, Captain Lynne Heyer insists hers is true.

Lynne gives joint credit for various aspects of this fly to several other captains in the area. She explains that a group of them were chartering in Florida and experimenting with yak hair. (Most people go to Florida to sit in the sun. Apparently, some go there to experiment with yak hair.) After trying out several patterns, they developed one to imitate a major food source for striped bass, amberjack and grouper. Because these fish swim deep in rips, holes and wrecks, Lynne uses sinking lines to get the Yak Hair Squid down to their level.

25% size

Length 30 cm (12 in)

Materials

Hook Tiemco 600SP, sizes 4/0–8/0

Thread Danville flat waxed nylon, 3/0, black

Body Pink Big Fiber Fly and blended yak hair; pink Grand Estaz

Eyes Large 3D moulded eyes with black pupils

Adhesives Softex and Goop

How to tie

1 Lay down a thread base from the hook eye to the hook bend.

2 At the hook eye, tie in some pink Big Fly Fiber and wrap a body back to the hook bend. Keep the length as long as possible.

3 Tie in pink Grand Estaz at the hook bend and wrap forward to just behind the hook eye.

4 Form the head (veil) by tying in a 15 cm (6-in) length of yak hair

behind the eye, tying it in the middle so that it looks like a moustache, with half above and half below the shank. Pull the hair back, around the Big Fly Fiber, making a head shape. Tie it in.

5 Whip finish the thread wraps.

6 Glue the eyes onto the body of the fly. Apply Goop to the

back of each eye so that the bottoms of the eyes just pinch the shank. Use a clothes-peg to pinch the eyes until the Goop dries.

7 Use a bodkin to work some Softex into the yak hair in front of the eyes. This gives the fly just enough stiffness to hold its shape.

Alberto Salvini

Alberto's Sand Crab

When fish see the same patterns over and over, they become harder to fool. Alberto's Sand Crab is the answer to that problem. This pattern has accounted for catching bonefish, permit, redfish and every other species that feasts on crab.

Alberto Salvini's credentials are impressive: former fashion model for numerous designers and world fly-fishing championship competitor. He has fished all around the world and is currently involved with several television programmes.

Most fly patterns are assembled by tying elements onto the hook in a specified order. This pattern is 'preassembled' and then fixed to the hook. As a result, if you need many copies, you can use an assembly-line process to speed up the process and complete them all at the same time.

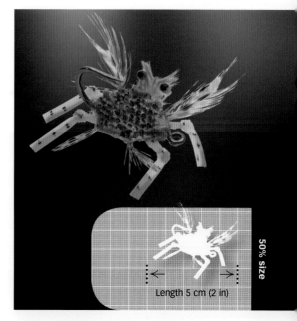

Length 5 cm (2 in)

50% size

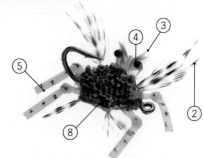

Materials

Hook Mustad C70SD, size 1/0

Thread Size 3/0, clear white

Weight Lead eyes, flattened, 19 g (⅗ oz) weight

Claws Two tan dyed grizzly hackle tips trimmed to a V-shape

Mouth Light brown filoplume

Eyes 1-mm (½₂-in) melted monofilament with black pupils

Marker pens Black and red

Legs Three strips of knotted cream medium round rubber

Carapace Alberto's Carapace, round

Swimmer legs Two tan dyed grizzly hackle tips, untrimmed

Abdomen White hot glue

Abdomen colour White correction fluid

Adhesives Superglue, one-step epoxy and hot glue

How to tie

1 Hammer two lead eyes flat.

2 Trim two tan dyed grizzly hackle tips to make claws. Leave one pair of tips untrimmed for the swimmer legs.

3 Trim the butt sections of a light brown filoplume into a V-shape to make mouth parts.

4 Melt the ends of two short lengths of monofilament to form eyes. Use a black permenent marker to colour the ends.

5 Separate three sections of medium round rubber legs. Trim to 2.5-cm (1-in) lengths and tie an overhand knot in the centre. You will need four legs.

6 Press the following materials onto the adhesive side of the carapace in the following order: mouth barbules, claws, monofilament eyes and legs. Apply a small drop of Superglue to fix all the materials together.

7 Hot glue the hammered lead eyes onto the top of the hook shank. Space them the same distance apart to match with the width of the carapace.

8 Under the hook shank, position the carapace (with parts attached) and attach with hot glue. Cover with one-step epoxy into a smooth, rounded belly shape. When the epoxy is dry, paint it white with white correction fluid.

William Faulkner

Back-country Bunny

The Back-country Bunny is straightforward, easy to tie and will catch fish in nearly all conditions. In stained or dirty water it projects a large profile with lots of wiggle. In clean or clear water it appears natural enough to fool even finicky fish.

50% size

Length 9 cm (3½ in)

The Back-country Bunny is a great pattern because it catches just about everything that swims in saltwater. It can be tied in a variety of sizes and colours, including chartreuse, yellow, black and red, white and red and all variations of browns and oranges. Bill, as he lets me call him, prefers to tie this fly on 1s and 1/0s for snook and redfish. However, when fishing deeper in the backcountry during the winter months, Bill will often cast 2/0s, because the possibility of encountering a 9-kg (20-lb) snook is always imminent. Tie this fly in black and purple on a 3/0 for laid-up tarpon during the spring months. Hook size is very important – not only because it will ultimately determine how large the fly appears in the water, but also because Bill always wants to be prepared for the biggest fish he could possibly encounter. Larger hooks instil the confidence to land big fish with cavernous mouths.

Materials

Hook Mustad All-round O'Shaughnessy S71S SS, size 1/0

Thread Danville 210 denier flat waxed nylon, black

Tail support Black bucktail

Flash Purple Flashabou

Wing Black rabbit magnum-cut zonker strip

Collar Purple marabou feather

Head Purple Estaz

Cement Griff's Thin Fly Tying Multi-Coat

How to tie

1 Wrap a short thread base on the shank just forward of the hook point.

2 Wrap the thread base forward a small amount and tie in a modest portion of black bucktail for support. Trim the bucktail just shorter than the intended length of the zonker strip tail.

3 In the same location, tie in 15 pieces of purple Flashabou.

4 Ahead of the Flashabou, tie in a black rabbit zonker strip as a wing long enough to make the fly 9 cm (3½ in)

in length. Then cement the thread wraps.

5 On top of the wing tie-in wraps, tie in and make three wraps of a purple marabou feather as a collar. Add more cement.

6 Ahead of the marabou collar, tie in a length of purple Estaz and wrap it forward to the hook eye as a head.

7 Cement the thread wraps.

Greg Morrison

Morrison's Mullet

The unusual characteristic of this pattern is the deer-hair head. Although more common in freshwater patterns, it is incorporated into Morrison's Mullet for its ability to move more water and create a larger disturbance that attracts striped bass.

Captain Greg Morrison has over 30 years' experience in saltwater fly fishing, because he was born and raised in it. Greg has won several awards in competitions for his innovative fly tying and has an impressive collection of original fly patterns that he has developed. Greg is a casting instructor at the Costal Guides Schools and is involved in seminars and private lessons.

Greg usually fishes this fly with floating lines along the jetty tips and sometimes in a chum slick made of ground bunker and spearing pieces. This is normally a daytime fly when used in the ocean and is primarily an autumn pattern. His largest striper, a fish weighing more than 13.6 kg (30 lb), was taken and released using this pattern. The fish was caught in knee-deep water at the New York Avenue Jetty, Sea Girt, New Jersey, on an October afternoon. This fly can also be dead drifted in currents from the jetty tips and beachheads.

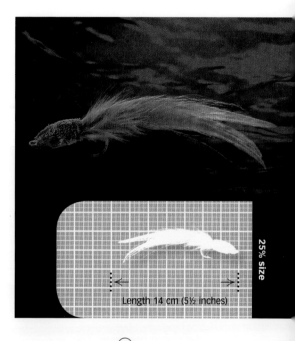

25% size

Length 14 cm (5½ inches)

Materials

Hook Mustad 34007 SS, size 2/0
Thread Monothread
Tail White bucktail and silver Krystal Flash
Wing Olive green saddle hackles
Head Green and grey deer hair
Sides White and green marabou
Eyes 6-mm (¼-in) glass eyes

How to tie

1 Tie in 7.5 cm (3 in) of white bucktail to the shank of the hook at the bend.

2 Tie in some sparse silver Krystal Flash above that.

3 Tie in a sparse amount of 7.5-cm (3-in) white bucktail above that.

4 Tie in two 10-cm (4-in) olive green hackles (wide webbing) on top of the flash.

5 Tie in some sparse green Krystal Flash alongside the hackles.

6 Tie in some white marabou to the bottom to match the bucktail, then add some green marabou to match the feathers and tie it off.

7 Spin some green deer hair on top and grey on the bottom. (Spin to three-quarters of the length of the hook.)

8 Add some glass eyes, then spin the deer hair around the eyes up to the eye of the hook and tie it off. You can use a little head cement or glue on the thread.

9 Trim the hair down close so that the fly swims better.

Barrett's Shrimp Fly

Shrimp Fly! It might sound like some kind of insult, but it isn't. The Shrimp Fly is a great go-to fly. It seems to be one fly that, day in and day out, catches those big black drum. It's also great on redfish. The fact that it is so quick and easy to tie makes it attractive.

50% size

Length 9 cm (3½ in)

If you had only one fly to use, this would cover you in most situations and conditions. You could fish from skinny grass-filled duck ponds to deeper shorelines over oyster shells. This pattern comes from Captain Barrett Brown from Metairie, Louisiana. Barrett ties it in numerous lighter shades for early morning and overcast days and in darker shades for bright, sunny conditions. The colours depend on water clarity and amount of sunlight.

Barrett reports you have to fish big 18-kg (40-lb) black drum differently than redfish. They won't chase a fly. You have to drag it right by their noses and let it drop. They will just suck it in. He's had clients say, 'You are going to put that gaudy fly on my line?' – but when they see the results, they become believers.

Materials

Hook Mustad 34007, size 1
Thread Size A, red
Eyes Red-centred large gold dumbbell eyes
Tentacles Crystal Flash
Mouth Red rabbit fur
Feelers Gold Mylar tubing
Body Red medium chenille
Hackle Red hackle
Adhesive Superglue

How to tie

1 Lay down a thread base from the hook eye to above the point of the hook.

2 Above the hook point on the top of the hook shank, tie in the dumbbell eyes. Superglue the thread for added strength.

3 Move the thread to the back-side of the eyes and tie on four strands of Crystal Flash folded in half as tentacles that are 2.5 times the length of the hook shank.

4 Tie in a patch of rabbit fur on each side of the tentacles.

Keep the rabbit fur the length of the hook shank.

5 Slide a 2-cm (¾-in) length of Mylar tubing over the hook, so that it covers the rabbit fur and Crystal Flash.

6 Take a bodkin and pull it through the Mylar tubing to open it all up. Pull the opened end of the Mylar one shank's length beyond the hook bend. Tie in the end of the Mylar in front of the dumbbell eyes.

7 At the hook bend, tie in a red hackle and leave it hanging.

8 At this same location, tie in red chenille and wrap the thread forward to the hook eye. Wrap the chenille to the hook eye and tie it down.

9 Wrap the hackle all the way forward to the eye. Tie it down and trim the excess.

10 Whip finish and Superglue the head.

Gary Dubiel

Dubiel's Red-ducer

This pattern fishes best in shallow flats and with a floating line. It is a great fly for fishing to feeding drum. The bead chain eyes give the fly an up-and-down motion that acts as a trigger to excite redfish. The Red-ducer is also productive on spotted sea trout, black drum, sheepshead and flounder.

Dubiel's Red-ducer is from Captain Gary Dubiel of Oriental, North Carolina, which has gained a reputation as an outstanding sport-fishing destination. Located on the widest river in North America, the Neuse, Oriental is the gateway to the vast Pamlico Sound Estuary.

Gary first adapted a Sea-ducer to fish on the grassy flats of Tampa Bay, when he was living in St Petersburg, Florida, back in the early 1990s. He needed a fly that he could swim a distance but that could also be stopped and allowed to fall into the grass. By adding the bead chain eyes to the head, many of his problems were solved. Over the years, he added the Estaz body, reduced the palmered hackle and created more flash.

The Red-ducer can be tied in many other colours. In addition to the tan version shown here, all-white, red-and-white and chartreuse versions have all been productive.

25% size

Length 11 cm (4½ in)

Materials

Hook Mustad 34007, size 1

Thread UNI size 3/0, red

Eyes Gold, large bead chain

Flash Copper Kreinik's Flash

Tail Grizzly tan-dyed whiting rooster hackle feathers

Body Tan Estaz

Adhesive Backcountry Laboratories Hard as Hull

How to tie

1 Wrap a short thread base close to the hook eye.

2 At this location, tie on the bead chain eyes to the top of the hook shaft.

3 Immediately behind the bead chain eyes, tie in ten strands of Kreinik's Flash, extending well behind the hook shank. These will be trimmed to match the length of the hackles that will be added next.

4 At this same location, tie in two grizzly saddle hackles on each side of the hook so that they splay outward.

5 At this same location, tie in another grizzly hackle.

6 At this same location, tie in a length of Estaz.

7 Wind the thread to the bead chain eyes.

8 Wrap the Estaz forward to the chain eyes and tie off. Trim the excess.

9 Wind the remaining saddle hackle over the Estaz to the bead chain eyes and secure. Trim the excess.

10 Build a small thread head in front of the bead chain eyes.

11 Whip finish the thread head and coat with Hard as Hull.

← Length 7.5 cm (3 inches) →

Alberto Salvini

Alberto's Shrimp

Alberto Salvini has been using this pattern since 1998 for Mediterranean sea bass in Italy, Spain, France, Greece, Croatia and the UK. It also works on sea trout in Denmark. The simplicity of the techniques means that anyone can reproduce this pattern.

Materials

Hook TMC 811S, sizes 6 and 4

Thread Size 3/0, white

Claws Grey dun rooster saddle hackles

Eyes 1-mm (1/32 in) nylon monofilament with melted ends

Marker pens Black, brown and yellow

Body/tail and front barbs Sandstone Antron yarn

Antennae Eight strands of copper Krystal Flash, eight strips of pearl Krystal Flash

Legs Tan Cactus Polar Chenille

Mouth barbs Bright amber synthetic fibres

Shell back/body Two layers of 5-minute epoxy

Alberto's Shrimp is especially effective in areas where shrimp are found, such as open beaches and jetties where a floating line works well. Other good areas are close to river mouths, harbours or canals, where an intermediate sinking line may be necessary due to the greater depths at which the shrimp are found. In tropical areas this fly works on bonefish, permit, redfish and baby tarpon. It is also excellent for striped bass in New England. In 2001, this pattern was used to win the First International Bonefish Tournament in Cuba.

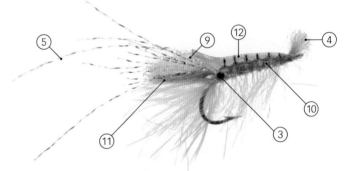

How to tie

1 Starting at the middle of the hook shank, wrap a short thread base almost to the hook bend and wrap back to the starting point.

2 At the bend, tie in the grey rooster saddle hackles on top of the hook. Wrap five wide turns of hackle with the fibres pointing towards the bend.

3 Carefully melt the ends of a short piece of monofilament to form eyes. Tie the monofilament in at the bend of the hook. Cement the thread wraps. Make black eye dots on the monofilament with black permanent marker pen.

4 At the hook eye, tie in a length of Antron yarn. Trim it to extend about 3 mm (1/8 in) beyond the hook eye. Push the fibres up at 90 degrees to the hook shank and secure with thread. Tie in at the bend of the hook.

5 Top the Antron with eight pieces of copper Krystal Flash. Tie one end at the hook eye. Trim the excess. Tie the other end in at the hook bend, but leave them sticking out beyond the hook bend by 5 cm (2 in). Trim four strands to 2.5 cm (1 in).

6 Repeat step 5 with pearl Krystal Flash.

7 Colour the tips of the four longest lengths of Krystal Flash using a black permanent marker pen.

8 Colour the pearl Krystal Flash with a yellow permanent marker pen.

9 At the monofilament eyes, tie in a length of sandstone Antron sticking out past the hook bend, equal to the length of the hook shank.

10 At the monofilament eyes, tie in tan Cactus Polar Chenille. Wind it in close turns over the Antron body to the hook eye.

11 At the bend, tie in amber fibres as a mouth on top of the hook shank. Trim to twice the hook gape.

12 Make the carapace by applying a coat of 5-minute epoxy over the back of the fly from the hook eye to just past the hook bend.

13 When the epoxy is dry, make shell lines with a brown permanent marker pen. Let them dry.

14 Apply a second coat of epoxy over the first, sealing in the brown markings.

Roan zumFelde

Rz's Back Country Booger

Woolly Buggers have a well-deserved reputation as great fish-getters. There is something about the sexy movement of the marabou that triggers strikes by gamefish. When another fly comes along that challenges the Woolly Bugger's reputation as a go-to fly, I pay attention.

50% size

Length 7.5 cm (3 in)

To me, Back Country Booger sounds like something Bigfoot hunters go looking for in the swamps of southern states.

Captain Roan zumFelde, from Naples, Florida, had something else in mind when he developed this pattern for snook, tarpon and redfish from the Everglades to Pine Island. Roan started tying this pattern several years ago. Prior to discovering the effectiveness of the Back Country Booger, he used Woolly Buggers for small snook in the 'Glades when he first started fly fishing. Now he relies on his creation more and more.

Put a few of these simple ties in your box and you'll come to rely on it, too. And keep a few extra-large ones handy – just in case Bigfoot shows up.

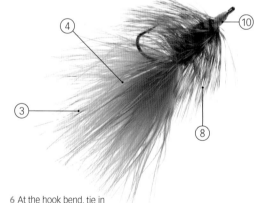

Materials

Hook Mustad Signature C52 S BLN, size 2/0

Thread Danville flat waxed nylon, orange

Weight (optional) Cone head

Tail Ginger marabou

Flash Yellow/pearl Polar Flash

Body Brown/yellow medium chenille

Hackle Yellow grizzly

Weed guard 9.5-kg (20-lb) hard monofilament

How to tie

1 Slide a cone head over the hook point and up to the hook eye (optional).

2 Lay a thread base from the cone head to the hook bend.

3 At the hook bend, tie in ginger marabou as a tail. It should be twice as long as the hook shank.

4 On each side of the tail, tie in ten strands of yellow/pearl Polar Flash.

5 At the hook bend, tie in a grizzly hackle for winding.

6 At the hook bend, tie in yellow/brown chenille and advance the thread to the cone head.

7 Wrap the chenille to the cone head as a body and tie off.

8 Wrap the hackle over the body and tie off at the cone head. Trim the excess.

9 Behind the cone head, tie in a monofilament weed guard that extends the same distance as the hook gape.

10 At the hook eye, make a thread head, whip finish and cement.

Gary Bulla

Gremmie

The Gremmie is an all-round surf fly. It casts easily in the wind and drops quickly into the feeding zone. It imitates shrimp, the pelagic red crab or the bloodworm. It's accounted for catching trout, blue trevally, salmon, redfish and calico, striped and white sea bass.

Captain Gary Bulla, from Santa Paula, California, is one of the California saltwater fly-fishing pioneers. He knew there was great fly-fishing potential for the California corbina, but they seemed impossible to catch on a fly. The old sand crab imitations were not live enough to fool them, so Gary tried marabou and it changed the game entirely. The Gremmie should be fished with straight casts and short 15–30-cm (6–12-in) strips on a 200- to 300- grain sink tip. This pattern is Gary's long-time favourite.

And the name? Back in the day, young wannabe surfers were called gremmies. They covered the water as thickly as the shrimp, crabs and bloodworms, so the name was a natural.

50% size

Length 6.5 cm (2½ in)

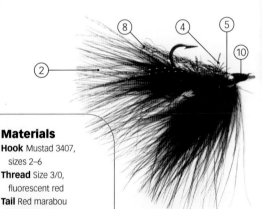

Materials

Hook Mustad 3407, sizes 2–6

Thread Size 3/0, fluorescent red

Tail Red marabou

Tail flash Pearl Krystal Flash

Abdomen Orange yarn

Eyes 2-mm (¹⁄₁₆-in) brass dumbbell eyes

Wing Red marabou tips

Throat Red dyed deer hair

How to tie

1 Lay down a thread base from the hook eye to the hook bend.

2 At the hook bend, tie in a tail of red marabou.

3 At the hook bend, tie in a topping of pearl Krystal Flash.

4 Ahead of the tail, tie in orange yarn and take two turns, forming an abdomen.

5 Ahead of the body, tie in brass dumbbell eyes to the top of the shank, one-third of the way back from the hook eye.

6 Just behind the brass eyes, tie in a wing of red marabou. It should reach just short of the tail. Tie the marabou butts down over the dumbbell eyes and wrap a thread head in front of the brass eyes.

7 Ahead of the brass eyes, tie in two strands of Krystal Flash to lay along each side of the shank.

8 Ahead of the brass eyes, tie in a throat of red deer hair directly behind the hook eye. The deer hair should extend just past the hook bend.

9 Just forward of the eyes, tie in a red marabou feather tip so that it stands straight up. When wet and folded back, the length should be shorter than the wing.

10 Wrap a small red thread head, whip finish and cement.

Charles Crue
Yak Fly

In late August, large sand eels are in the Merrimack River estuary in Massachusetts. Striped bass feed on this bait. Charles Crue created the Yak Fly because yak hair provides the 12.5–18-cm (5–7-in) length needed to imitate this bait.

Materials

Hook Mustad 34011, size 3/0

Thread Danville flat waxed nylon, white

Internal cone and head 3-cm (1¼-in) length of Corsair braid, 1.25 cm (½ in) in diameter

Wing Olive and white yak hair with pearl Krystal Flash

Head 4-cm (1½-in) length of Corsair braid, 1.25 cm (½ in) in diameter

Marker pens Brown and olive

Eyes 6-mm (¼-in) stick-on 3D moulded holographic eyes

Adhesives Superglue and 30-minute epoxy

Equipment Rotating dryer

Charles tried his new Yak Fly, but made a messy cast and ended up with a wind knot to untangle. As he began to work out the knot, his line suddenly took off, pulling the knotted line out of his hand and through the fly rod guides. All he could do was hold onto the rod handle and let the fish fight the drag.

Charles and his friend 'calmly' discussed how to bring this obviously big striper in with a knotted fly line. Gradually the striper tired and Charles was able to get line back to the reel. During a lull in the fight, he cranked the knot onto the reel. Charles was able to bring the fish to the side of the boat. It was a beautiful 90-cm (36-in) striper with his new Yak Fly hanging from its jaw.

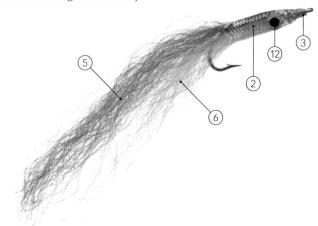

How to tie

1 Wrap a thread base from the hook eye to the hook bend.

2 Tie in a 3-cm (1¼-in) length of Corsair braid behind the eye, with the braid extending over the eye.

3 Push the end of the braid back over the eye so that it rolls over itself. Pinch it down on the hook and tie it down, forming a cone.

4 Put a couple of drops of Superglue on the thread to lock it to the hook shank.

5 Tie in a clump of olive yak hair just ahead of the cone on the bottom side.

6 Tie a clump of white yak hair on the top, distributing the yak hair evenly so that it surrounds the cone.

7 Tie in eight or ten strands of pearl Krystal Flash on each side.

8 Slide a 4-cm (1½-in) length of Corsair braid over the inner cone and yak hair and tie it down just behind the hook

eye to form a bullet-shaped head. Trim any excess braid that covers the hook eye.

9 Put a couple of drops of Superglue on the threads.

10 Colour the top and sides of the braid with brown permanent marker pen.

11 Colour the top with olive permanent marker pen over the brown.

12 Attach stick-on eyes to each side of the braid, just beyond the tapered section of the head.

13 Coat the head with 30-minute epoxy.

14 Put the fly on a rotating dryer to distribute the epoxy.

15 Add a second coat of epoxy after the first is dry.

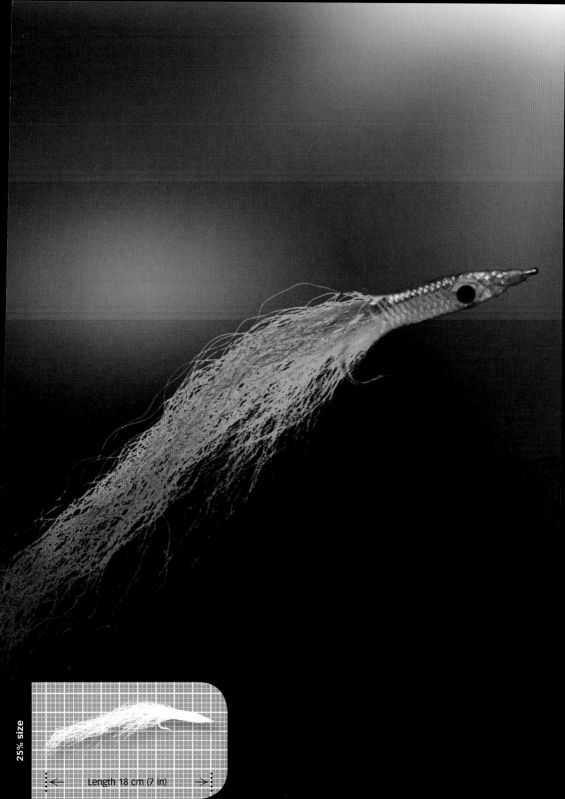

Length 18 cm (7 in)

Wirianto Ng

WN Cobra

We often hear about the everyday benefits of the space programme. Here's a pattern developed from modern materials found in home electronics stores. It results in a bombproof jungle perch fly that defies fish to destroy it.

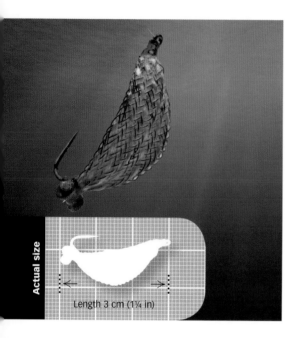

Actual size

Length 3 cm (1¼ in)

Wirianto Ng from Indonesia discovered this sleeve material while window-shopping at an electronics shop. The cable sleeve material is hard, unlike Mylar tubing, but it can be formed just like Mylar tubing.

Once Wirianto arrived home, he started experimenting with it, pressing and twisting the material. Soon he discovered the teardrop shape that is suitable for making a spoon fly. This was his initial pattern, and it worked so well that no improvements were necessary. The only optional step might be the addition of a monofilament loop weed guard for fishing in snag-filled areas.

The action of the fly as it flutters to the bottom is a trigger for this fly. Another feature is the fluorescent finish covering the cable. It will shine in the dark if it is 'charged' with a torch beam prior to casting. This makes for a fly that can be fished in the dark as it gives off its glow.

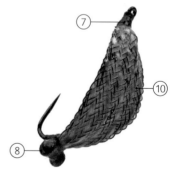

Materials

Hook Gamakatsu Worm 321, size 1
Thread UNI size 3/0, black
Body Silver tinsel and cable sleeve
Head Extra-small dumbbell with eyes painted red
Adhesive Fluorescent Loon Hard Head

How to tie

1 Lay down a thread base from the hook eye to past the hook bend.

2 Tie in silver tinsel at the bend and wrap it to the hook eye. Tie off and trim both the tinsel and the thread.

3 Restart the thread at the bend.

4 Slide the open end of the cable sleeve over the hook eye to the hook bend.

5 Tie the end of the cable down and trim the thread.

6 Pinch the cable between your thumb and first finger to flatten it into a teardrop shape. You may need to push extra cable onto the hook to get the shape you want.

7 At the hook eye, tie in the cable. Trim the excess.

8 On the end of the cable, near the bend, tie on a small dumbbell for the head, using figure-of-eight wraps.

9 Make a small thread head over the cable end. Cement the thread.

10 Apply three coats of fluorescent Loon Hard Head, making sure that each coat dries before the next one is applied.

Greg Morrison

Lead Head Bunker

The Lead Head Bunker works well for stripers, blues, weakfish and fluke. It can be tied 15–30 cm (6–12 in) in length, depending on the size of the bunkers in residence. This pattern fishes well in all water clarities for stripers, but works best in clear to lightly roiled seas for the other species.

Captain Greg Morrison from New Jersey can attribute his prowess with fur and feather to his lineage: Greg's dad is Eddy Morrison, one of the sport's earliest pioneers and an East Coast fly-casting champion in his youth.

The Lead Head Bunker is designed for a quick descent to reach fish that are holding in 4.5–9-m (15–30-ft) depths, and should be used with either full sinking lines or shooting head systems ranging from 350 to 750 grains, depending on tides and rod weights.

Couple your shooting head to a 1.5-m (5-ft) leader in 6.5–9-kg (15–20-lb) test and use a Duncan, Perfection Loop or similar knot to increase the action of this fly. Greg likes to cast out and count down to the desired depth, then begin retrieving with three short strips followed by a roll cast of the fly line retrieved into the basket. Repeat the three strips and roll cast method until the fly reaches the boat or is taken by a gamefish.

25% size

Length 15 cm (6 in)

Materials

Hook Mustad 34011 SS, size 4/0

Thread Monothread

Tail White bucktail and pearl Angel Hair

Body Silver tinsel, white bucktail, blue marabou and red fox tail

Flash Cobalt Flashabou, pearl Angel Hair and polar bear hair

Weight Stainless dumbbell

Marker pens Black and yellow

Sparkle Silver glitter

Adhesive 5-minute epoxy

How to tie

1 Lay down a thread base from the hook eye to the hook bend.

2 At the hook bend, tie in the tail of white bucktail and pearl Angel Hair.

3 At the hook bend, tie in the flat silver tinsel and build the body, wrapping up one-quarter of the way from the hook bend to the hook eye. Do not cut off the tinsel.

4 At the middle of the shank tie in 20-cm (8-in) lengths of white bucktail in equal proportions on the top and

bottom of the hook. This gives a larger profile.

5 Continue wrapping the body tinsel forward towards the hook eye and over the wing.

6 Repeat steps 4 and 5 three-quarters of the way to the eye.

7 Ahead of the body tie in some flash mixture, top and bottom, with more on the top and less on the belly.

8 Ahead of the body, tie in some blue marabou on each side.

9 At this same location, tie in some short red fox tail for gills.

10 Ahead of the body, tie on a stainless dumbbell with painted (yellow/black) eyes.

11 Coat the head with 5-minute epoxy and add silver glitter. Let dry.

Length 20 cm (8 in)

Pedro Pablo Yañez Duran

GT Candy Fire Tiger

Big fish require big flies that can be seen from a distance. The GT Candy Fire Tiger represents a tying technique that results in a thick body easily seen from below. The colours and size can be adapted to imitate baitfish in any location.

Materials

Hook TMC 600 SP, size 8/0

Thread UNI size 3/0 mono thread

Rattle 6-mm (¼-in) Pyrex rattle and 6-cm (2½-in) piece of pearl medium Minnow Body

Tail Electric yellow Slinky Fibers

Core body and belly Blend of electric yellow Slinky Fibers, ice blue/opal Mirage Flashabou, electric yellow Angel Hair

Throat Blend of hot orange Slinky Fibers, fluorescent red EP Sparkle, mirage opal Flashabou

Back Blend of chartreuse Slinky Fibers, fluorescent chartreuse EP Sparkle, ice blue/opal Mirage Flashabou

Back highlights Blend of Polar rainbow black, marine blue and marine green Flashabou

Belly Pre-tapered, blend of 30-cm (12-in) electric yellow Slinky Fibers blended with ice blue/opal Mirage Flashabou

Marker pen Permanent black

Eyes 1.25 cm (½ in) 3D eyes

Adhesive Clear Cure Goo Tack Free

Pedro Duran designed this pattern for giant trevally off the Seychelles, Tonga, New Caledonia and the Cook Islands.

He prefers a 12-weight rod or larger, with 1.8-m (6-ft) leaders of 36–59-kg (80–130-lb) fluorocarbon tippet. A super-high-quality large arbor reel with a powerful break is also required to land these heavy fish.

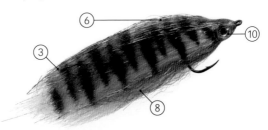

How to tie

Note: Several parts of this fly are made of blended materials. To accomplish this, lay the materials on a sheet of paper in thin layers. Repeat layering three times. Raise one side of the paper, allowing the materials to roll over each other and mix.

1 Cut a 6-cm (2½-in) section of Minnow Body. Make a few tight wraps in one end and introduce the rattle. Tie the front half of the rattle capsule to the middle of the hook shank and cover with a layer of adhesive.

2 Ahead of the capsule, tie in a tail of electric yellow Slinky Fibers completely surrounding the hook shank. The total length of the fly should be 20 cm (8 in).

3 Ahead of the tail and on each side of the hook shank, tie in 40 pieces of blended Flashabou Mirage. Cover the first 6 cm (2½ in) of the tail with adhesive.

4 Form the core body by tying the materials around the hook shank just in front of the tail and one-third of the way back from the hook eye. Brush the fibres with a comb to equally distribute the fibres. Cover the first 6 cm (2½ in) of these fibres with adhesive. Do not trim the ends.

5 Ahead of the core body, form the belly by tying the blend by the centre of the length. Then fold the forward half backward, evenly distributing the materials on each side of the hook bend. Comb the fibres. Do not trim off the butt ends.

6 To form the back, attach a length of the fibre-and-flash blend at its middle with four wraps. Fold back and catch the tip of the fold with four more wraps.

7 Add highlights to the back by tying in the mix of six strands of each highlight material. The highlights should nearly reach the end of the back.

8 On the bottom of the hook shank, tie in the throat mixture so that it reaches slightly more than halfway to the end of the fly.

9 Lay the fly on a flat surface and add a few black marker stripes to create a tiger-stripe pattern. Alternate long and short stripes.

10 Secure the eyes with adhesive. Cover the eyes with thin layers of adhesive to form the head.

Kenji Shrimp Fly

In Java, Indonesia, many people use live shrimp as bait for a simple reason – shrimp are the favourite forage fish for predators anywhere shrimp are found. They are plentiful and easy for barramundi and grouper to catch. The Kenji Shrimp Fly looks alive and has materials that yield a lot of movement.

Materials

Hook Maguro mackerel, size 2/0
Thread Clear 4.5-kg (10-lb) monofilament
Weight Wapsi medium lead eyes
Eyes 45-kg (100-lb) melted monofilament
Marker pen Permanent black
Tail and mouth parts White Slinky Fiber
Legs Black and white banded rubber legs
Flash Krystal Flash
Body Black and white bucktail
Adhesive 5-minute epoxy

Many moulded shrimp patterns use epoxy or other resin-based materials. The Kenji Shrimp Fly does not use epoxy to form the body, so it does not give off any epoxy odour or taste.

Kenji Sekiguchi reports one of his first trials of the Kenji Shrimp. At dusk, he hooked a fish that took off for the open ocean. After ten minutes Kenji's 7-weight rod beat the 3-kg (6½-lb) barramundi without breaking off the 9-kg (20-lb) leader.

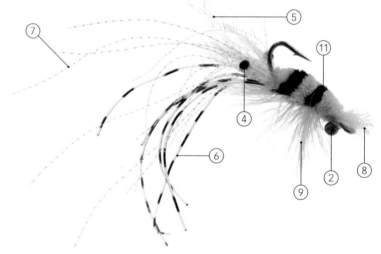

How to tie

1 Lay down a thread base from the hook eye to the hook bend.

2 Behind the hook eye and on top of the hook shank, tie on the lead eyes. Use criss-cross thread wraps and coat the thread wraps with 5-minute epoxy. Wrap the hook shank with the monofilament to the hook bend.

3 Use a flame to melt the ends of two short strands of 45-kg (100-lb) monofilament into a ball. Darken the melted ends with a black permanent marker pen.

4 At the bend, tie in the two monofilament eye stems so that they stick out beyond the hook bend.

5 At the hook bend and between the monofilament eyes, tie in a sparse bunch of white Slinky Fiber sticking out past the hook twice the length of the hook shank.

6 At the same location, tie in six rubber legs long enough to make the overall length of the fly 14 cm (5½ in).

7 At the same location, tie in 15 strands of Krystal Flash

equal to the length of the rubber legs.

8 Advance the thread to the lead eyes and tie in white Slinky Fiber as a tail that sticks out 1.25 cm (½ in) beyond the hook eye.

9 Return the thread to the hook bend and tie in a white hackle. Wrap it forward to the lead eyes and tie off, but do not cut the thread.

10 Bring the thread to the hook bend again without trapping white hackle fibres under the thread.

11 Tie in and spin small bunches of alternating white and black bucktail from the bend to the lead eyes. Whip finish the thread.

12 Trim the bucktail down to a tapered cylinder, making it thin at each end.

Length 14 cm (5½ in)

Audrey Ciurca

AC Pearl Fly

Audrey Ciurca learned to incorporate epoxy into existing patterns, and she decided to combine that with the characteristics of a marlin trolling bait called the Sevenstrand Green Machine. The problem was how to incorporate beads covered by epoxy while keeping it light enough to be fly cast.

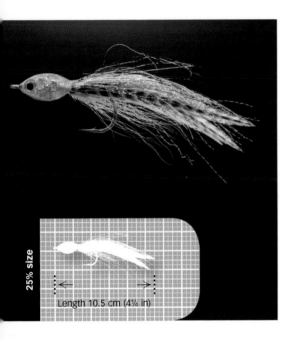

25% size

Length 10.5 cm (4¼ in)

The AC Pearl Fly can be tied in several sizes and colours to match your local baitfish. The two or three drops of alcohol serve two important purposes. First, the alcohol eliminates bubbles. Second, it keeps the epoxy from turning yellow and opaque over time.

The pearls are low density, and for this reason the fly has almost neutral buoyancy. This allows you to make even a slow retrieve without changing the depth of the fly. You can find strung pearls in that last bastion of manly fly-tying supplies – the craft shop.

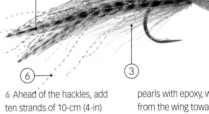

Materials

Hook Mustad 34011, size 2/0
Thread Silver Gudebrod HTA
Head Strung silver 2-mm (¹⁄₁₆-in) plastic pearls
Body White and grey bucktail
Tail Cream and grizzly saddle hackles
Flash Silver Krystal Flash and blue Polar Flash
Eyes Silver with black centre
Adhesives Superglue and 5-minute epoxy (with alcohol added)
Equipment Rotating dryer

How to tie

1 Lay down a thread base from the hook eye to just past the midpoint of the shank.

2 At this location, tie in 10-cm (4-in) white bucktail on top of the shank as the body.

3 At this same location, tie in grey bucktail under the shank.

4 Just ahead of the bucktail, tie in two 12.5-cm (5-in) cream hackles. They should make the fly 10.5 cm (4¼ in) long.

5 Outside of the white hackles tie in two 12.5-cm (5-in) grizzly hackles.

6 Ahead of the hackles, add ten strands of 10-cm (4-in) silver Krystal Flash and ten strands of 10-cm (4-in) blue Polar Flash surrounding the top half of the hook shank.

7 About 1.25 cm (½ in) from the eye, tie in a strand of pearls. Wrapping away from the eye, take four wraps as tightly as possible. Tie off and add Superglue to the hook and the pearls.

8 Add several drops of alcohol to 5-minute epoxy. Work quickly and do not allow the epoxy to harden. Cover the

pearls with epoxy, working from the wing towards the eye. Keep rotating the epoxy to avoid sags.

9 When the head shape is formed but before it hardens, stick the eyes to the epoxy head and also cover the eyes with epoxy.

10 Once you've created a well-shaped head that entirely covers the pearls, remove the fly and place it in a rotating dryer until it sets hard.

Dave McCoy

McCoy's Herring Popper

Herring, when under attack, gather into 'bait balls' so thick that a predator fish may not be able to see your fly. A special design is necessary if you are to successfully entice a predator away from the centre of the bait ball to strike your fly.

This pattern comes from Dave McCoy, owner of Emerald Water Anglers in Seattle. His company guides primarily in Oregon and Washington but regularly hosts trips internationally. Puget Sound is his local saltwater home.

Dave notes that this fly is the product of watching bait balls being crashed on the surface in Puget Sound.

When coho are crashing the surface, they take this fly with reckless abandon – as do other species. What's been taken on this pattern? Albacore tuna off the Oregon coast near Winchester Bay; blues and stripers off the New England coast; barracuda around Andros, Belize and Grand Bahamas; and roosters off Mexico and Costa Rica.

25% size

Length 17.5 cm (7 in)

Materials

Hook Wapsi popper, size 1/0
Thread UNI clear monofilament
Tail White and herring yak hair, silver Gliss'N'Glow, pearl Saltwater Flashabou, chartreuse and white saddle hackles, black and chartreuse schlappen feathers
Body Pencil popper size 2/0 or Edgewater Boiler Maker size 2/0, Delta Ceramcoat or similar acrylic paints in colours of your choice, Delta Sparkle Glaze
Adhesive Zap-A-Gap, 20-minute epoxy or Backcountry Laboratories Hard as Hull

How to tie

1 Wrap a thread base of clear monofilament from the hook eye to the hook bend.

2 Blend equal parts of white and herring yak hair.

3 At the bend, tie in the yak hair. Wrap it forward, stopping 6 mm (¼ in) from the eye. Do not trim the excess.

4 Repeat step 3 with six strands of silver Gliss'N'Glow. Do not trim the excess. Then do the same with two strands of pearl Saltwater Flashabou. Do not trim the excess.

5 At the hook bend, tie in two chartreuse and two white schlappen hackle feathers. Do not trim.

6 Simultaneously wrap both the black and chartreuse schlappen feather bases. Trim.

7 Apply Zap-A-Gap to the front half of the fly materials on the hook shank. Slide a painted popper body onto the shank until it butts up against the palmered schlappen feathers.

8 Using Delta Ceramcoat or similar acrylic paint, paint the body as desired.

9 Paint the entire body with Delta Sparkle Glaze and leave to dry.

10 Coat the entire body with 20-minute epoxy or three layers of Hard as Hull.

Length 3 cm (1¼ in)

Billy Trimble

Mai Tai Crab

Many crabs live in shallow water within oyster beds. Flies used to fish in these situations must not only imitate the natural, but must also be capable of swimming among the hazards and not fouling on the oysters. The Mai Tai Crab's construction also allows it to be fished in grass without hanging up.

Materials

Hook Tiemco 811S, size 6
Thread UTC, 210 denier, black
Cone 2-mm (¹⁄₁₆-in) red Hot Cone
Eyes Black plastic shrimp eyes
Mouth parts Blue saddle hackle
Face Orange Ice Chenille
Claws Red and blue saddle hackle tips
Body Olive- and blue-dyed deer hair

Billy Trimble, from Austin, Texas, developed the Mai Tai Crab for fishing among oyster beds on the coast of Texas. The reason this redfish fly is successful is that it will sit with its point up, and it can crawl carefully through oysters or grass. It can be fished slowly or stripped fast over the top of a grass bed.

The pattern name? Billy noticed (he claims, after only two drinks) that the little umbrellas that came in each drink looked a whole lot like a mud crab, and in that moment he knew he had a name for the pattern.

How to tie

1 Slide a red cone onto the hook, up to the eye.

2 Attach thread at the cone and wrap a thread base to the hook bend.

3 At the hook bend, tie in plastic shrimp eyes so that they stick out at 90 degrees to the hook shank.

4 At the hook bend, tie in one blue saddle hackle by its tip.

5 At the hook bend, tie in orange Ice Chenille, then wrap the chenille around the plastic shrimp eyes in a criss-cross

fashion. Tie off the chenille behind the plastic eyes and trim the excess.

6 Do the same with the saddle hackle, first making a couple of turns of hackle in front of the eyes, on the hook bend side of the eyes, then cross the eyes and tie off. Trim the excess hackle.

7 Next, match up one red and one blue hackle tip. Place the blue hackle on top of the red hackle, so that the blue hackle will be on the inside when tied in. Repeat for the opposite set of claws. The claws should be

about the same length as the hook shank. At the hook bend, tie them in behind the eyes with the tips pointing down. Push the hackles up against the plastic eyes, causing them to stay in place at 90 degrees to the hook shank.

8 Next, invert the fly. Move the thread to the middle of the hook shank and flare a good-sized clump of olive deer hair with evened tips pointing back towards and just covering the point and bend of the hook.

9 Turn the fly back over and flare a clump of blue deer hair on top of the hook shank.

10 Work the thread through the deer hair to the back of the cone and wrap thread up into the cone's cup. Whip finish.

11 Now trim the olive deer-hair butts, leaving the tips covering the hook, and shave the blue deer-hair flat.

12 Work a liberal amount of head cement into the deer hair.

Sean Mills

Pilchard Block Fly

Chumming is the practice of throwing chopped baitfish overboard to attract gamefish close to the boat so that an angler can cast to them. The Pilchard Block Fly has proven its effectiveness in the chumming situation. Now, even the fly fisher can take advantage of this technique.

25% size

Length 9 cm (3½ in)

Sean Mills, from Cape Town, South Africa, says the pilchard block is used offshore of the Western Cape for yellowfin tuna, longfin tuna and blue sharks in the chum line, and is designed to look like a block of pilchard. It sinks very slowly, like the rest of the chum.

Sean has watched yellowfin, bluefin and mako sharks eat in the chum line. Drawing them in is easy. The hard part is landing the fish once they take the fly. He once hooked a mako of about 59 kg (130 lb) on the Pilchard Block fly and he was stunned by its speed. It picked up the fly and Sean set the hook – but for a few seconds it continued eating in the chum line as if nothing was wrong. An instant later, it was 46 m (150 ft) away before it jumped and then was another 46 m (150 ft) further before going deep. After about 15 minutes his leader parted, leaving Sean to marvel at the speed and strength of this species.

Materials

Hook Gamakatsu S112s Trey Combs Big Game, size 8/0

Thread UTC, 140 denier, red

Body 1.25-cm (½-in) white foam block, strip of Mylar stick-on strip

Tail White and brown marabou

Marker pens Blue and red

Adhesives Superglue and clear silicone

How to tie

1 Cut a 1.25- × 5-cm (½- × 2-in) block of white foam.

2 Cut a slit in the foam and Superglue the block onto the hook shank.

3 Fold a strip of stick-on Mylar sheet over and stick it onto both sides of the foam.

4 Add markings with a blue permanent marker pen.

5 Fill the inside of the fly with clear silicone.

6 Push some white and brown marabou into the silicone before it sets up.

7 Colour the marabou with a red permanent marker.

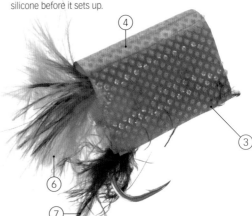

Barrett Brown

Spoon Fly Wobbler

The Spoon Fly is a natural for redfish because the Johnson Spoon is one of the most productive lures used for redfish. The Spoon Fly Wobbler is very flashy, and wobbles back and forth giving off good sound vibration.

Barrett Brown, from Metairie, Louisiana, owns E-Z Fly Guide Service. He credits Jon Cave with 'the spoon fly' pattern. Barrett adapted the pattern in order for it to cope with all the grass found in his local area.

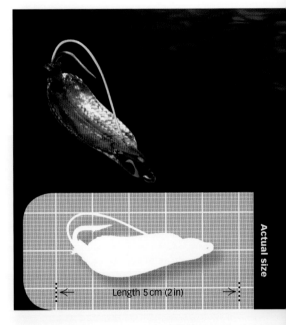

Actual size

Length 5 cm (2 in)

Materials

Hook Mustad #34007, size 1
Weed guard 9-kg (20-lb) hard Mason monofilament
Lead wire 2 mm (1⁄16 in)
Thread Red saltwater, size A
Mylar tubing XL
Epoxy 30-minute
Marker pens Marks-A-Lot
Form Foil leaf
Paint Acrylic
Adhesives Superglue, glue stick and epoxy

How to tie

1 Bend the hook shank behind the eye to a slight upward angle.

2 Wrap the hook shank with thread from the bent angle to below the barb.

3 Tie in the monofilament below the barb so it points away from the hook shank.

4 Make ten wraps of lead wire, starting over the thread behind the eye.

5 Reverse the fly, with the eye of the hook now in the vice jaws.

6 Superglue the foil leaf down the centreline and attach it to the bottom of the hook shank from the bent angle to the monofilament.

7 Coat the foil form with glue stick.

8 Restart the thread at the bent angle.

9 Immediately slide the Mylar tubing over the form. Tie it in at the monofilament.

10 Put two loose wraps around the tubing. While pinching the wraps and tubing with forefinger and thumb, slowly cinch the thread, closing the Mylar around the form. Add loop knots and cut off the thread.

11 Restart your thread in front of the bent angle. Repeat step 10 for the front side.

12 Pull the end of the weed guard through the eye of the hook and fold back over the fly. Put enough wraps over the weed guard to cover well and build up a nice-size thread head.

13 Whip finish, cut the thread off, take the fly out of the vice and use your fingers to shape the Mylar around the form. You need a cupped form to make it wobble.

14 Use your markers to give whatever colouring you want.

15 Mix your epoxy and paint the fly.

16 Let the epoxy dry and paint eyes on the head.

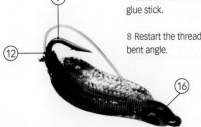

Length 26.5 cm (10½ in)

Brian Thielicke

Pink Frenzy Billfish

When billfish charge a fly, they often slash at it without taking. Flies that get 'billed' are often ruined. Brian Thielicke decided to develop a fly with slick materials that would not be ruined each time a fish slashed at it. His creation has proven itself in many tournaments.

Brian's experience with this tube fly pattern includes four or more sailfish in a single day. The winning team for the Memorial Sailfish Tournament in Costa Rica has also used this fly exclusively the past few years, winning the Best Angler Award in each of the past two years. In addition, the second-place team in the Jake Jordan Sailfish Tournament in Guatemala used this fly in 2011.

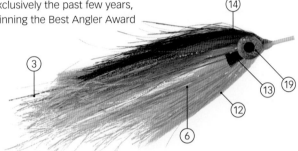

Materials

Tube 7.5-cm (3-in) length of rigid plastic tubing, 3 mm (⅛ in) in diameter

Thread Medium, clear monofilament and white size A flat waxed thread

Body Multiple layers of XXXL pearl Mylar tubing, saltwater magnum silver holographic Flashabou, saltwater pearl Flashabou dyed pink, pearl Lazer Flash

Lateral line Pearlescent Crinkle Mirror Flash

Gills Red Flashabou

Wing Pink Unique Hair

Topping Pink holographic Flashabou

Belly White Unique Hair

Eyes 2-cm (¾-in) pearl 3D eyes

Adhesives Superglue, Softex, Sally Hansen Hard As Nails, hot glue

Marker pen Pink

How to tie

1 Using monofilament, starting at the midpoint of the tube, make a 1.25-cm (½-in) thread base.

2 Tie the body materials above and below the tube, using blunt end cuts and 6-mm (¼-in) thread wraps. This will result in a 'bump' to lift and create a broader profile, both above and below the hook shank.

3 Above the tube tie in 20 cm (8 in) of unravelled pearl Mylar tubing. Note there is no bottom layer for this step.

4 Immediately in front of the last materials and on top of the tube, tie in 20 cm (8 in) of unravelled pearl Mylar tubing.

5 Below the tube, tie in 17.5 cm (7 in) of unravelled pearl Mylar tubing.

6 Repeat step 5 with 20 cm (8 in) of magnum holographic silver Flashabou.

7 Below the tube, tie in 15 cm (6 in) of unravelled pearl Mylar tubing.

8 Repeat step 5 with 17.5 cm (7 in) of pearl Lazer Flash.

9 Below the tube, tie in 12.5 cm (5 in) of unravelled pearl Mylar tubing.

10 Immediately in front of the last materials and on top of the shank, tie in 17.5 cm (7 in) of pearl Flashabou dyed pink.

11 Below the tube, tie in 12.5 cm (5 in) of white Unique Hair.

12 On each side tie in 20 cm (8 in) of pearlescent Crinkle Mirror Flash as a lateral line.

13 On each side, tie in 2.5 cm (1 in) of red Flashabou.

14 Switch to white size A flat waxed thread. Immediately in front of the last materials and on top of the tube, tie in 12.5 cm (5 in) of pink Unique Hair. Above this, tie in 10 cm (4 in) of pink holographic Flashabou.

15 Below the tube, tie in 12.5 cm (5 in) of white Unique Hair.

16 Wrap a small tapered head and coat with Hard as Nails.

17 When dry, colour the top of the thread head pink.

18 Hot glue the 2-cm (¾-in) pearl 3D eyes directly behind the thread head.

19 Coat Softex over the thread head, eyes, and 6 mm (¼ in) behind the eyes.

20 When dry, coat all the Softex areas with Hard As Nails.

Mike Corblies

Weaky Whistler

Dr Frankenstein made his creation from various parts. This fly pattern is also the result of part scavenging, but for a more noble purpose – to entice short-striking weakfish fished by inexperienced fly rod clients.

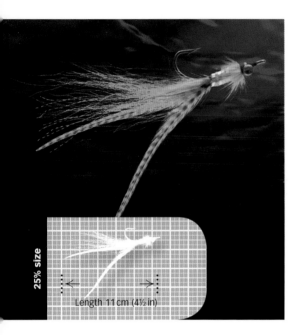

25% size

Length 11 cm (4½ in)

Mike Corblies is the original saltwater fly-fishing captain of the New York/New Jersey metropolitan area. He has set world records and won several tournaments in and around the area. One area in particular, Barnegat Bay, has a strong run of weakfish. It also has a strong run of tourists who would like to catch weakfish on a fly but who lack the experience to hook short-striking fish.

The retrieve method Mike uses with this pattern is to raise the rod tip up to a position pointing at 11 o'clock and then put the line in as he lowers the rod tip down to 8 o'clock. He raises back up to 11 o'clock and repeats the cycle until he has the fly back at the boat. He finishes the last few retrieve strips by pointing the rod tip at the water. This method of following the strip down with the rod tip minimizes the slack in the line on the retrieve, but still imparts the right jigging action.

Weakfish are notorious for short striking. If you think you feel something funny, strike it: you may be pleasantly surprised.

Materials

Hook Stainless steel saltwater, size 2/0
Thread Monothread and Danville flat waxed nylon, red
Tail Yellow 12.5-cm (5-in) grizzly hackles and white bucktail
Tail flash Pink Krystal Flash
Body Pink Estaz
Rib Silver tinsel
Head Gold barbells, medium
Collar Pink hackle feather

How to tie

1 Wrap a monothread base from the hook eye to halfway down the shank.

2 At the end of the thread base, tie in two yellow 12.5-cm (5-in) grizzly hackles, white bucktail and pink Krystal Flash.

3 At the same location, tie in a length of pink Estaz and a length of silver tinsel.

4 Wrap the pink Estaz forward almost to the hook eye as a body. Tie off and trim.

5 Wrap the silver tinsel forward, leaving gaps so that the body material shows through. Trim the excess.

6 Tie the barbells on top of the hook shank slightly behind the hook eye with

monothread, then cover the monothread with red flat waxed nylon thread. Trim the excess threads.

7 Wrap a thread head forward of the dumbbell.

8 Apply a light coat of epoxy to the threads and the body area.

9 Tie in a pink hackle behind the dumbbell eyes and make three wraps. Trim the excess and tie off.

Wills Burger

White Bad Breath

This version of the Bad Breath works quite well as an imitation of small squid and even shrimp. In the warm waters of the Arabian Gulf, it is not uncommon to see squid just lazing about close to, or over, shallow reefs. The White Bad Breath is most successful in bright conditions over a light-coloured bottom.

White Bad Breath sounds really nasty, but don't leave before reading what Wills Burger from Dubai in the United Arab Emirates has to say about this adaptation he developed for trevally and queenfish in the coastal waters of the Arabian Gulf.

Wills has used this fly with great success at the entrance to the port of Ajman, and also at the entrance to the port of Umm Al Quwain. Off the beach at Hamriya, he successfully tempted some groupers over the shallow reefs and then managed to coerce a nice emperorfish on the sandy bottom right next to the reef. In Musandam, the Omani enclave at the northern tip of the Arabian Peninsula, he has also used it with great success in the bays and rocky fjords.

The retrieve should start slow with a smooth movement, gradually increasing the speed and changing the movement to long 'jerks' that imitate the movement of squid when chased. Wills usually gets the most success on long casts, allowing the fish to follow for a long time.

50% size

Length 6 cm (2½ in)

Materials

Hook VMC O'Shaughnessy Classic, size 2

Thread White 2/0

Eyes Medium bead chain

Legs White Super Hair

Body White medium chenille

Adhesive White EZ Sparkle Body

Sparkle Glaze

Adhesive Zap-A-Gap, 20-minute epoxy, or Backcountry Laboratories Hard as Hull

How to tie

1 Starting one-third of the way down the shank length from the hook eye, wrap a thread base that stops three-quarters of the way down the shank and before the hook bend.

2 At this point, tie in the bead chain eyes.

3 Tie in a small bunch of white Super Hair over the eyes and secure the Super Hair to the hook just before the bend. Make the legs as long as the hook shank.

4 Tie in white medium chenille below the eyes and wrap forward, making a tapered body that ends near the hook eye.

5 Whip finish and secure the knot with a dab of white EZ Sparkle Body.

6 Trim the Super Hair to leave a length about equal to the hook length.

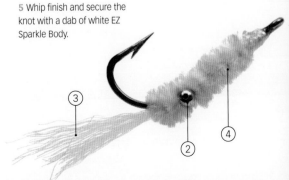

Jim White

White Ghost Squid

Captain Jim White was asked by none other than Lefty Kreh to tie this one to use during an episode of Bass Pro Shop Outdoor World. On that particular day, Jim had Lefty casting to stripers in the 13.6-kg (30-lb) range, right up tight to the shoreline where the bass were herding 17.5-cm (7-in) squid.

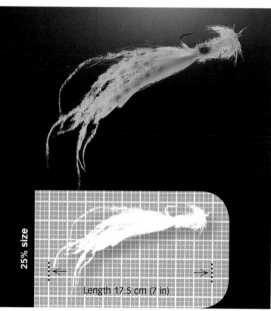

25% size

Length 17.5 cm (7 in)

Jim White, from Coventry, Rhode Island, fishes Narragansett Bay almost exclusively. There are so many areas to fish in the bay that it would take someone years to fish them all. He uses this pattern because the short-fin squid is such a big part of the striped bass' diet.

Jim's clients like this fly because it is easy to cast, relatively lightweight and it has great action. The fly should be fished beneath the surface and stripped in with short, quick strips with a pause in between.

If your arm and elbow don't get tired or start to ache a bit, then you aren't fishing it properly. If you fish it slow and steady, you will cut down dramatically on the number of hits that you get. Squid don't swim slowly when they are frightened or when pursued by a hungry striper or other gamefish.

Materials

Hook Matzuo black/chrome hook, size 4/0
Thread White flat waxed, size 3/0
Tail White bucktail, white hackle feathers and white ostrich plumes
Tail flash Pearl Flashabou
Body Pearl Estaz
Eyes 3-mm (⅛-in) red doll's eyes (with black centres)
Hackle Pink saddle hackle feather
Adhesive 5-minute epoxy
Marker pen Permanent black

How to tie

1 Wrap a thread base from the hook eye to the hook bend.

2 At the hook bend, tie on a small amount of long white bucktail on top of the hook.

3 At the bend, tie on 15 long white ostrich plumes on the top and sides of the hook shank.

4 At the hook bend, tie in four long white hackle feathers (thin) on each side, so that they flare out to the sides.

5 At the hook shank, tie in eight strands of pearl Flashabou equal to the length of the white hackles.

6 At the hook bend, tie in a small amount of long white bucktail over the pearl Flashabou.

7 At the hook bend, tie in a length of pearl Estaz and make a hump to receive the eyes. Wrap the pearl Estaz down to the hook eye, tapering it thinner as it approaches the hook eye.

8 Use 5-minute epoxy to stick the doll's eyes onto the head and the hump made earlier.

9 Palmer a pink hackle feather on the head, just in back of the hook eye.

10 Using a black permanent marker, make dots on the white hackle feathers.

Ed Lepore

Ed's Bonito Bandit

Ed's Bonito Bandit imitates sand eels and silversides found in abundance in the waters around Martha's Vineyard off Massachusetts.

Here's a case where the original fly was a proven producer, but not as durable as it could have been. Ed Lepore, from Martha's Vineyard, Massachusetts, wanted his time at the vice to be better spent, so he made some improvements that resulted in an improved more-fish-per-fly ratio. Now he fishes more and ties less. Sounds good to me.

Ed fishes Middle Ground, West Chop and the North Shore for bonito and bass. He uses this fly with a clear intermediate sinking line. The neutral buoyancy of the materials helps this fly stay suspended, near the quieter waters.

This pattern fishes well both day and night. At night, it's good fished slowly for striped bass when fishing from the beach. Daytime, it works well for bonito, false albacore and bluefish when using a fast retrieve. But, that's not all: it's also responsible for a world record Spanish mackerel on a 5.4-kg (12-lb) tippet.

50% size

Length 7.5 cm (3 in)

Materials

Hook TMC 811S, size 1/0
Thread Danville flat waxed nylon, white
Tail Four thin white saddle hackles
Body White Pearl Bill's Bodi Braid
Belly and wing Sparse white bucktail
Head White thread coated with epoxy
Gills Red tying thread or red Krystal Flash
Eyes Witchcraft 2-mm (1/16-in) silver eyes
Adhesives Head cement, 5-minute epoxy and Dave's Flexament

How to tie

1 Lay down a thread base from the hook eye to the hook bend and coat it with head cement.

2 At the hook bend, tie in a tail of four short white saddle hackles about 1.5 times the shank length.

3 Apply a drop of Dave's Flexament at the base of the hackles. This makes them stiff yet flexible, and stops them from fouling around the hook. Allow to dry.

4 At the hook bend, tie in a strip of pearl Bill's Bodi Braid. Cover the hook shank with

Flexament and then move the thread to the hook eye.

5 Wrap the Bodi Braid forward along the shank to the eye and tie off.

6 Ahead of the body, tie in sparse white bucktail for both the belly and wing. They should be slightly longer than the hook. Build up a thread head with white thread. Cut off the white thread.

7 Switch to red thread and make a narrow wrap between the wing and the thread.

8 Apply a coat of 5-minute epoxy to the thread head. Before it dries, press on two 2-mm (1/16-in) silver eyes.

9 Coat the entire head and the eyes with epoxy.

Length 5 cm (2 in)

Will Casella

Will's Skettel

Will Casella created this fly while he was fishing manager at El Pescador lodge in Belize. He found that no single pattern could consistently catch permit. This was Will's solution.

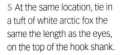

Materials

Hook Gamakatsu saltwater hook, sizes 6–4/0

Thread Clear monothread

Eyes Silver bead chain; 22.6-kg (50-lb) clear monofilament

Feelers Black Krystal Flash

Mouth parts White arctic fox

Legs Pink Flashabou Wiggle Legs

Shell back Any translucent synthetic hair mixed with craft fur

Body Pink Ice Chenille and matching Polar Chenille

Pincers Light pink cross-cut rabbit strips

The fly is excellent on bonefish anytime and anywhere and has proven to be very successful on cruising/schooling Yucatan permit.

How to tie

1 Wrap a thread base from the hook eye to halfway down the hook bend.

2 Tie in bead chain eyes halfway down the hook shank.

3 At the same location, tie in two pieces of 22.6-kg (50-lb) monofilament with the ends melted. The eyes must extend at least half the length of the hook shank past the bend.

4 At the same location, tie two strands of black Krystal Flash out past the bend of the hook.

5 At the same location, tie in a tuft of white arctic fox the same the length as the eyes, on the top of the hook shank.

6 On each side of the monofilament eyes, tie in one Wiggle Leg a little longer than the length of the hook shank.

7 At the hook bend, tie the shell back onto the top of the hook with the material sticking out past the hook bend.

8 Turn the hook over in the vice.

9 At the hook bend, tie in the pink Ice Chenille and make one wrap. Trim the excess.

10 At the hook bend, tie in a 10-cm (4-in) piece of pink Polar Chenille. Do not trim the excess.

11 Cut two 2-cm (¾-in) wide pieces of rabbit strip. Tie one on each side of the hook next to the Polar Chenille, so that the grain is pointing towards the hook eye with the leather side facing out. Do not trim.

12 Wrap the Polar Chenille up to the bead chain eyes, tie off, and trim the excess.

13 Tightly pull one piece of rabbit strip towards the hook eye. Separate the fibres to a length just short of where the weighted eyes are and tie off. Repeat with the other piece of rabbit strip.

14 Cut another 2-cm (¾-in) wide piece of rabbit strip. Tie in on top of the bead chain eyes in the same reverse way as the other pieces of rabbit.

15 Turn your hook so that the point is facing up.

16 Fold back the shell back and place a few half hitches behind the bead chain eyes. This is the carapace. Do not trim off.

17 In front of the bead chain eyes, make a few thread wraps over the shell back to create a segmented tail section.

18 Turn the hook so that the point is again facing down.

19 Pull the rabbit strip tight and tie off right before the hook eye. Trim the excess.

20 Make another tail section segment in front of the hook eye. Bend the shell back over the hook eye and make a few wraps to secure the fibres, with the fibres facing out from the bottom of the fly (top of the hook). This will be the tail.

21 Tie off the thread and cement the wraps.

22 Trim the synthetic fibres of the tail to approximately 6 mm (¼ in). This will be the flipping tail section of a shrimp.

23 Trim the back three-quarters of the rabbit strip that lies on top, so that it is parallel to the hook shank.

24 Repeat the same process with the rabbit strips on the side of the hook, but leave the guard hairs in on the 6 mm (¼ in) closest to the hook end to act as pincers.

25 Trim the Krystal Flash feelers so that they are a bit longer then the legs.

Length 10 cm (4 in)

Wirianto Ng

WN Fast'n'Furious

After successfully experimenting with woven bodies for smaller flies, Wirianto Ng wanted to try the same technique with a streamer. The result is an indestructible fly that will stand up to the teeth of major saltwater predators.

Materials

Hook Tiemco TMC811S, size 4
Thread Danville 210 denier, chartreuse
Eyes Extra-small dumbbell eyes, painted black
Tail Chartreuse bucktail
Body Luminous Rainbow Sheet, gold tinsel, fluorescent chartreuse rabbit zonker strip, red rabbit zonker fur
Rib Gold tinsel and 9-kg (20-lb) monofilament
Flash White Glow Flashabou
Glue Phosphorescent Loon Hard Head

Wirianto uses this pattern for barramundi, Indo-Pacific tarpon and jungle perch. He is confident that other species such as mangrove jacks, threadfin salmon and grouper will also take his Fast'n'Furious. His fishing areas include Indonesia and Malaysia. He fishes mangrove areas, estuaries and brackish rivers. He reports that the success of this pattern is due to its action in the water and to the glowing materials that allow it to be used in the dark. Wirianto recommends casting to where strong currents enter mangrove areas. He uses a combination of fast and slow strips, interspersed with pauses. Another method is to cast directly to tarpon feeding on baitfish at the surface.

How to tie

1 Lay down a short thread base behind the hook eye.

2 On top of the hook shank and next to the hook eye, tie on the lead eyes.

3 Lay down a thread base to the bend of the hook.

4 At the bend, tie in a small bunch of chartreuse bucktail as a tail. The tail should be three times the length of the hook.

5 Cut a strip of Luminous Rainbow Sheeting 1.25 cm (1 in) wide. Tie it in at the hook bend.

6 At the bend, tie in a length of gold tinsel.

7 At the bend, tie in two lengths of 9-kg (20-lb) monofilament.

8 Advance the thread to the dumbbell eyes.

9 Wrap the tinsel with open wraps to the eyes. Trim the excess.

10 Wrap the Luminous Rainbow Sheeting strip next to the tinsel without covering it. Trim the excess.

11 Counter-wrap one length of monofilament over the body to the eyes. Trim and tie down one piece of monofilament. Leave one piece for later use.

12 Cut a 5-cm (2-in) strip of fluorescent chartreuse rabbit zonker strip. Pierce the hook point through the end of the zonker strip.

13 Pull the zonker strip over the body to the eyes. Secure it with thread wraps.

14 Wrap the remaining length of monofilament over the zonker strip with four turns, and secure the monofilament with thread at the lead eyes.

15 At the hook eye and under the hook, tie in two strands of Glow Flashabou on each side of the fly. Trim them to slightly longer than the bucktail.

16 Ahead of the eyes, tie in a bunch of red zonker fur cut from the zonker strip.

17 Build a thread head and whip finish. Coat the head threads with Loon Hard Head.

Randy Sigler

Yak Attack

Unlike some other materials, less is more with yak hair. The material has great body and seems to fish best when it is very translucent. The bottom line is that the Yak Attack is a classic 'guide's fly'. It is fast to tie, uses inexpensive materials, has outrageous durability and, most importantly, the fish love it.

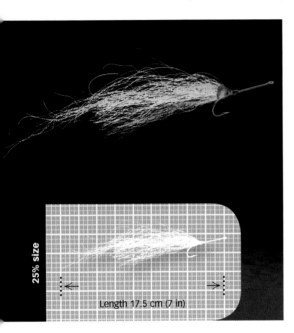

25% size

Length 17.5 cm (7 in)

Guides are often expected to provide flies for clients. This can require lots of time at the vice unless a solution is found. According to Captain Randy Sigler, his hectic lifestyle, combined with high-volume fly usage, created a need for an attractive, durable, easy-to-tie fly pattern. His needs have been met in spades with the Yak Attack. If you tie it as described, you won't need a wire leader.

Materials

Hook Muslad 34007, size 1/0
Thread Olive Big Fly
Wing Dark green yak hair over chartreuse over white
Flash A few strands of sparkle between wing layers
Eyes 1.25-cm (½-in) holographic eyes
Adhesives Superglue and 5-minute epoxy
Equipment Rotating dryer

How to tie

1 Start a thread base three-quarters of the way towards the hook bend and apply a drop of Superglue to help bind it to the hook.

2 At this location, tie in a small bunch of white yak hair. (The length of the yak hair is up you: it can be just past the bend or 25 cm (10 in) beyond. Tie off with strong pressure at the head. Place a drop of Superglue over the wraps.

3 At the same location, tie in six strands of your favourite flash material over the white wing.

4 At the same location, tie in a smaller bunch of chartreuse yak hair above the flash. Keep the thread wraps confined to the front of the fly. Apply a drop of Superglue to the thread wraps.

5 Repeat step 2 with some yellow, green or chartreuse flash.

6 At the same location, top the fly with a bunch of dark green yak hair. Use firm pressure on your thread wraps.

7 Whip finish the head and again apply a drop of Superglue.

8 Creating the head is a two-step process with epoxy. A rotating dryer is helpful in that it allows you to make more than two or three flies at a

time. Mix up some 5-minute epoxy and dab some through the yak hair, just behind the thread wraps. Allow it to dry for about four minutes until the epoxy is starting to firm up and has just lost its tackiness. Hang the fly upside down while the epoxy hardens so that the wing is being pulled down, creating a broader profile.

9 When the epoxy is almost dry, place an eye on each side of the fly and pinch the epoxy so that it flattens out and up, giving the fly a broad, flat, vertical profile. Let the epoxy dry fully.

10 Once the first coat of epoxy is fully dry, mix another batch and give the fly a second coat to form a nice, smooth, round tapered head.

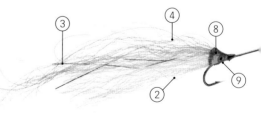

Fabrice Boucher

Crystal Gurgler

Fabrice Boucher owns Aspe Angler Fly Shop and Guiding Service in the western Pyrenees of southwestern France. As a professional guide, he had to find a way to bring success to his clients in a heavily fished area known as the oyster park.

Fabrice noticed that the sea bass were striking traditional gurglers short when they were feeding on small, translucent baitfish. He knew he needed a more realistic imitation. He selected Ice Dub because it is translucent. He also discovered Crystal Foam, which is used to package electronic equipment and is especially light and flexible.

When fish are feeding over oyster beds, the water's depth may be only a few inches. A heavier fly would spook the feeding fish. The Crystal Gurgler is so light that it lands softly and does not frighten the sea bass away.

The characteristics of the Crystal Gurgler are such that it will attract sea bass from a great distance, even when the water surface is glass-flat. Landing softly, it will not put sea bass down.

50% size

Length 7 cm (2¾ in)

Materials

Hook O'Shaughnessy style, size 1
Thread UNI size 3/0, white
Tail White yak hair
Tail flash Pearl Crystal Flash
Gurgler top Crystal Foam
Body Pink Ice Dubbing

How to tie

1 Wrap a thread base from the hook eye to the point above the barb.

2 At this location, tie in a small bunch of white yak hair so that the total length of the fly is 7 cm (2¾ in).

3 At this same location, tie in four pieces of pearl Crystal Flash the same length as the yak hair.

4 At this same point, tie in an 8-mm (⅜-in) wide strip of Crystal Foam so it hangs out over the hook bend.

5 At this same point, dub a length of pink Ice Dubbing. Wrap it forward to the hook eye. Tie it down and trim the excess.

6 Pull the Crystal Foam over the top of the body and tie it in at the hook eye. Trim it so there is a short section sticking up and out over the hook eye.

7 Make a small thread head, whip finish, and cement the thread wraps.

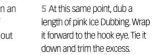

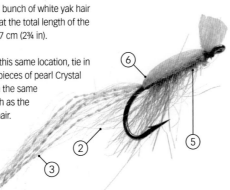

Joe Mattioli

Virtual Bunker Chartreuse

Here's a pattern that's obviously the real deal. It's a big fly designed for big fish and cast with a big rod. Big fish prefer a full meal, not a snack. If your imitation is to be successful, it has to ring the dinner bell. What's the big deal? Read on.

Materials

Hook Owner 5111-181 offset hook, size 8/0

Thread 4.5-kg (10-lb) monofilament

Tail and body White Slinky Hair

Wing and head Chartreuse Slinky Hair

Throat Pink Slinky Hair

Body accent Pearl Sparkle Flash

Sides Silver Polar Flash

Eyes 1.25-cm (½-in) 3D prismatic eyes

Adhesives Goop and 5-minute epoxy

Captain Joe Mattioli, from Staten Island, New York, reports that Raritan Bay receives large schools of menhaden every spring, and striped bass love them. Here's his medicine for fooling stripers virtually every time.

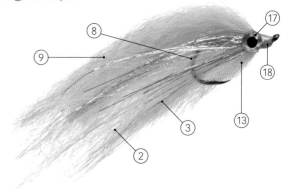

How to tie

1 Starting at the hook eye, wrap the hook shank with a 1.25-cm (½-in) monofilament thread base.

2 At the same location, tie in a tail made of one clump (about the diameter of a pencil) of 17.5-cm/7-in white Slinky Hair.

3 At the same location, tie in the body accent made of one clump of 17.5-cm (7-in) pearl Sparkle Flash.

4 At the same location, tie in one clump of 15-cm (6-in) white Slinky Hair.

5 At the same location but under the hook shank, tie in one 15-cm (6-in) clump of white Slinky Hair.

6 Ahead of the tail, tie in the mid-wing top made of one clump of 12.5-cm (5-in) chartreuse Slinky Hair.

7 At the same location, tie in the bottom of the mid-wing on the bottom of the hook shank made from one clump of 12.5-cm (5-in) white Slinky Hair.

8 At the same location, add the body accent flash to the bottom of the hook shank, using half a clump of 12.5-cm (5-in) pearl Sparkle Flash.

9 At the same location, tie in the wing top made of one clump of 10-cm (4-in) chartreuse Slinky Hair.

10 At the same location but on the bottom of the hook shank, tie in the wing bottom made of one clump of 10-cm (4-in) white Slinky Hair.

11 Just behind the hook eye, tie in one clump of 12.5-cm (5-in) chartreuse Slinky Hair, in front of the wing top. Tie it in so that 7.5 cm (3 in) hangs over the hook eye and then fold it over and tie it down.

12 At the same location, tie in one clump of 7.5-cm (3-in) white Slinky Hair in front of the wing bottom.

13 At the same location, tie in a throat made of one clump of 7.5-cm (3-in) pink Slinky Hair.

14 With scissors, finish shaping the entire fly to obtain the desired profile.

15 At the same location, tie in one clump of 22.5-cm (9-in) Silver Flash at the eye of the hook.

16 Repeat step 13 for the other side.

17 Use Goop to stick on the 3D prismatic eyes and leave to dry.

18 Epoxy between the eyes and then cover the entire head wrappings.

25% size

Length 22.5 cm (9 in)

Eric Wallace

Captain Eric's Flat Wing Herring

Captain Eric Wallace needed an effective striper and bluefish fly for a specific situation involving spawning forage fish. This is what he developed.

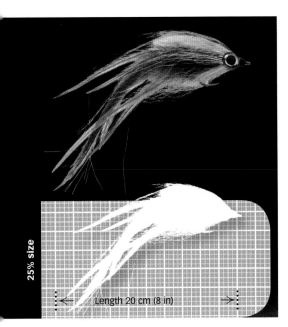

25% size

Length 20 cm (8 in)

This fly was tied to have a lot of action and flash. Eric fishes it with a couple of short quick strips, then long pauses, hoping it looks like a dying baitfish. Get it down deep and work it slowly. If you want to fish it in shallower water, lose some of the flash and go a little smaller on the eyes. Replace the purple with olive and you have a Flats Deceiver.

Match the fly's colour to your local needs. Remember that when baitfish are just coming in from the sea they are bright, but they quickly start to brown or yellow out after spending time in brackish water.

When big baitfish are just entering the river to spawn, they ball up, and stripers are there to work them over. The bait ball could run deep, and often it's in the lower water column that you will find the larger feeders.

Materials

Hook Gamakatsu SC15, size 3/0
Thread Fine monofilament
Tail Long, thin, purple saltwater hackles and Flashabou Mirage
Body Flashabou
Belly White and purple bucktail and some Flashabou Mirage
Wing Purple bucktail, with black DNA Holo Fusion as a topping
Eyes Prismatic silver moulded eyes
Adhesive Epoxy

How to tie

1 Lay down a thread base from the eye of the hook to the bend.

2 At the bend, make a body/tail by tying in long, thin, purple saltwater hackles and Flashabou Mirage.

3 Ahead of the body, tie in some Flashabou Mirage the same length as the hackles.

4 At the same point, tie in some white and then purple bucktail as a belly. Add some Flashabou Mirage.

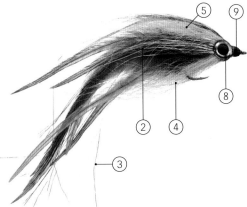

5 Tie in a wing of purple bucktail.

6 Top the wing with some black DNA Holo Fusion.

7 Make a thread head.

8 Cement the moulded eyes in place with epoxy.

9 Wrap a thread head and coat the head wraps with epoxy.

Gene Dickson

Copperhead

This pattern comes courtesy of Gene Dickson, from Georgetown, South Carolina. This fly was originally tied just because redfish seem to like gold or copper – the colours found in the Johnson Gold Spoon and other flies that are like it.

One of this fly's endearing qualities is that when you wet it, it seems to stick together and it casts really well. But when you put it in the water, it 'fluffs' back out into a large profile. As you strip and stop the retrieve, the body seems to pulse; Gene believes this makes it appear more lifelike.

As for the reds, Gene normally uses medium or large dumbbell eyes to get the fly to sink more rapidly. Redfish spend most of their time looking down for their meals, so it makes sense to keep the bait on or near the bottom.

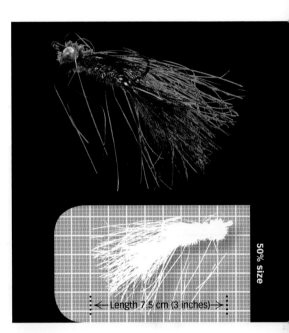

50% size

←— Length 7.5 cm (3 inches) —→

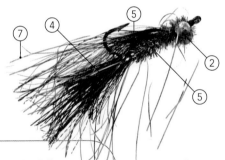

Materials

Hook Gamakatsu SC15, size 1/0 or 2/0

Thread UNI size 6/0, brown

Eyes Medium chrome dumbbell eyes

Tail Copper Flashabou

Body Copper Crystal Chenille

Underwing Copper K-flash

Wing Copper Flashabou

How to tie

1 Lay down a thread base from the eye of the hook to the hook.

2 Wrap the thread forward and lay the dumbbell eyes onto the top of the shank, Clouser style. Attach the eyes by wrapping thread in a figure-of-eight pattern around the hook shank and eyes.

3 Apply a generous amount of your favourite head cement to the thread wraps.

4 Wrap the thread back to the bend of the hook. Cut ten strands of copper Flashabou about 2.5 cm (1 in) in length.

Attach the Flashabou for the tail and apply more head cement to your wraps.

5 At the bend, tie in a 7.5-cm (3-in) strand of copper Crystal Chenille and wrap the thread forward to the back of the eyes. Wrap the chenille forward to just behind the eyes. Tie it off. Leave the remaining chenille hanging for use later.

6 Turn the hook upside down.

7 Cut ten 7.5-cm (3-in) strands of copper K-flash. Tie in the strands of K-flash just behind the eyes.

8 Cut 20 7.5-cm (3-in) strands of copper Flashabou and tie them in just behind the eyes.

9 Advance the thread ahead of the eyes.

10 Wrap the remaining Crystal Chenille twice behind the eyes and then in a figure-of-eight over the eyes. Finish by taking two wraps in front of the eyes. Trim the excess.

11 Whip finish and cement.

Justin Sander

Pink Moe Joe

The Pink Moe Joe mimics nothing in nature, but is suggestive of any generic, small baitfish. It works wonders on pink salmon in the Pacific Ocean near British Columbia.

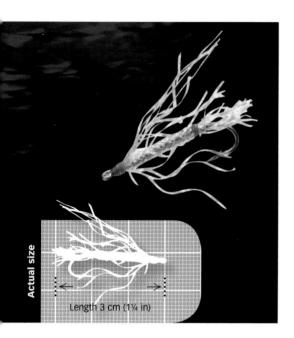

Actual size

Length 3 cm (1¼ in)

Justin Sander is a fly designer for Sandpiper Fly Fishing. He believes that the Pink Moe Joe is effective because of its pink colour, tons of flash and a sleek profile that suggests any number of small baitfish upon which the pink salmon feed.

Justin fishes this fly pattern when the pink salmon are starting to run in middle to late July and into August. It is equally effective whether fished from shore, from a boat, in the open water or at the mouth of a river. In any situation, it is fished with a slow retrieve.

He recalls fishing one evening after dinner, just to work for a few minutes on his casting. A seal surfaced not far from where his fly landed in the water. The seal was busy chasing fish. The next thing Justin knew, he had a good strike and reeled in a nice-sized pink salmon. That convinced him to continue fishing until the sun set.

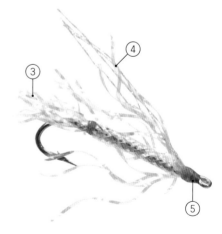

Materials

Hook Tiemco 777 SP, sizes 6 and 8
Thread Pink 6/0
Underbody Pink floss
Tail Pearl Super Weave Mylar Piping
Overbody Pearl Super Weave Mylar Piping
Collar Pearl Super Weave Mylar Piping – unwoven

How to tie

1 Tie thread in at the bend of the hook.

2 Tie in pink floss at the bend. Wrap it forward almost to the eye, then wrap it back to the tie-in point, making an underbody. Tie off and trim the excess.

3 Cut a length of pearl Super Weave Mylar Piping twice as long as the hook shank. Slide the piping over the hook eye and over the underbody to beyond the bend of the hook. Unravel a short section, making a short tail. Tie it down, whip finish and cut the thread.

4 Reverse the piping so that it turns inside out and forms a collar around the hook shank. Tease the piping apart so that the filaments form the collar. The collar should extend to the end of the tail.

5 Tie in the thread 6 mm (¼ in) from the hook eye and cover the forward section of the piping.

6 Wrap a thread head, whip finish and cement to hold it in place.

George Harris

Super Fly Alewife

Captains can't spend too much time at the vice – it cuts into tavern time. Here's a workhorse pattern that takes less than five minutes to tie and works very well.

This fly is an early-season workhorse on the St George and Kennebec Rivers in Maine. When the alewives and blueback herring are running thick in the rivers, this is the fly that 'matches the hatch' for feeding stripers.

It's from Captain George Harris of Warren, Maine. He uses it off Maine and Florida. No reason to think it wouldn't work at all points in between.

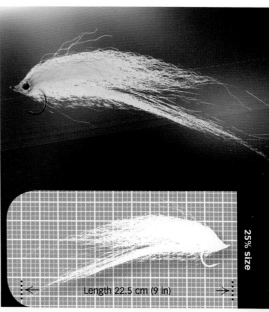

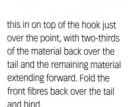

Length 22.5 cm (9 in)

25% size

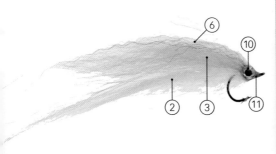

Materials

Hook Gamakatsu Finesse Wide Gap, size 3/0

Thread Danville 0.1-mm (0.006-in) fine monofilament (clear)

Tail wing Lavender over white polar Ultra Hair

Top wing Metz Flash 'N Slinky (seaweed over light purple over light pink)

Bottom wing White Metz Flash 'N Slinky

Flash Pearl Fire Fly

Eyes Gold prism eyes

Head Sally Hansen Hard As Nails and 5-minute epoxy

Adhesive Goop

How to tie

1 Start a thread base over the barb of the hook.

2 Take a sparse bunch of white polar Ultra Hair and trim it to 20 cm (8 in). Tie it in on top of the hook shank, just over the barb of the hook.

3 Tie in a bunch of lavender Ultra Hair the same size and length as the first over the white fibres. Apply head cement to the thread wraps.

4 Tie in a dozen strands of pearl Fire Fly flash over the Ultra Hair.

5 Move the thread to over the hook point. Take a bunch of light pink Flash 'N Slinky. Tie this in on top of the hook just over the point, with two-thirds of the material back over the tail and the remaining material extending forward. Fold the front fibres back over the tail and bind.

6 Repeat step 5 with a slightly shorter pinch of light purple Flash 'N Slinky, tying it in just forward of the previous bunch. At this point, your thread should be roughly 6 mm (¼ in) behind the eye of the hook.

7 Take a slightly shorter bunch of seaweed Flash 'N Slinky and repeat step 6.

8 Turn the fly upside down. Take a 12.5-cm (5-in) bunch of white Flash 'N Slinky. Find the middle and tie it in, with half the material on one side of the fly and the other pulled back down the other side of the fly. This forms the belly.

9 Build a thread head and whip finish.

10 Place a dab of Goop on the back of each prism eye and stick them in place.

11 Mix a small amount of 5-minute epoxy and coat the thread head and eyes.

Useful information

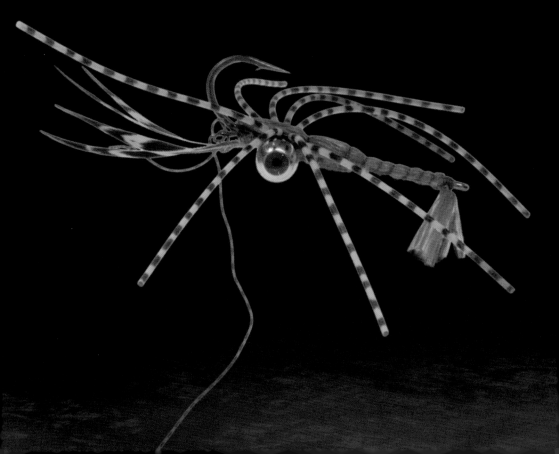

Starting and finishing techniques

There are a number of basic techniques common to the majority of fly patterns, primarily the methods used for starting and finishing a fly. Casting a fly can be tough on the materials secured around the hook, and many gamefish are equipped with enough teeth to do a fly a great deal of damage. For this reason, it is important to know how to start a fly off properly and, more importantly, how to finish it so that it stays in one piece. There is little point in going to all the trouble of creating an elaborate and beautifully tied fly for it to unravel after only a few casts.

Unless otherwise stated, always begin a fly with tight, close turns of tying thread to build a solid base onto which the various materials can be secured. Then, when all the materials have been added, complete it with a strong, secure whip finish.

In the following sequences, a large hook and thick thread have been used to help illustrate the techniques.

Fixing the hook in the vice

The hook must be held firmly and securely before you begin tying. In the past, tiers used their fingers to hold the hook, but today it is recognized that using a specially designed vice is the best method of achieving stability.

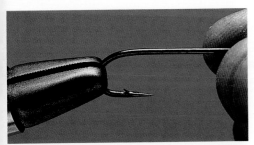

1 Adjust the vice so that the gap between the jaws is slightly greater than the thickness of the hook.

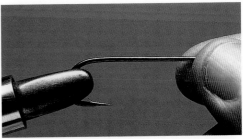

2 Slip the hook bend into the jaws, holding the hook so that the shank is perfectly horizontal.

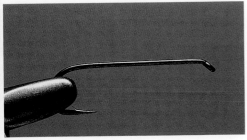

3 Tighten the vice jaws around the hook. If you are using a vice with a lever-action, push the lever down firmly.

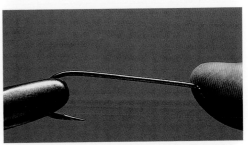

4 Check that the hook is held firmly by lightly depressing it. If it can still be moved up and down slightly, then the jaws require further tightening

Attaching the tying thread

When tying most flies, the tying thread not only binds the materials onto the hook, it also forms a solid base for those materials. Smooth metal hooks don't offer a lot of grip, so to stop the dressing from sliding along the shank, close thread turns are first applied. The thread is usually run on just behind the eye, then wound in close turns along the hook shank. The thread itself is normally fed from its spool, using a purpose-designed bobbin holder. The thread colour is usually chosen to match the main body of the fly. However, it is sometimes chosen to contrast and stand out if it is being used to tie a bright head or thorax.

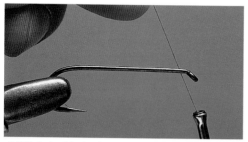

1 With the hook in the vice, hold the tying thread on the far side of the hook with the loose end above the shank and the bobbin holder below.

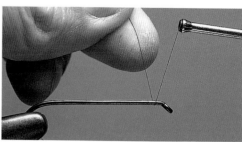

2 Holding the loose end tight, bring the bobbin holder in front of and above the shank to form a V-shape.

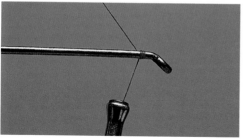

3 While still holding the loose end of the thread upright and tight, begin to wind the bobbin holder end of the thread down the shank.

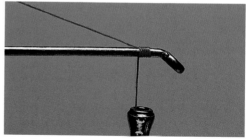

4 As the thread is wound down the shank, it will begin to cover the loose end, locking it in place.

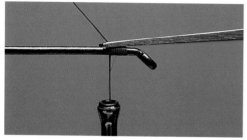

5 After five or six turns of thread have been made, the loose end of the thread will be secure. Put the bobbin holder down and trim the waste end of the thread.

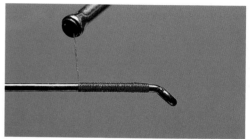

6 Continue winding the thread down the shank, feeding it from its spool with the bobbin holder. Close turns will form the required base.

Whip finish

Once the fly is complete, it is important that the thread is cast off properly. The whip finish is a secure method for finishing off a fly. It involves forming a series of slipping loops that are pulled tight over the loose end of the thread, locking it in place. On very small flies, a three-turn whip finish is usually adequate, but on larger patterns, especially where thick threads are used, five turns give a more secure finish. It is possible to produce a whip finish with the fingers alone, but many tiers use a specially designed tool called a whip-finish tool (see page 11). The tying thread is positioned over the tool's hook and the loop is then wound perfectly around the fly hook.

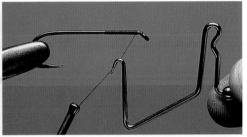

1 With the tying thread positioned just behind the eye, feed a short length of the thread off the bobbin. Hold the thread tight and place the front hook of the whip-finish tool over it.

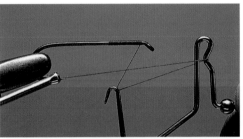

2 Feed through more thread and pass it around the back of the tool's arm. Loop the thread around the arm and carry it back in a line parallel to the hook shank.

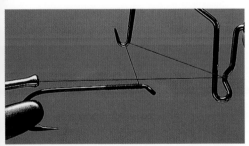

3 Retaining tension on the thread at all times, flip the tool over so that both it and the loose end of the thread are above the hook and form a figure four.

4 Rotate the whip-finish tool. The first couple of turns are the most important, because these hold the loose end of the tying thread against the hook. Five turns are normally made, but one or two more are perfectly acceptable.

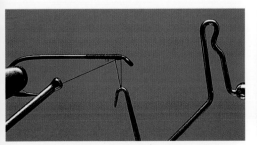

5 Once the required number of turns has been made, the loop must be drawn tight. Carefully flip the thread off the rear arm, retaining tension with the front hook. Pulling the bobbin end of the thread closes the loop.

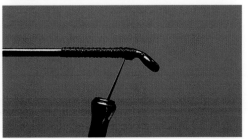

6 Continue pulling the bobbin end of the thread until the loop is almost closed and the tool's hook is tight against the hook shank. Remove the hook and pull the thread tight. The loose end can now be removed.

Forming the head

The base for a head is created by adding repeated turns of thread to build a neat, slightly tapered profile. Once the whip finish has been made, coats of lacquer are added to the turns, both to protect them and to form a shiny, aesthetically pleasing finish to the fly. Various colours of lacquer can be used, but the more usual colours are black or clear. Clear allows the colour of the thread to come through and won't discolour the materials closest to the head.

Lacquer is normally applied in one to three coats. The more coats are used, the shinier the effect.

1 Complete the dressing for the fly. Use the tying thread to cover the roots of the wing and build up a neat, slightly tapered profile. Cast off the thread with a whip finish.

2 Apply a drop of clear lacquer with a dubbing needle to the head. Always apply in small drops to avoid it running. Allow the lacquer to soak into the turns, then leave it to dry.

3 Use the point of a dubbing needle to apply black lacquer to the head. Make sure that the coloured lacquer does not bleed into the surrounding materials. Allow to dry.

4 Once again, use the point of a dubbing needle to add clear lacquer to make the third coat, making sure that the lacquer is spread evenly over the head.

5 Before the head dries, run a short length of nylon monofilament through the eye. This ensures that the eye remains unblocked and means that the fly can be tied on easily when waterside.

6 Remove the fly from the vice and leave to dry overnight.

Dubbing

Dubbing is the application of fur to the tying thread. The yarn that dubbing creates is then wound over the hook shank to form the body or thorax of the fly. The finer the fur, the easier it is to grip onto the tying thread. Getting coarse furs to stick can be a problem, but there are two ways to alleviate this. The first is to apply a thin coat of beeswax to the tying thread before offering the fur up to it. The wax acts as an adhesive, though the application should always be sparing. The second is to make sure that the direction of the dubbing fibre is well mixed so that the fibres mesh together and are less likely to fall in line with the thread.

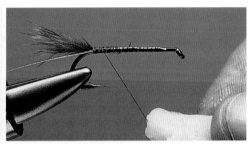

1 With the tying thread positioned to the rear of the hook, and with any tail and ribbing materials already added, apply a thin coat of beeswax to the thread.

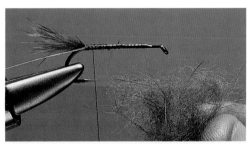

2 Take a small pinch of fur, in this case muskrat – enough to cover the tip of one finger. Tease it out slightly.

3 Offer the fur up to the tying thread and spread it thinly along a short length. Make sure the spread is even and that there are no thick spots.

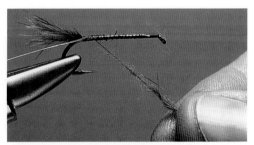

4 Begin to twist the fur between finger and thumb. As you do so, the fur will begin to compact, at the same time gripping onto the thread. Always twist in the same direction, otherwise the fur will not adhere to the thread.

5 Continue twisting, creating the required yarn as you do so. Try to achieve a slight taper to the rear of the yarn, the end nearest the hook, so that the finished body will increase in thickness towards the front end.

6 Wind the dubbing in close turns so that it covers the hook shank. If the pattern has a wing, stop well back from the eye to allow space for the other materials to be added.

Winging loop

When tying in a winging material, whether feather or hair, it is important that the finished wing sits straight and directly on top of the hook shank, to ensure that the fly swims straight when it is pulled through the water. However, there is a tendency for the wing to twist as it is being tied in, caused by the dragging action of winding the thread. The winging loop is the technique used to alleviate this problem. A loose turn of thread is wound over the wing's base, then carried around in the normal way until it is directly below the hook shank. Only at this point is it pulled straight down and tight onto the wing.

1 Position the tying thread at the eye and collect the wing materials. Here, the body and hackle have been omitted to help illustrate the method clearly.

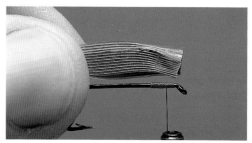

2 Make sure the slips are of equal width and place them so that the tips are level. Hold the slips so that the butts are over the eye and the tips project just past the hook bend.

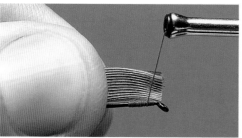

3 drop the slips so that they sit on top of the hook. Raise the tying thread above the wing slips so that it forms a straight line in front of them.

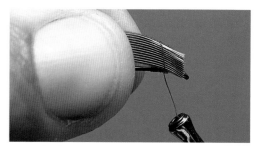

4 Keeping the tying thread loose, drop it behind the wing slips. Do not pull the thread tight at this point but position it directly beneath the hook shank and wing.

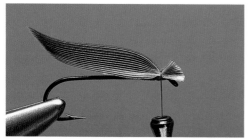

5 Still holding the wing slip in place, pull the thread tight in a straight, downward motion. This will compress the wing fibres directly onto the top of the hook. Remove the fingers and check the wing position.

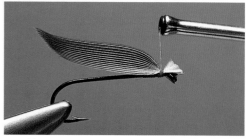

6 Add two more winging loops to make sure that the wing doesn't twist, then fix the wing in place with normal, tight thread wraps.

Forming a collar hackle

A collar hackle is used on many types of flies. Even where other styles of hackle are employed – such as a throat hackle – the base is often still a collar hackle. Therefore, it is important to have a basic grounding in this technique. When tying any type of wound hackle, choosing the correct feather for the job is crucial. For dry flies this usually means a stiff-fibred cock hackle, while for wet flies and other subsurface patterns a softer-fibred cock or hen hackle is required. For each of the flies featured in the book that includes a collar hackle, the correct feather is specified.

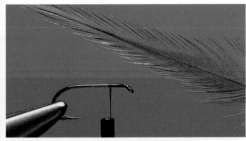

1 Choose the hackle, making sure that the fibre length is right for the hook. For most dry flies it is around one-and-a-half to twice the width of the hook gape.

2 If you find it difficult to judge the fibre length, bending the hackle will cause the fibres to flare so that they can be seen more easily against the hook.

3 Remove the fibres from a short length of the stem. Tear off any broken or otherwise damaged fibres.

4 With scissors, remove most of the bare stem to leave a short stub.

5 Using the bare stub of hackle stem, catch the hackle in position with two or three turns of tying thread. Take hold of the hackle tip with hackle pliers, clamping them firmly but gently onto the tip.

6 Wind on the hackle in closely butted turns towards the eye. Do not let the turns overlap since this will cause the fibres to twist out of position. To complete, secure the tip with thread and remove the excess hackle tip with scissors.

Fly tier information

This book would not have been possible without the generosity of the fly tiers who shared their hard-earned knowledge. Their skills were developed through imagination, dedication, experimentation and observation. Visit their websites and learn more about their expertise. And, if you find yourself visiting their countries, contact them for their recommendations about where to fish. These are professional guides who can provide experiences that will be remembered for a lifetime.

Page 75

Page 204

Guide: Algar, Mike
Flies: Dunce Cap
Bowser
Flashy Floozy
Country of origin:
Canada
Website:
freestoneflyfishers.com

Page 74

Page 80

Guide: Andersen, Pål
Flies: Andersen
Multipurpose Pupa
Heggeil Streamer
Country of origin:
Norway
Website:
flyfishnorway.com

Page 21

Page 15

Guide: Ångnell, Martin
Flies: Ångnell's
Floating Cased Caddis
Ångnell's Floating
Damselfly Nymph
Country of origin:
Sweden
Website: angnell.se

Page 82

Page 84

Guide: Araki, Masa
Flies: Higenaga Dry
Mouse
Country of origin:
Japan
Website: maxtreamfly.
com

Page 87

Guide: Atli, Gudmundur
Fly: Rainbow Ghost
Streamer
Country of origin:
Iceland
Website:
flyfishingiceland.com

Page 104

Guide: Bayer, Walter
"Wolly"
Fly: Facocchi Mayfly
Country of origin:
Ireland
Website:
outlawflyfisher.com

Page 128

Guide: Befus, Brad
Flies: Glass Bead Ultra
Midge
Country of origin:
United States
Website:
frontrangeanglers.com

Page 174

Guide: Beilinson, Daniel
Fly: DB Brown Crab
Country of origin:
Patagonia
Website:
flyfishingcaribe.com

Page 119

Page 110

Guide: Bithell, Alan
Flies: BiColoured
Nymph
Little Black Bug
Country of origin:
Scotland
Website: crackaigflies.
co.uk

Page 166

Guide: Bitters, David
Fly: Baymen Universal
Country of origin:
United States
Website:
baymenoutfitters.com

Page 189

Guide: Blinken, David
Fly: Jellyfish
Country of origin:
United States
Website: northflats.
com

Page 259

Guide: Boucher, Fabrice
Fly: Crystal Gurgler
Country of origin:
France
Website: blog.aspe-angler.com/

Page 228

Page 247

Guide: Brown, Barrett
Flies: Barrett's
Shrimp Fly
Spoon Fly Wobbler
Country of origin:
United States
Website: e-sfly.com

Page 233

Guide: Bulla, Gary
Fly: Gremmie
Country of origin:
United States
Website: garybulla.
com

Page 251

Guide: Burger, Wills
Fly: White Bad Breath
Country of origin:
United Arab Emirates
Email: wills_burger@
yahoo.com

Page 167

Guide: Cabrera, Ariel
Fly: Bullethead
Country of origin:
United States
Website: captainariel.
com

Page 177

Guide: Carver, Tom
Fly: Tom's Redfish
Magic
Country of origin:
United States
Website: flataddicted.
com

Page 217

Page 211

Guide: Casella, Will
Fly: Will's Skettel
Country of origin:
Belize
Website:
shackletoninternational.
com

Guide: Celeschi, Ezio
Flies: Ezio's Mullett
Ezio's Needlefish
Country of origin:
Italy
Website: ecflytier.it

Page 212

Guide: Churchill, Gordon
Fly: Scrab
Country of origin:
United States
Website: geocities.
com/~flyfishnc

Page 164

Page 242

Guide: Ciurca, Audrey
Flies: AC Diamond Fly
AC Pearl Fly
Country of origin:
United States
Website: saltflyfish.
com

Page 188

Guide: Clover, Keith
Fly: Flipper
Country of origin:
Mozambique
Website:
tourettefishing.com

Page 152

Guide: Cook, Mike
Fly: Ron's Red Eyed
Shrimp
Country of origin:
United States
Website:
cooksguideservice.com

Page 165

Guide: Cooley, Butch
Fly: 911
Country of origin:
Panama
Website: butchcooley.
com

Page 29

Guide: Cooney, Jason
Fly: Cooney's Mudeye
Country of origin:
Australia
Website: flymad.com

Page 182

Page 205

Page 250

Guide: Corblies, Mike
Flies: E-Z Eel
Simple Shrimp
Weaky Whistler
Country of origin:
United States
Website:
coastalguides.com

Page 32

Page 33

Page 70

Guide: Corps, Mark H. V.
Flies: Corr Shrimp
Elaine Shrimp
Tara
Country of origin:
Ireland
Website: mark.corps@
fisheriesireland.ie

Page 109

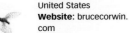

Page 103

Guide: Corwin, Bruce
Flies: Organza Softy
Wally Wing Peccary
Spinner
Country of origin:
United States
Website: brucecorwin.
com

Page 183

Page 234

Guide: Crue, Charles
Flies: Epoxy Sand Eel
Yak Fly
Country of origin:
United States
Website:
channeledgecharters.
com

Guide: Damm Petersen, Kennet
Fly: Pink Godbid
Country of origin: Denmark
Website: dammsflydesign.dk

Page 201

Page 73

Page 72

Guide: Dessaigne, Jean Paul
Flies: Boxite
Futura Mayfly
Country of origin: France
Website: jpdessaigne.com

Page 263

Page 213

Guide: Dickson, Gene
Flies: Copperhead
Spoon Fly
Country of origin: United States
Website: deltaguideservice.com

Page 181

Page 229

Guide: Dubiel, Gary
Flies: Dubiel's Lil'haden
Dubiel's Red-ducer
Country of origin: United States
Website: specfever.com

Page 162

Guide: Duff, Coach
Fly: Spam and Eggs
Country of origin: United States
Website: hawaiibonefishing.com

Page 218

Guide: Duggan, Justin
Fly: Duggan's Suspender Shrimp
Country of origin: Australia
Website: sydneyflyfishing.com.au

Page 185

Guide: Dussias, Jim
Fly: Duke's Diver
Country of origin: United States
Website: oasisangling.com

Page 121

Guide: Edmund, Silvio
Fly: Pinky
Country of origin: New Zealand
Website: fishnewzealand.com

Page 65

Page 26

Guide: Ehnström, Leif
Flies: Red Eye Corixa
Sililegs Chamois
Dragon Nymph
Country of origin: Sweden
Website: fishingflies.ehnstrom.se/

Page 60

Page 62

Guide: Eriksson, Pontus
Flies: Flipside Mayfly
PCL Nymph
Country of origin: Sweden
Website: pontus.sinklair@gmail.com

Page 226

Guide: Faulkner, William
Fly: Back-country Bunny
Country of origin: United States
Website: gulfcoastguideservices.com

Page 105

Page 111

Guide: Feuerstein, Günter
Flies: Minky Mouse
Pin-Ki
Country of origin: Austria
Website: g-feuerstein.com

Page 40

Guide: Finney, Lawrence
Fly: Finney Woven Wire Nymph
Country of origin: Ireland
Website: finneysflies.com

Page 18

Page 25

Guide: Flåten, Tore
Flies: Bekkoira Special
Brufoss Special
Country of origin: Norway
Website: waterproof.as

Page 97

Guide: FlyKrouss Belanger, Christian
Fly: EZ Crayfish
Country of origin: Canada
Email: christianbelanger78@hotmail.com

Page 178

Guide: Ford, John
Fly: Dressed To Kill
Country of origin: United States
Website: mainesaltwaterfishing.com

Page 78

Guide: Freeman, Glyn
Fly: Sewinmeister
Country of origin: England
Website: cumbriaflyfishing.co.uk

Page 69

Page 139

Guide: Gajardoni, Fabrizio
Flies: Gaja's Olive Emerger
Gaja's Orange Shrimp
Country of origin: Italy
Website: gajaflies.it

Page 71

Guide: Gamet, David
Fly: Turkey Biot Yellow Sally
Country of origin: United States
Website: flyfishsd.com

Page 132

Page 136

Guide: Ginevri, Mauro
Flies: Avalon Bonefish Fly
Avalon Permit Fly
Country of origin: Cuba
Website: cubanfishingcenters. com

Page 47

Guide: Gordon, John
Fly: Gordon's BWO Hackle Stacker
Country of origin: United States
Website: www.danica. com/flytier/jgordon/ jgordon.htm

Page 140

Guide: Graham, Gary
Fly: Baja Wasabi Deepdiver
Country of origin: Mexico
Website: bajafly.com

Page 16

Page 30

Page 57

Guide: Hall, Mick
Flies: Aussie Black Water Beetle
Compressed Aussie
March Brown Emerger
Red-Orange Spinner
Country of origin: Australia
Website: kossiedun.comau

Page 265

Page 214

Guide: Harris, George
Flies: Super Fly Alewife
Super Fly Gurglebug
Country of origin: United States
Website: superfly-charters.com

Page 51

Guide: Henley, Howard
Fly: Howard's Fly
Country of origin: Kenya
Email: jcat@ africaonline.co.ke

Page 224

Page 176

Guide: Heyer, Lynne
Flies: Lynne
Yak Hair Squid
Yak Hair Baitfish
Country of origin: United States
Website: crossrip.com

Page 22

Guide: Hintzman, Doug
Fly: Bonnie Belle
Country of origin: Canada
Website: www. wilsonscamps.nb.ca

Page 23

Page 50

Guide: Högberg Robertsdotter, Mikael
Flies: Brown Foam Ant
Grey and Blue Zonker
Country of origin: Sweden
Website: classicflysweden. wordpress.com

Page 54

Guide: Hyde, Gary
Fly: Horsehair Klinkhammer
Country of origin: England
Website: westyorkshireflyfishing services.co.uk

Page 117

Guide: Hytönen, Harri
Fly: Harri's Sipsipussi (Harri's Chip Bag)
Country of origin: Finland
Website: hahytonen@ gmail.com

Page 24

Page 68

Guide: Illana, Laszlo
Flies: CDC and Elk
Yellow Spider Variant
Country of origin: Romania
Website: flytying.ro

Page 36

Guide: Ishimura, Misako
Fly: Eboshi
Country of origin: Japan
Website: misakoishimura.com

Page 102

Guide: Juskovic, Mladjen
Fly: Lim River Yellow Stonefly
Country of origin: Montenegro
Website: musicarenje. net/sr

Page 216

Guide: Kashner, Chuck
Fly: Kashner Striper Bunny
Country of origin: United States
Website: vermontfishingtrips. com

Page 39

Guide: Kasuya, Masamitsu
Fly: Foam Emerger
Country of origin: Japan
Website: www.d1. dion.ne.jp/~k_kasuya

Page 203

Guide: Kelsey, John
Fly: Ray's Fly Flatwing
Country of origin: United States
Email: wkdi@comcast. net

Guide: King, David
Fly: King's Chimera
Country of origin:
England
Website: thatfly.co.uk

Page 151

Page 123

Guide: Kitis, Jim
Fly: Jimki Marron
Country of origin:
Australia
Website:
australisfishing.com.au

Page 190

Guide: Klug, James
Fly: Klug's Ranger
Burrito
Country of origin:
Belize
Website:
yellowdogflyfishing.
com

Guide: Laatsch, Kelly
Fly: Laatsch's Attractor
Stone Fly
Country of origin:
Canada
Website:
stmaryangler.com

Page 55

Page 157

Guide: Laviada, Enrique
Fly: Turish
Country of origin:
Mexico
Website:
mayanfishingtours.com

Page 253

Guide: Lepore, Ed
Fly: Ed's Bonito Bandit
Country of origin:
United States
Email: bonitoed22@aol.
com

Guide: Loe, Tom
Fly: Crystal Tiger Midge
Country of origin:
United States
Website: sierradrifters.
com

Page 101

Page 199

Guide: Loercher, Jeremy
Fly: Nine Mile Shrimp
Country of origin: Little
Cayman
Website:
LittleCaymanFishingClub.
com

Page 120

Page 129

Guide: Ludkin, Joseph
Flies: Tiger Fly
Reel Daddy
Country of origin:
England
Website: reelwings.
co.uk

Guide: Lustrik, Rok
Flies: Lustrik Nymph
Lustrik Streamer
Country of origin:
Slovenia
Website: lustrik.com

Page 59

Page 14

Page 76

Page 94

Guide: Malventano,
Marcelo
Flies: Realistic CDC
Emerger
Realistic Soft Hackle
Country of origin:
Argentina
Website:
laesenciadelatado.com

Page 192

Page 260

Guide: Mattioli, Joe
Flies: Magnum Minnow
Virtual Bunker
Chartreuse
Country of origin:
United States
Website: flyfishingnyc.
com

Page 243

Page 209

Guide: McCoy, Dave
Flies: McCoy's Herring
Popper
Sound Advice
Country of origin:
United States
Website:
emeraldwateranglers.
com

Page 168

Page 208

Guide: McGowan, Bryan
Flies: Blackbone
Silhouette Shrimp
Country of origin:
United States
Website: saltyfeather.
com

Page 147

Guide: McLeod, Peter
Fly: Pete's Cheat
Country of origin:
England
Website:
aardvarkmcleod.com

Page 196

Guide: Mendelson, John
Fly: Mud Dog Bunny
Bunker
Country of origin:
United States
Website: bostonfishstix.
com

Page 17

Page 158

Guide: Menz, Christof
Flies: Backpack Emerger
Cuban Crab
Country of origin:
Austria
Website: pro-guides.
com

Page 184

Page 223

Guide: Michaels, Edward
Flies: Michaels' Big Cake
Michaels' Permit Pro
Choice
Country of origin:
United States
Website:
flyfishingguidekeywest.
com

Page 124

Guide: Miller, Todd
Fly: Credit Card Hell
Country of origin:
United States
Website: ToMi_
BlkFlies@msn.com

Page 246

Guide: Mills, Sean
Fly: Pilchard Block Fly
Country of origin:
South Africa
Website: flywaters.
co.za

Page 180

Page 237

Page 227

Guide: Morrison, Greg
Flies: Dorado Delight
Lead Head Bunker
Morrison's Mullet
Country of origin:
United States
Website: flyrod.tv

Page 198

Guide: Mullet Dickinson,
Josh
Fly: Mullet's Fry
Country of origin:
Honduras
Website: bajafly.com

Page 92

Page 86

Guide: Munn, Stevie
Flies: Black and Blue
Jam
Munn's Mayfly
Country of origin:
Ireland
Website: irishangler.
co.uk

Page 48

Page 64

Guide: Murray-Orr,
David
Flies: CDC Emerger
Quill Emerger
Country of origin:
New Zealand
Website: mataura.
co.nz

Page 236

Page 256

Guide: Ng, Wirianto
Flies: WN Cobra
WN Fast 'n' Furious
Country of origin:
Indonesia
Email: wirianto.ng@
gmail.com

Page 146

Guide: Noël, Paul
Fly: Click-Clack
Country of origin:
United States
Website: captpaul.com

Page 122

Guide: O'Keefe, Pat
Fly: Damsel Nymph
Country of origin:
New Zealand
Website: blarneylodge.
co.nz

Page 98

Page 96

Guide: Oishi, Todd
Flies: Todd's Czech
Nymph
Todd's Vampire Leech
Country of origin:
Canada
Website:
innovativeflyfisher.com/
forum

Page 238

Page 141

Guide: Pablo Yañez
Duran, Pedro
Flies: GT Candy Fire
Tiger
Xtreme Squid
Country of origin:
Chile
Email: Peter@
xtremefly.cl

Page 66

Guide: Perrone, Pepe
Fly: Reversed Frog
Country of origin:
Argentina
Website: peppeflycast.
com

Page 150

Guide: Petersen, Lance
Fly: Mona Lisa
Country of origin:
Mexico
Website: lpandch@juno.
com

Page 175

Page 210

Guide: Poness, Ralph
Flies: Abused Mackerel
Thatcher's Island
Zonker
Country of origin:
United States
Website: olfc.com

Page 38

Page 56

Guide: Pop, Adrian
Flies: F-Fly
Olive Epoxy Minnow
Country of origin:
Romania
Website: www.danica.
com/flytier/apop/apop.
htm.

Page 106

Page 114

Guide: Popov, Aco
Flies: New Village
Popov Gammarus
Country of origin:
Macedonia
Website:
grandepescatore.com

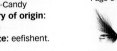

Page 191

Page 186

Page 142

Page 154

Guide: Priest, Jeff
Flies: Baby Mole Crab
Flatiron Herring
Ghost Sardina
Rock-N-Candy
Country of origin:
Mexico
Website: eefishent.
com

Page 34

Page 61

Guide: Putz, Sacha
Flies: Dark Queen
Orange Angel
Country of origin:
Sweden
Website: puetz-
hemer@t-online.de

Guide: Ramirez, Juan
Fly: Juan's Hopper
Country of origin:
United States
Website: Hopperjuan.
blogspot.com

Page 52

Guide: Re, Giuseppe
Flies: Gold Bead
Krystal CDC
Grayling Jig Fly
Country of origin:
Italy
Website: giuseppero.
com

Page 46

Page 49

Guide: Reeves, Chris
Fly: Bluefish Soda
Country of origin:
England
Website: fishingclass.
co.uk

Page 144

Guide: Rice, Mike
Flies: Cichetti's Sand
Eel
Yak Hair Deceiver—
Herring
Country of origin:
United States
Website: muddogflies.
com

Page 138

Page 160

Guide: Ruiz Pérez, José
Manuel
Fly: Cholo's Orange
Emerger
Country of origin:
Spain
Website:
moscasorbigo.com

Page 28

Guide: Salomonsson,
Roger
Flies: Roger's
Damsel Nymph
Roger's Wasp
Country of origin:
Sweden
Website: imitationflies.
com

Page 88

Page 90

Guide: Salvini, Alberto
Flies: Alberto's Sand
Crab
Alberto's Shrimp
Country of origin:
Italy
Website: theitalians.
net

Page 225

Page 230

Guide: Sander, Justin
Flies: Pink Moe Joe
Super Scud
Country of origin:
Canada
Website:
sandpiperflyfishing.
com/our-flies.html

Page 264

Page 93

Guide: Sekiguchi, Kenji
Flies: Kenji's Devil May
Cry
Kenji Shrimp Fly
Country of origin:
Indonesia
Website: flyrodder.org

Page 222

Page 240

Guide: Sellers, Warren
Fly: Murderous
Marshmallow
Country of origin:
Costa Rica
Website:
wssportfishing.com

Page 148

Guide: Shirley, Vic
Fly: Jamaican Salty
Shrimp
Country of origin:
Jamaica
Website:
flyfishingjamaica.com

Page 145

Guide: Sigler, Randy
Fly: Yak Attack
Country of origin:
United States
Website: striper.com

Page 258

Guide: Simmons,
Dexter
Fly: Sandy Merkin
Country of origin:
United States
Website:
keywestflyfishing.com

Page 221

Guide: Simpson, Jack
Flies: Cripple Midge
Root Beer Leech
Country of origin:
Canada
Website:
sandpiperflyfishing.
com

Page 85

Page 81

Guide: Smith, Jeff
Flies: Buffy the Striper
Slayer
Meatball
Country of origin:
United States
Website: finaddiction.
com

Page 170

Page 194

Guide: Statler, Fox
Fly: Fox's Mudbug
Country of origin:
United States
Website:
fishinwhattheysee.com

Page 42

Guide: Suominen, Jarkko
Fly: Olive Shuttlecock
Country of origin:
Finland
Email: suominen.j@
gmail.com

Page 107

Guide: Thielicke, Brian
Fly: Pink Frenzy Billfish
Country of origin:
Costa Rica
Website:
brianthielicke@aol.com

Page 248

Page 172

Page 206

Guide: Thomas, Eric
Flies: Cam's Fly
Rhody Flatwing
Country of origin:
United States
Website: fishteezer.
com

Page 108

Guide: Toivonen, Olli
Fly: Olli's Damsel
Country of origin:
Finland
Email: ollitoivonen9@
hotmail.com

Page 63

Guide: Toldi, Nick
Fly: Peute
Country of origin:
France
Website: gourmetfly.
com

Page 134

Page 244

Guide: Trimble, Billy
Flies: Blind Chicken
Mai Tai Crab
Country of origin:
United States
Website:
trimbleflyfishing.com

Page 116

Guide: Tripet, Lambert
Fly: Tubestream
Orange
Country of origin:
Switzerland
Website:
flyfishinglifestyle.com

Page 112

Guide: Tripoli, Abel
Fly: Pajarito Alemàn
Country of origin:
Argentina
Website: abeltri@
hotmail.com

Page 126

Guide: Tutalo, Ken
Fly: Delaware Baby
Brown
Country of origin:
United States
Website: baxterhouse.
net

Page 118

Guide: Vainio, Ville
Fly: Ville's Peacock
Rubber Leg Nymph
Country of origin:
Finland
Website: www.
flyfishingteamfinland.
com

Page 100

Guide: Vallerotonda,
Alessandro
Fly: Blue Wing Olive
Cripple
Country of origin: Italy
Email: Alexfly76@
hotmail.it

Page 44

Page 58

Guide: van den
Driesche, Paul
Flies: Foam Wasp
Loop Fly
Country of origin: The
Netherlands
Website:
kickassflytying.com

Page 202

Guide: van Mook,
Laurenz
Fly: Pos Chiquito
Shrimp
Country of origin:
Aruba
Website: www.
flyfishingaruba.com

Page 262

Guide: Wallace, Eric
Fly: Captain Eric's Flat
Wing Herring
Country of origin:
United States
Website:
costalflyangler.com

Page 220

Guide: Weissman, Eric
Fly: Eric's Ugly Coho
Killer
Country of origin:
Canada
Website:
exploreflyfishing.com

Page 252

Guide: White, Jim
Fly: White Ghost Squid
Country of origin:
United States
Website:
whiteghostcharters.
com

Page 20

Guide: White, Philip
Fly: Blown-over Dun
Country of origin:
England
Website:
peakdistrictflyfishing.
com

Page 200

Guide: Yelverton, Basil
Fly: Original Pompano
Rocket
Country of origin: United
States
Website:
gulfbreezeguideservice.
com

Page 156

Guide: Young, Simon
Fly: Sparkle Charlie
Country of origin:
Venezuela
Website: simonyoung@
hotmail.com

Page 232

Page 135

Guide: zumFelde, Roan
Flies: Rz's Back Country
Booger
Rz's Mangrove Slider
Country of origin:
United States
Website:
fishingextremes.com

Glossary

Bobbin A tool for holding a thread spool, preventing the thread from unwrapping.

Bobbin threader A thin loop of wire inserted into the tube of a bobbin to facilitate running the thread from the spool through the bobbin.

Bodkin A pointed tool used to pick out fibres.

Dub The technique of twisting fur onto tying thread so it can be wound around the hook shank as a body.

Dubbing twister A weighted pair of wires used to keep the thread dubbing loop open while fibres are placed inside the thread loop. Turning the twister tightens the thread loop, capturing the dubbing fibres and preventing them from falling out as the body is wound around the hook.

Hackle gauge A scale for measuring the length of fibres on hackle feathers. Each size of dry fly requires a corresponding length of fibres.

Hackle pliers A tool for grasping a hackle feather while it is wound around the hook.

Hair stacker A hollow cylinder used to even the natural, tapered ends of hair.

Half hitch A simple overhand knot used to hold materials in between tying steps.

Loose loop A thread wrap that does not secure material in place when pulled tightly. It is often used when spinning deer hair to keep the hairs in place without flaring them outward.

Palmer To wind a feather around the hook shank in open turns allowing the body to show.

Rib Wrapping material in open turns over a fly body so it shows through. A rib also reinforces otherwise fragile bodies and prevents them from falling apart.

Rotating dryer A motor-driven disk that slowly turns, preventing adhesives from drying in an unequal thickness around the hook shank.

Thorax The part of an insect between the head and abdomen.

Tube A hollow plastic, brass or metal straw upon which the fly is tied. A leader is then run through the tube and a hook is attached.

UV light A lamp generating ultraviolet wavelengths. Certain adhesives require a UV light source to cure in seconds rather than relying on sunshine to cure in several minutes.

Whip-finish tool Completes the head of a fly so the final thread wraps are wound under, thus preventing unraveling.

Materials glossary

Bead Ring or globe-shaped metal, plastic or glass added for weight and intended to sink the fly.

Biot An individual fibre of a bird's wing feather often wound around the hook shank to create a body.

CA cement Cyanoacrylate glue, known by trade names such as Superglue or Krazy Glue.

CDC (cul-de-canard) Feathers found on waterfowl near the oil gland. Due to their structure and the presence of oil, CDC feathers float very well.

Cement Also known as head cement or head lacquer, used to prevent the thread head from unravelling.

Chenille A tufted cord or yarn wrapped around a hook shank to make a body with a segmented profile.

Collar Feather hackle wound at the front of a fly. It often suggests the legs of an insect.

Cone A bullet-shaped weight that sinks a fly quickly and gives an up-and-down movement as it is retrieved.

Downwing Wings tied in so they lay flat against the body.

Embossed tinsel Tinsel with reflective indentions.

Epoxy A two-part cement known for its durability. It is available in various cure rates.

Eyes This can refer to metal hourglass-shaped eyes added for weight or plastic imitations of fish eyes.

Herl The long fibres with fuzz found on peacock, ostrich and emu. They give the appearance of bulk without adding weight.

Marabou Originally soft feathers of the marabou stork, now substituted by turkey feathers. The ease of movement of the long fibres attracts fish.

Monocord A flat, untwisted nylon thread. Its advantage is that it lays flat and smooth.

Mylar A synthetic product made to add shine to flies. Can be purchased in sheets, on spools or as a dubbing. Its purpose is to flash and attract fish.

Oval tinsel Tinsel wrapped around a cloth center. It is oval in cross-section.

Overbody Materials wrapped so as to cover the body's foundation and give the desired colour.

Overwing The very top material of a compound wing. It is often dark in colour to mimic the dark dorsal side of a baitfish.

Quill The center rib of a feather from which the feather's fibres grow. When stripped and dyed, it is wound around the hook to create a body.

Rubber hackle Round legs made from rubber. They move easily in the water and attract fish.

Saddle hackle The extra-long cock hackles from the 'saddle' (back) of the rooster are often used as wings on baitfish imitations. Their long thin shape forms a fish body silhouette.

Tinsel A thin strip of metallic foil often used to add sparkle.

UV adhesive A bonding agent that requires ultraviolet light to cure. It cures quickly and keeps all loose fibres in place, preventing the fibres from twisting around the hook.

Vinyl cement A thin, viscous adhesive often used to coat feathers, preventing the feather fibres from separating.

Zonker strip A length of tanned rabbit hide with the hair on. The strip can be tied in as a tail or wrapped around the hook. The soft hairs wave enticingly in the water.

Index

Credits

Quarto would like to thank the following agencies and manufacturers for supplying images for inclusion in this book:

Mario Tarello/Shutterstock
Strejman/Shutterstock
keren-seg/Shutterstock

All other images are the copyright of Quarto Publishing plc. While every effort has been made to credit contributors, Quarto would like to apologize should there have been any omissions or errors – and would be pleased to make the appropriate correction for future editions of the book.